P9-EEA-987

OUR BIT OF TRUTH

An Anthology of Canadian Native Literature

Agnes Grant, editor

Pemmican Publications Inc. gratefully acknowledges the assistance accorded to its publishing program by the Manitoba Arts Council and Canada Council.

Printed and Bound in Canada - Hignell Printers Ltd., Winnipeg

Canadian Cataloguing in Publication Data

Grant, Agnes
Our bit of truth

ISBN: 0-921827-10-5
1. Canadian Literature (English) - Indian authors
2. Canadian Literature (English) - Inuit authors
3. Canadian Literature (English) - Metis authors
4. Canadian Literature (English) - 20th century
I. Grant, Agnes, 1933 -

PS8235.I6086 1990 C810.8'0897 C90-097003-0
PR9194.5.I5086 1990

412 McGregor Street / Winnipeg, Manitoba / Canada R2W 4X5

TABLE OF CONTENTS

Chapter IV - Biography and Autobiography

Chapter V - Short Stories

Chapter VI - Novels

Chapter VII - Contemporary Poetry

In Conclusion

PREFACE

Over the past thirty years, more and more Aboriginal students in Canada have graduated from high school and university, and then chosen careers as teachers and writers wanting to share their appreciation of traditional Métis and Native culture and values.

At the same time, the love of oral storytelling tradition has enriched the styles of Aboriginal writers exploring contemporary concerns through poetry, short stories, drama and novels.

This volume takes readers from coast to coast in Canada, and offers a rich sampling of Aboriginal writing past and present. The editor, Professor Agnes Grant of Brandon University, has been teacher and friend to Aboriginal students in rural, urban, and remote locations throughout Manitoba. Because of her long-standing devotion, Dr. Grant has been entrusted with material handed down from generation to generation. Her encouragement has helped many aspiring storytellers to find inspiration for their own creativity by drawing upon legends and original stories.

The authors in these pages have tried to capture and retain the voices of their people, including that true humour which is often overlooked or lost in translation from an Aboriginal language into English. This is especially important because many people have lost the Aboriginal tongue of their ancestors and now have English as their first language.

The importance of a collection such as this for school use cannot be overestimated. Native and Métis students will gain a strengthening of their identity as people with a rich and varied background and cultural traditions. Amongst non-Aboriginal students the creativity of the contributors in these pages can promote the broadening of horizons and greater respect for people of different backgrounds, particularly the Aboriginal population of Manitoba.

For readers of all ages and identities, the book can provide enriching ways of seeing and understanding the world in terms which may be quite different from their own. At this point in Canadian history nothing could be more timely or important.

Flora Zaharia

INTRODUCTION

This anthology is a showcase of Canadian aboriginal writing: the authors and poets are all of Métis or Native ancestry.* In a few cases their words were taken down and edited by a non-Native person. There are also some integral pieces of information - original songs, ballads, and legends - which were put in writing by non-Native researchers with as much accuracy as possible. As shown in this anthology, a considerable body of writing by aboriginal people exists, but only a few books by aboriginal writers are found in Canadian classrooms.

Today, aboriginal students are completing school in unprecedented numbers, so the inclusion of Métis and Native literature in programs of study is of increasing importance to enhance their self-image and provide accurate information about their people. It is also important that non-Native students receive greater insight into aboriginal cultures if Canada is to fulfill its potential as a truly multicultural society.

Concern for relevant curricula has been expressed in almost every statement aboriginal people have made concerning education in the last twenty years. Some changes in history courses are evident and numerous cultural activities have been incorporated into school programs. There are, however, no real changes in literature programs at any level of education. Too often books about Métis and Native people by non-Native writers are still viewed as the best interpretation of aboriginal cultures. Aboriginal readers have a right to expect that masterpieces of their living tradition be a part of the country's language arts study. No Canadian literature course can be truly representative of Canada without literature written by aboriginal Canadians themselves.

Literature is generally considered an effective vehicle for the transmission and understanding of a culture. It has the power

* "Native" is commonly used in such terms as "Native literature" and "Native Studies", and in these contexts it refers to both Native and Métis, though the term "Métis" refers to a distinct society of Canadians who are of Native and European ancestry.

to recreate reality and combine insights in a manner that may be lacking in other disciplines. Art and music may achieve the same results, but unlike language arts, they are not a required component of every student's school day. Some literature is used in every reading program, and every student should have the opportunity to explore literature with familiar cultural content. It is also important that students from different cultures explore each others' literature.

The significance of literature can best be understood in terms of the culture from which it springs. It is understandable that school programs rely heavily on the literary traditions of Europe because those are the culture bases of most of the teachers and curriculum developers, the literary traditions in which they have been trained. It is not, however, appropriate to continue this practice as Canadians increasingly attempt to define what "Canadian" is in terms of our multicultural reality. At such a time, as more and more aboriginal writers publish their work, ignorance of the culture can no longer be used as an excuse for not teaching Native literature. It is of considerable importance to readers of all ages to have access to literature which enables them to understand and accept the principles upon which the values and traditions of their particular culture are based.

A fundamental reason that traditional Native literature is not included in many programs is that looking at Native literature, and literature of all minority cultures, requires a change in perspective by the reader. The absence of the familiar European form, style, and content, too often leads to the criticism that such literature is inferior. The possibility of different but equal merit is seldom, if at all, entertained. In contrast, Native art, once considered bizarre, is now identified as uniquely Canadian; in fact, much that is considered Canadian is recognizable by its very Nativeness. No such phenomenon has happened in literature.

In the same way, much contemporary writing by Métis and Native people is rejected because it does not fit the literary criteria used in English literature studies. Moreover, its content is often disturbing to mainstream readers because it comments on the experience of being aboriginal within an atmosphere of rejection by the larger society. Certainly, the history of Canadian aboriginal people in contact with Europeans is not a proud one; even today racism, in its many forms, affects them, and society, in many ways. A recognition of Native literature could go a long way towards healing the rift by helping aboriginal and other people to come to terms with the past and cope with the present. Until this happens aboriginal writers may well continue to produce material that is generally disturbing for mainstream readers.

Validating aboriginal literary expression is often viewed by teachers, who have been educated in one tradition only, as invalidating a revered canon of European literature. Native literature does not challenge the style and content of masterpieces from European culture, but it does offer an alternative way of thinking and it can add new dimensions to existing thought patterns.

Before Native literature can be fully appreciated for its unique qualities it is imperative to identify assumptions underlying the cultural beliefs and practices of Métis and Native societies. Native mythology underlies much contemporary writing; visions and dreams played a vital role in the lives of traditional people, and their influences are still felt in contemporary writing. The style of the literature is influenced by the shape and content of mythology, so literary devices which reflect this creative source of oral expression are used. It may be difficult for the teacher trained in European literary tradition to recognize these devices, because what was meaningful to North American aboriginal people was not familiar to Shakespeare and Wordsworth.

Students need to be given an alternative approach to understanding this distinctive literature. Evident in the writings is a profound spiritualism, whether traditional or Christian, an intense reverence and respect for nature, a strong sense of community and a love of life, laughter, and harmony as aboriginal people tell their own stories disclosing their culture's richness and revealing the beauty of this world, beauty that is often invisible to or ignored by an observer from outside the culture. Points of view familiar to Métis and Native people will be expressed. A particular brand of humour which is prevalent, and vital, in aboriginal cultures will be found. The value of a life of mingling, caring, and sharing will emerge in the portrayal of the community and its rituals. There is a sense of place and the characters have a dependence on that place. In the land imagery which pervades the writings the readers will discover that the land is a spiritual and moral idea, a unifying force, and the memories, chants, and rituals of the community tie the people to the land. The rugged individualism of heroes in non-Native North American folklore is antithetical to this sense of community. The sense of alienation from society is strong, but there is also healing; the quest themes always lead back home where elders wait to teach traditional ways to the young who may be floundering in alien cultures or questioning their identity.

Traditional poetry portrays a profound spiritualism, a reverence for nature and a particular reverence for the world. The composers took no credit, for it was believed that nature's poems were discovered, not composed; the poet merely nourished them and gave them back to the people, thus remaining humble before nature and the tribe. This anonymity left the poet unassuming and dignified. Contemporary poetry, though credited to the poet, expresses many of the same attitudes in modern times.

Literary devices such as dualism, paired phrases, repetition, understatement, significant pauses, synecdoche, precision of detail, fragmentation of thought and associational imagery are found in Native literature. Perhaps the most unique feature of the literature is the influence of oral tradition. Few cultures have been able to retain an oral and a written tradition simultaneously. This leads not only to a unique style but often the old stories, or fragments thereof, are incorporated into the new stories. Shape-shifting, the transformation of the body form, which is found in myths and legends, was not merely a literary device; it was an article of belief, and it surfaces in contemporary writing. Visions and the importance of dreams still play an important role in some contemporary societies so they too are reflected in the literature.

For non-Native readers the beliefs and customs may be unfamiliar but they will recognize the strength, beauty, and common themes of the literature. For aboriginal readers the literature may be an unprecedented source of strength and an avenue for personal development that has not been utilized to its fullest potential yet.

An attempt has been made in this anthology to include literature from the main Canadian Native cultures. There were six major groups at the time of contact and the geographic regions they occupy today have remained largely unchanged. The migratory tribes of the woodlands hunted and gathered in what is now the Maritimes, Quebec, Ontario, and northern Manitoba, and some pushed into northern Saskatchewan. These tribes spoke Algonkian languages as did the Blackfoot tribe and the Plains Cree. The plains tribes lived largely in what is now the United States but the Blackfoot, Peigan, Blood, Sarcee, Assiniboine, and Plains Cree lived in what is now southern Manitoba, Saskatchewan, and Alberta. The Five Nations of the Iroquois and the Hurons hunted and farmed in the St. Lawrence Lowlands and the Niagara Peninsula. Tribes of the Cordilleran Region such as the Chilcotin, Carriers and Tahltan lived in the valleys and plateaus between the ranges of the Rocky Mountains. The West Coast Indians, known for their daring whale hunts and magnificent potlatches, lived on the coast and the gulf islands; their territory ranged from the Tlinkits in the north to the Haida, Kwakewlth, and Salish in the south. Tribes such as the Chipeweyan and Dogrib lived in the sparsely populated Mackenzie and Yukon River basins, while the far north was the land of the Inuit.

The following myths, legends, traditional poetry and contemporary writings reflect the cultures in pre-European contact time as well as the present. A traditional Ojibway poet sang, "Verily the sky clears when my Mide drum sounds" (See page 98). Just as surely misunderstandings and misconceptions about aboriginal cultures will disappear as non-Natives become familiar with the literature of the Aboriginal People.

ACKNOWLEDGEMENTS

Grateful acknowledgement is extended to the following for permission to use material quoted.

Chapter I

Ethel Gardner for “Ack-koo’s Song”.

From *Swampy Cree Legends* as told to Charles Clay by Kushapatchees, the Smoky One, “How the World was Made Again”, “Why the Moose’s Skin is Loose”. Used by permission of Charlotte Clay.

From *Indian Legends of Canada* by Ella Elizabeth Clark, “Legend of the Qu’Appelle River #2”, “The Creation of the Northern Rocky Mountains”, “The Creation Myth of the Hurons and the Iroquois”, “The Little People”. Used by permission of the Canadian publishers, McClelland and Stewart, Toronto.

From *Great Leader of the Ojibway: Mis-quona-queb* by James Redsky, “Shaking Tents”. Used by permission of the Canadian publishers, McClelland and Stewart, Toronto.

From *Sacred Legends of the Sandy Lake Cree* by Carl Ray and James Stevens, “Wee-sa-kay-jac and the Ducks”, “The Windigo Spirit”. Used by permission of the Canadian publishers, McClelland and Stewart, Toronto.

From *Ojibway Heritage* by Basil Johnston, “Nanabush Kitchi Manitou’s Emissary”. Used by permission of the Canadian publishers, McClelland and Stewart, Toronto.

From *Son of Raven, Son of Deer* by George Clutesi, “How the Human People First Got Fire”. Used by permission of Gray’s Publishing, Victoria.

From *Legendes Indiennes Du Canada* by Claude Mélançon, “A Piegan Indian Myth”. Used by permission of Editions du Jour, Montreal.

From *The Wishing Bone Cycle* by Howard Norman.

pp. 133-148. Used by permission of Ross-Erikson, Santa Barbara, CA.

From *Where the Chill Came From*, "The Wrong Chill Windigo", Copyright (c) 1982, edited by Howard Norman. Published by North Point Press and reprinted by permission.

From *Blackfoot Lodge Tales* by George Bird Grinnel. Used by permission of the University of Nebraska Press, Lincoln, IL.

From *Tales of the Mohawks* by Alma Greene / Forbidden Voice, "The West Wind". Used by permission of J.M. Dent & Sons, Markham, Ontario.

From *I Am an Indian* edited by Kent Gooderham, "Wesakachak and the Geese". Used by permission of Paula Beardy.

From *Recollections of an Assiniboine Chief* by Dan Kennedy. Used by permission of Gloria Gordon-Timm.

Chapter II

From *Songs of the Indians I* by Robert John Columbo. "Hunter's Song", "Prayer for Food", "Song of the Returning Warriors", "Treaty Song", "Invocations of the Sun and Moon", "Dance Song", "Love Song", "War Song", "Songs of the Hunt 1-6", "We will Go", "Paddle Song", "Winter Song", "Drinking Song", "Buffalo Song 1-3", "Battle Song", "I Will Walk", "Love Song 1-4", "Dawn Song", "Love Song: A Black Haired Girl", "Oh I Am Thinking", "My Love Has Departed", "Lover's Lament", "Song of the Snow", "Animals 1-3", "The Hare and the Lynx", "Hunter's Song", "A Song of Spring", "Corn Husking Song", "A Woman's Song", "Where the Fight Was", "The Sky Clears", "Vision Song", "Canadian Medicine Song", "Medicine Song for War", "Prayer to the Four Quarters", "Song of A Maiden Disappointed in Love", "Song of the Mother of a Certain Young Girl", "Coyote Medicine Song", "Woman's Song", "The Song of the Tree", "Buffalo Chant", "Crow Song", "Song of the Great Spirit", "Sung After Battle", "Cradle Songs 1-3", "Charming Songs", "Invocation to the Sun Dance", "Warpath Song", "Gambler's Song", "Lover's Songs 1-3",

"Crossing the Ice", "Caughnawaga Song", "Rainmaking", "Hawk Dream Song", "Petition", "A Helpless Babe", "The Buds of Spring", "Peace Song", "Shaman's Song", "Victory Celebration", "Gambling Song", "White Man's Dances." Reprinted by permission of Oberon Press, Ottawa.

From *Songs of the Indians II* by Robert John Columbo. "Prayer for the Field", "Prayer for the Spirit of the Slain Bear", "Prayer of a Woman in Labour", "Prayer of the Stone Carver", "The Lonesome Youth", "For Relief from Rain", "For Abundance of Food", "They Say I Loved Her", "The Birds are Beginning", "Look Down and Make it Calm", "Send Us a Rainbow", "Weather Chant", "A Prayer Before Whaling", "Courtesy Song", "Bear Song", "Divorce Song", "Boastfulness", "Hamatsa Song", "#14", "Cradle Song 1-5", "Cradle Songs For Girls 1-7", "Song of Ridicule", "Stop all this Idle Chatter", "Song of an Old Woman", "Song of the Departed", "Song of Mourning", "Chinook Songs 4-9." Reprinted by permission of Oberon Press, Ottawa.

Reprinted from *The Sky Clears: Poetry of the American Indians* by A. Grove Day, by permission of University of Nebraska Press. Copyright 1951 by A. Grove Day. "Walrus Hunting", "Petting Song", "Complaint Over Bad Hunting", "Cradle Song of a Boy".

Chapter III

From *Voices of the Plains Cree* by Edward Ahenakew, "The Foot Race", "The Buffalo Chase". Used by permission of Ruth M. Buck.

From *Vanishing Spaces: Memoirs of Louis Goulet* by Guillaume Charette, "The Buffalo Hunt". Used by permission of Pemmican Publications, Winnipeg.

From *The Days of Augusta* by Jean E. Speare, "The Holdup", "Christmas at the Mission", "Doctor's Book". Used by permission of Jean E. Speare.

From *An Indian Remembers* by Tom Boulanger, pp. 37-39. Used by permission of Peguis Publishers, Winnipeg.

Chapter IV

From *Forty Years a Chief* by George Barker, pp. 10-17. Used by permission of Peguis Publishers, Winnipeg.

From *I Walk in Two Worlds* by Eleanor Brass, pp. 5, 13-17. Used by permission of Eleanor Brass and Glenbow Museum.

From *My Name is Masak* by Alice French, "Winter Studies". Used by permission of Peguis publishers, Winnipeg.

From *Halfbreed* by Maria Campbell, pp.19-22, 57-59. Used by permission of the Canadian publisher, McClelland and Stewart, Toronto.

From *Chief Peguis and His Descendants* by Chief Albert Edward Thompson, pp. 1-5. Used by permission of Peguis publishers, Winnipeg.

From *The Metis: Canada's Forgotten People* by D.B. Sealey and Antoine S. Lussier, pp. 101-102. Used by permission of Pemmican Publications, Winnipeg.

From *Fifty Dollar Bride: Marie Rose Smith. A Chronicle of Metis Life in the 19th Century* by Jock Carpenter, pp. 44-48, 53-56. Used by permission of Gray's Publishing, Victoria.

From *I Am Nokomis, Too* by R.M. Vanderburg, pp.148-155. Used by permission of General Publishing, Don Mills, Ontario.

From *Defeathering the Indian* by Emma LaRocque. Used by permission of Stoddard Publishing, Don Mills, Ontario.

Chapter V

From *Stories of the Métis* by D. Bruce Sealey, ed., "An Act of God". Used by permission of Pemmican Publications, Winnipeg.

From *The Moccasin Maker* by Pauline Johnson, "Catharine of the Crow's Nest". Used by permission of the Ryerson Press and the University of Arizona Press (1987), Tucson.

From *Wild Drums* by Nan Shipley, ed., "Torch Woman". Used by permission of Peguis Publishers, Winnipeg.

From *Medicine Boy and Other Cree Tales* by Eleanor Brass, "Abandoned". Used by permission of Eleanor Brass and Glenbow Museum.

From *Indians Don't Cry* by George Kenny, "On the Shooting of a Beaver", "Sunset on Portage", "Old Daniel". Used by permission of New Canada Publications, Toronto.

Herbert Gunn for "A Question of Rights" and "A Lamp to Read By".

Basil Johnston for "The Kiss and the Moonshine".

D. Bruce Sealey for "Joe Bignell's Fight with the Weetigo".

Gilbert Oskaboose and Canadian Dimension, vol. 22, no. 1 (February, 1988) for "The Serpent's Egg".

Chapter VI

From *Harpoon of the Hunter* by Markoosie, pp. 17-25. Used by permission of the publisher, McGill-Queen's University Press, Montreal.

From *In Search of April Raintree* by Beatrice Culleton, pp. 63-69. Used by permission of Pemmican Publications, Winnipeg.

From *Honour the Sun* by Ruby Slipperjack, "The Last Row". Used by permission of Pemmican Publications, Winnipeg.

From *Slash* by Jeanette Armstrong, pp.36-93. Used by permission of Theytus Books, Penticton, B.C. and Jeanette Armstrong.

From *Brothers In Arms* by Jordan Wheeler, "Exposure", pp. 164-175 and 218-223. Used by permission of Pemmican Publications, Winnipeg.

Chapter VII

From *Flint and Feather* by Pauline Johnson, "The Cattle Thief", "The Corn Husker". Used by permission of Hodder & Sloughton, London.

From *Red on White: The Biography of Duke Redbrid* by Marty Dunn, "My Mocassins Have Not Walked". Reprinted with permission of Stoddart Publishing, Don Mills.

From *Many Voices: An Anthology of Contemporary Canadian Indian Poetry* by David Day and Marilyn Bowering, eds., "My Nokum". Used by permission of Marilyn Bowering.

From *Notice, This is an Indian Reserve* by Kent Gooderham, ed., "Don't Rhyme the Words Too Closely", "I Hear the Gods are Crying in the Night", "My Camera Catch the Light". Used by permission of Kent Gooderham.

From *Native Sons* by Ken George Batisse and others, "Pottery", "Someone", "Ordinary Man". Used by permission of Highway Book Shop, Cobalt, Ontario.

From *Poems of Rita Joe* by Rita Joe, "There is a tale of men of peace", "We Make the Baskets", "When I was Small". Used by permission of Rita Joe.

Native Education Branch, Department of Education, Manitoba, for "What Colour is Love", "Walk Slowly, Little One".

Roslea Prosser for "My Leighton".

From *My Heart Soars* by Chief Dan George, "They Say We Do Not Show Our Feelings". Used by permission of Hancock House, Surrey, British Columbia.

From *I Am Woman* by Lee Maracle, "Creation", "Ghosts". Used by permission of Lee Maracle and Write-On Press, Vancouver.

In Conclusion

From *Why Women's Studies?* by Agnes Grant and Ingrid Makus, eds., pp. 51-57. Used by permission of Eva McKay.

Every effort has been made to trace the owners of the following. If anyone has knowledge of the copyright owners we would be grateful for this information.

From *Trapping is My Life* by John Tetso, "Inviting a Moose for a Picture".

From *Geniesh: An Indian Girlhood* by Jane Willis, pp. 1-11.

Chapter One

Myths and Legends

Introduction

Native literature, like any other literature, is based on mythologies which shape its underlying beliefs. The ability to create myths was found in all early societies. In the twentieth century we rely on science which sets absolute standards by which to judge truth. We are skeptical of anything that cannot be proven. This has led to a common degeneration of the term "myth" to mean fiction or invention. This definition, however, grossly misrepresents the true meaning and importance of myths and legends.

Myths are the histories of early humanity created by people who were naturally creative. Like all art, myths are a way of coping with reality, and they have their beginnings in the attempts of people to explain and understand their surroundings. Some scholars believe that myths arose as a response to local conditions and interests. They were an attempt to explain what otherwise would be unexplainable. For them climate, landscape, history, and social conditions are the primary forces shaping humanity's ideals, fantasies, and emotions. Myths and legends were created to explain these conditions. As such, myths created the foundation for the social customs of the societies. They represent a mature and sophisticated way of knowing and understanding information. Like present-day Jungian psychology they are based on the belief that there are two kinds of knowledge: knowledge of the conscious, external world of everyday life and a knowledge of the subconscious workings of the human mind. It is this subconscious knowledge that mythology tries to explore and explain.

These scholars explain myths in terms of "archetypes." They believe that literature goes beyond the definite meanings conveyed and has an emotional appeal to the subconscious stirrings of a reader's mind. They believe all humanity has innumerable experiences of the same type, experiences that have not happened to themselves but to their ancestors. The results of these experiences form brain patterns which are passed on as inherited memory. These stories are deeply imbedded in the memory of a people; they clarify and identify cultural patterns. The archetypes are the same for all cultures, but the ways they are interpreted and understood form the different cultural beliefs.

Whatever the theory of origin of mythology, similar themes are found in all cultures. Two of the most common are the idea of a nurturing Great Mother (Mother Earth) and the concept of a rebirth (the death of one person who later returns, perhaps in a different form, and benefits all humanity). These themes are developed in widely different ways, creating profound differences in cultures.

Native myths and legends must not be confused with fairy tales. Fairy tales are a product of Western culture and are structurally and thematically different. While they all take place at some point in the past, a fairy tale has an ambiguous, dreamy beginning - "Once upon a time" - whereas Native myths and legends have more down-to-earth starting points like "One day Nanabush went walking." In addition, a fairy tale has an abrupt and conclusive ending: "And they were married and lived happily ever after", whereas the ending of a myth or legend may be almost a non-ending; indeed, the ending of one story may well be the beginning of the next, joined by an extension of images and experiences. The magic number three is replaced by the sacred number four which has spiritual significance. There are no child heroes in myths or legends who must overcome evil adults. The expectations in reading a fairy tale are that the reader will be entertained through fantastic experiences; the expectations of a myth or legend are that the reader will learn about the culture's history, beliefs or moral insights.

Native mythology is unique in North America in that it not only dates back to ancient times, but it is still developed and transmitted orally today wherever oral story telling is a way of life. Myths arise out of dreams and visions, a practice common in all North American Native societies in traditional times and still found in many today. These myths are sacred, spiritual expressions treated with the utmost respect.

The influence of Christianity has been widespread among Métis and Native people, and often the Christian and the traditional beliefs have combined to create a new kind of story. Maria Campbell, a Métis, said of her grandmother,

Grannie was a combination of a very strict Catholic and a superstitious Indian, which made her the greatest storyteller in the world.[1]

Aboriginal parents and grandparents have transmitted these myths and legends from generation to generation with little interruption. There are, however, some Métis and Native people who have no knowledge of their mythology, especially those who have lost their languages. Fortunately, many myths and legends have been recorded in writing and most communities still have people who can tell the old stories.

An attempt has been made in this anthology to include different kinds of myths and legends, as well as representative stories from different culture areas. Many different storytellers are included, so styles will necessarily vary. They range from the carefully transcribed oral narrative by a non-Native listener to skillfully crafted stories by Native writers. Johnston, Kennedy, Clutesi, Green, Red Sky and Beardy all submitted their stories to earlier publications. Gardner's story appears in print for the first time in this anthology. Norman listened to oral narrative sessions in northern Manitoba in the 1960s and he describes the events as well as recording the stories, whereas other stories come from collections where the actual listening event is not described. Whatever the mode of transmitting the stories has been, the characteristics of the stories show many similarities and delight readers of all ages.

1. Maria Campbell, **Halfbreed**. (Toronto: McLelland and Stewart, 1976) p.80.

Kinds of Myths and Legends

Native folklore can be divided into three general categories. Usually included under the broad term "myth" are the origin tales and the trickster cycles, while "legends" are those incidents which develop partly or entirely in human society.

Origin Myths

These myths deal with the changes from a mythological to a modern age. The mythological world of earth, water, fire, sun, moon, stars, seasons, and animals did exist, but not in the forms possessed today. Or some part of the world, vital to the good of humanity, was jealously guarded in some place, inaccessible to human beings. The idea of creation in the Biblical sense did not exist; the belief was much more evolutionary. Everything always existed but perhaps in hazy or incomplete form. Origin myths tell how the world as we know it today came to be. The following origin myths include how the Tse-shaht people got fire, the creation myths of the Piegan, Hurons, and Iroquois, how the Rocky Mountains were created according to the Dogrib oral tradition and the Ojibway myth of the origin of the Thunder.

How the Human People Got the First Fire (Tse-shaht)
Son of Raven, Son of Deer (Sidney, B.C.: Gray, 1967)
by George Clutesi

George Clutesi was an honoured singer, dancer, storyteller, and illustrator. He collected the Tse-shaht myths in a book called *Son of Raven, Son of Deer.*

> It has been said there was no fire at all amongst the human people. No one had fire, except the Wolf people.
>
> The Wolf people were the most dreaded people in all the land.
>
> "No other people shall ever have our fire," they would say, and they guarded it with care, for they alone owned the precious fire.
>
> "No one shall have it," they declared.

The human people wanted and needed the fire very much. Great chiefs and their wise councillors would sit and make plans, and more plans to find a way in which to capture the wondrous fire.

"Let us call all the strong and brave men," the wise men would say.

So the great chiefs from all the land would command that all men come forward and try to capture the fire. The strongest would boast that he would go forth to the land of the Wolf people and force his way into their village and bring the fire back. He was strong. The brave knew no fear. He would go forth and capture the fire.

The wise one would say, "I will find a way to win the fire. I am wise."

The fastest would boast, "I will run off with the fire and bring it here to you all. I am fast."

One by one they would go out to capture the fire, and one by one they would come back with the same story. It cannot be done!

The strongest would say, "I could not even get near the village of the dreadful Wolves. They have guards all over the place of the fire. No one can ever enter their village. We can never have the fire. The Wolves are too smart for us."

The fastest would say, "I got so close to their village that I could smell the food roasting in their great fires, but I could not enter their great house."

The wise old one would say, "I'll think of a way."

The great chief was very sad. His best men had failed him and all the people of the land.

"What shall we do? What can we do? We shall be cold again this winter. We shall again eat cold, raw food. We shall be blind by night when the moon will not give us light, and there is no fire to light the way. We must have fire! We must!" cried the great chief in despair.

No one spoke. No one moved. All eyes were cast down. All had tried and all had failed. All the people were very sad indeed.

But there was really no great need for sadness, for all the while the great council had met - the many trials to capture the fire -

young Ah-tush-mit, Son of Deer, had the real secret of how to procure the fire from the Wolf people.

All throughout the great struggle for the possession of the fire Ah-tush-mit had been gambolling about the beach, racing, leaping and hopping about on his long spindly legs. He had seemingly paid no heed to all the great fuss about the fire.

He was racing past the people, as he had done so many times before, when suddenly he stopped directly in front of the chief and announced very simply in a small, small voice, "I'll get you the fire."

"You will what? What did that little boy say?"

There was anger in the loud queries from the great braves and the strong men.

Then from the foolhardy ones a loud hee-haw went up - "Ho-ho-ho-ho-ho-ho."

"I'll get you the fire," the small boy repeated quite unabashed and not a bit frightened of the braves and the strong men, for he knew they had all tried and had failed to capture the fire.

Looking the great chief full in the face, Ah-tush-mit repeated again, "I'll get you the fire."

The little boy stood there, so small, so tiny and foolish looking among the great strong men. The wise chief was solemn while the others chuckled and laughed.

Ah-tush-mit, the Son of Deer, began twitching his long, long ears and rolling his big eyes as he looked this way and that way - but still he held his ground.

"I'll get you the fire," he persisted.

At last the great chief looked up and said, "Choo - all right - Ah-tush-mit, my strongest, bravest, fastest and wisest have all failed. Do the best you can."

Ah-tush-mit called the womenfolk together.

"Make me the most colorful costume you can," he commanded. "I am going to dance for the great Wolf chief."

"Dance? Who wants to dance at a time like this?" all the women wanted to know. "The boy is really foolish. He is wasting our time," they all declared.

"Obey and do everything Ah-tush-mit says," the wise old chief commanded his people. "Let the boy try. Give him a chance as I did to all of you," he continued.

Thus the womenfolk made him a red head-band, a sash for his belt, bands for his knees and elbows, and for his ankles too. All these were made from the inner bark of the cedar tree, and dyed the colour of the young cohoe salmon - as red as red can be.

Ah-tush-mit fitted and worked with his regalia until it was just right. He paid especial attention to the bands for his knees. He kept remarking these knee-bands had to fit exactly right - not too tight, not too loose - just right so that he could dance well for the great Wolves.

While he was paying special attention to the knee-bands no one noticed that he tucked something into them between the bark and the skin. He worked with the knee-bands and finally they were smooth and exactly to his liking.

"Now I want the best drummers and singers," he announced. "Come with me to the outskirts of the Wolf village. Do not enter with me. When I give the signal you must all run back home as fast as you can."

"We shall go before dark so that you can reach your homes before the night blinds you," he assured the brave men and women drummers and singers who were to risk their very lives to accompany him to the outskirts of the Wolf village.

At last everything was in readiness. Evening came. Ah-tush-mit sallied forth to capture the fire for the human people from the most dreaded people in the land, the Wolf people.

"Show yourselves. Do not hide or sneak in any manner," he warned. "The Wolf people are wise and cunning. They would be sure to see us anyway, even if we were to try and sneak in by the dark of the night."

So the odd little company sang and beat their drums with all their might and main. The Wolf people heard them from a long distance off they sang so lustily. One strange thing took place. Ah-tush-mit did not take the lead as everyone had expected. Instead he hid himself behind the company of the drummers.

"Ah, the foolish boy is now too frightened to show himself?" the women asked one another.

Finally the group of singers and drummers reached the outskirts of the great village of the dreaded Wolves. The huge doors of the house opened slowly, and the biggest, fiercest-looking Wolves bounded out to see what all the noise and din was about.

The humans could see the large fire burning and blazing inside the great house of the Wolves. They could almost feel the heat and the smoke smelled so sweet as they inhaled with all their might, for they had never before seen or smelled the fire.

What a wondrous beautiful sight! Great sparks burst and escaped through the smoke hole on the top of the great roof. What a wonderful thing! So bright and beautiful in the gathering gloom of the dark night. These were the thoughts that ran through the minds of the awe-stricken humans.

Suddenly Ah-tush-mit sprang forward from his place of concealment. He was on all fours as he began his dance. He sidled towards the door of the great Wolf house. It was fast getting dark. The flickering light from the fire reached out to him and cast pleasing shadows all around as he danced and sprang about on his four spindly legs. Suddenly, he made the signal and the singers and drumers stopped their din abruptly and fled for home as they had been instructed.

Little Ah-tush-mit was left all alone with the fire and the fierce Wolves. There were no more drums nor singers to give him courage, and he was very frightened. He was very, very frightened indeed.

He could hear the Wolf chief asking, "What is all the noise about?"

A Wolf guard answered, "It is only young Ah-tush-mit dancing."

"Send him away," the chief growled.

"Ah, what a jolly little boy! Bring him in. Do let him in," the Wolf chief's wife called out.

"Let us see him dance for awhile, then send him home," the chief agreed.

Ah-tush-mit increased the pace of his dance. Towards the great doors he pranced, hopping straight up and down, with no bend to his knees. Hop, hop, hop, hop, he went, sidling ever closer to the opening of the doorway, and as he circled around he sang a rollicking ditty:

Kiyaaa tlin, tlin, tlin, tlin,
Kiyaaa tlin, tlin, tlin, tlin,

Ooo nootl sahshh keeyah-qwa-yup qwatlin,
Hee yah ahh haaa ya-yaulk tah khaus ti-nah-is,
Kiyaaa tlin, tlin, tlin, tlin,
Kiyaaa tlin, tlin, tlin, tlin,

Break, crack, crack, crack, crack,
Break, crack, crack, crack, crack,
Do I break yon stakes with these I wear?
My flints, my sandstone hooves,
Break, crack, crack, crack, crack,
Break, crack, crack, crack, crack,

Ah-tush-mit's voice was small, but he sang with all his heart. He sang with all his might. He was singing to capture a spark. Ah-tush-mit was singing for his life!

Hop, hop, hop, hop, stiff-legged, he entered the doors. Once inside he could see the fire burning brightly and all about it was a bed of stakes made of broken bones implanted into the earth, as sharp as mussel shells they were. This is what his little song was all about. Up to this very minute no human who had ever tried to get past that awful bed of bone stakes had lived to tell the tale.

Ah-tush-mit danced with all his heart. He danced as he had never danced before. He danced so he might capture a tiny spark. Ah-tush-mit danced for his life.

"Kiyaaa tlin, tlin, tlin, tlin," he sang as he sidled ever closer towards the awful trap made with broken bones. Skirting its edges in a half circle, he danced towards a far corner, closer to the fire, but where the bones were neither so large nor too plentiful in the ground.

Suddenly he had arrived at his chosen spot and with a mighty leap he was among the broken bones, hopping higher and ever higher as he picked his way among the sharp spear-like bones. His sharp little feet seemed to fit around and pass between the dangerous bones harmlessly. His long shanks and slim legs kept his plump little body safely away from the sharp, sharp points and thus he was saved from being torn to shreds.

"Do I break yon stakes of bones with these I wear? My flints, my sandstone hooves?" he sang.

The Wolf people were completely fascinated. Their big and awful jaws hung open in wonderment. Ah-tush-mit had won the cheer and applause of the Wolf people.

The little fellow's bright costume glowed in the firelight.

"Break, crack, crack, crack, crack," his little song floated over the great fire. "With these I wear my flints, my sandstone hooves," he carolled as he suddenly sprang right beside the great fire.

Ah-tush-mit sang louder and louder; he leaped higher and ever higher; he was dancing to capture a spark; he was dancing for his very life.

"Ah, what a jolly little boy! He is a dancer, a good dancer," the mamma Wolf beamed.

Then it happened - as quick as a flash - before your eyes could blink. Ah-tush-mit had turned towards the roaring fire and with a mighty leap he sailed into the air - right over the roaring fire sailed he.

"Ho-ho-ho-ho-ho," roared the Wolves. "Ah-tush-mit is on fire. Ho-ho-ho-ho-ho."

Ah-tush-mit had indeed caught on fire. His little legs smouldered between the knees. He stopped his dancing and bounded through the great doors with a mighty leap. Once clear of the great Wolf house he raced for his life towards home as fast as he could run.

All around the leaping, roaring fire the Wolves sat bemused. The whole action of the little Ah-tush-mit had happened so quickly and seemingly without intent that they were taken completely by surprise. Before they realized what had occurred Ah-tush-mit was well away from the Wolf village. Ah-tush-mit, the Son of Deer, the fleetest of them all, had completely outsmarted the Wolves, the most dreaded people of the land.

With a spark smouldering between his knees he had captured the fire! With his sharp pointed feet, his flints and sandstone hooves he had successfully run the sharp broken stakes of bones.

Yes indeed, with his colourful costume, his captivating dance, he had outwitted the most cunning people of the land. Ah-tush-mit, Son of Deer, the small one, had captured the fire for the human people.

The secret something Ah-tush-mit had tucked between his knees had been a small bundle of very dry sticks he had gathered from the undermost branches of the spruce tree. It was this that had caught fire since it was dry as dry can be, and even some of the spruce gum still stuck to the twigs. When the sticks caught fire the cedar bark bands had smouldered until he reached home with the tiny sparks of fire. This was where the tinder had come from and where the human people first came to know about fire.

But Ah-tush-mit had burned himself. The inside of his knees were badly scorched. Thus it is to this day that the inside of all deers' knees are singed black. That is how the human people got their first fire.

In the growing season, when all living things burst out in bloom
Sit in the glade of the wood at even-tide.
If your own heart be open to love be there for Ah-tush-mit
You will hear the thump and the beat of his little song:
Thump, thump, thump, thump.

A Piegan Creation Myth
Indian Legends of Canada (Toronto: Gage, 1974)
by Claude Mélançon

Long ago, the Spirits above sent the Great Water to flood the world below where men and women used to live. Afterwards Napiwa, the Old Man, created our floating island from a grain of sand in the following manner. When the time came to look for this grain of sand, Napiwa was floating on a raft with Nanoss, the Old Woman, and all the animals. He sent the otter down first. She dived at sunrise and when she surfaced at sunset she was dead. The Old Man examined her paws but didn't find anything, so he told the beaver it was his turn to dive. Two days later, the beaver surfaced lifeless, his paws empty. The loon was next. He stayed under water for three days before he died and he brought back nothing. Napiwa then asked the muskrat to go, and he stayed under for four days. When he floated back up to the surface he, too, was dead. However, one of his front paws was closed. Napiwa opened it, removed the grain of sand hidden inside, and from it made our island.

When he thought our island was big enough, Napiwa sent a young wolf to find out where it ended, but the wolf died of old age before he got there. Nevertheless, the Old Man was satisfied and set out on a journey with the Old Woman.

The two of them were walking beside a river with banks of clay when the Old Woman said to the Old Man,

"Your island is big and beautiful, but something's missing. How about filling it up with some people?"

"That's fine by me," said the Old Man, "but I'll have the first word."

"All right," said the Old Woman. "And I'll have the last word."

"I'll get started then," announced Napiwa. "Men will be made of wood and they'll grow like trees."

"No!" said Nanoss. "They'll be made of flesh and will reproduce their kind like animals."

"Let it be so," said the Old Man. "But they'll have square faces, with the mouth running up and down and the eyes above, one on top of the other, and an ear on either side of the nose."

"I don't like that design," said Nanoss. "Men will have round faces, with the mouth horizontal, and an eye on either side of the nose. Their ears will be placed on each side of their head. Otherwise, they won't be able to hear their enemies coming without getting a noseful of dirt."

"Let it be so," said the Old Man. "But they'll have four arms and four legs, and ten fingers on each hand."

"That's far too many," said Nanoss. "They won't work any better if they have four arms rather than two, and four legs won't let them walk any more quickly. They'll have two arms, two legs, and four fingers and a thumb on each hand."

"Let it be so," said Napiwa. "But men won't have to eat or wear clothes. They and their wives will spend all their time together playing with their children."

"No! No!" said Nanoss. "Men will become bored doing nothing, and their wives will get tired of having them around all the time. Men will hunt all day and won't return to the teepee until sunset. While they're gone, women will gather wood and nuts, pick fruit, and dig up roots. They will also dry meat and tan hides. While they work, they'll think of their men and be glad to see them come home."

"Let it be so," said the Old Man. "But men and women will not die. They will live forever and will never part."

"No," said Nanoss. "It's better that they die. Otherwise your island will have too many people, and there won't be enough food for everybody."

"I don't think it should be so," replied the Old Man.

"But we agreed," insisted the Old Woman.

" 'No', I tell you," replied the Old Man.

"And I'm telling you 'Yes'," shouted the Old Woman.

"All right! All right!" said Napiwa. "We'll settle this another way. I'm going to throw this chip of wood into the water. If it floats, men will remain dead for four days and then come back to life."

He threw the chip of wood into the water, and it floated.

"There, you see," said Napiwa.

"No," replied Nanoss, "we're not going to settle it like that. I'm going to throw a stone into the water. If it floats, men will remain dead for four days and then continue to live. If it sinks, they'll be dead forever."

She threw the stone in, and it sank immediately.

"There we are," said Nanoss. "Now men will feel a little sympathy for one other."

"Let it be so," said the Old Man.

Several moons later, Nanoss gave birth to a little girl whom she loved very much. But when the child was old enough to help her mother with the chores, she died. Nanoss regretted having wanted men to remain dead forever. She went to find the Old Man and said to him,

"Can't we go over that problem we disagreed about last time?"

"No," said the Old Man. "That problem's settled. What's done is done."

The Creation Myth of the Hurons and the Iroquois

Indian Legends of Canada (Toronto: McClelland and Stewart, 1960)
by Ella Elizabeth Clark

In the beginning, there was nothing but water - nothing but a wide, wide sea. The only people in the world were the animals that live in and on water.

Then down from the sky world a woman fell, a divine person. Two loons flying over the water happened to look up and see her falling. Quickly they placed themselves beneath her and joined their bodies to make a cushion for her to rest upon. Thus they saved her from drowning.

While they held her, they cried with a loud voice to the other animals, asking their help. Now the cry of the loon can be heard at a great distance over water, and so the other creatures gathered quickly.

As soon as Great Turtle learned the reason for the call, he stepped forth from the council.

"Give her to me," he said to the loons. "Put her on my back. My back is broad."

And so the loons were relieved of their burden. Then the council, discussing what they should do to save the life of the woman, decided that she must have earth to live on. So Great Turtle sent the creatures, one by one, to dive to the bottom of the sea and bring up some earth. Beaver, Muskrat, Diver, and others made the attempt. Some remained below so long that when they rose they were dead. Great Turtle looked at the mouth of each one, but could find no trace of earth. At last Toad dived. After a long time he arose, almost dead from weariness. Searching Toad's mouth, Great Turtle found some earth. This he gave to the woman.

She took the earth and placed it carefully around the edge of Great Turtle's shell. There it became the beginning of dry land. On all sides, the land grew larger and larger, until at last it formed a great country, one where trees and other plants could live and grow. All this country was borne on the back of Great Turtle, and it is yet today. Great Turtle still bears the earth on his back.

After a while, the woman gave birth to twins, who had very different dispositions. Even before they were born, they struggled and disputed. The mother heard one of them say that he was willing to be born in the usual manner; the other angrily refused to be born in that way. So he broke through his mother's side and killed her.

She was buried in the earth, and from her body grew the plants that the new earth needed for the people who were to be created. From her head grew the pumpkin vine, from her breasts the corn, and from her limbs the bean.

The twins were not men, but supernatural beings; they were to prepare the new earth to be the home of man. As they grew up, they showed their different dispositions in everything they did. Finding that they could not live together, each went his own way and took his portion of the earth. Their first act was to create animals of different kinds.

Evil Brother, whose name means "flint-like," created fierce and monstrous animals, to terrify and destroy mankind. He created serpents, panthers, wolves, bears - all of enormous size - and huge mosquitoes that were as large as turkeys. And he made an immense toad that drank up all the fresh water that was on the earth.

Good Brother, at the same time, was creating the harmless and useful animals - the dog, the deer, the elk, the buffalo, and many birds. Among them was the partridge. To the surprise of Good Brother, Partridge rose in the air and flew toward the country of Evil Brother.

"Where are you going?" asked Good Brother.

"I am going to look for water," answered Partridge. "There is none here, and I have heard that there is some in the land of Flint."

Good Brother followed Partridge, and soon he reached the land of Evil Brother. There he was met by the giant snakes, the fierce beasts, and the enormous insects his brother had created. Good Brother overcame them. He could not destroy them, but he made them smaller and less fierce, so that human beings would be able to master them.

Then Good Brother came to the giant toad. He cut open the toad and let the water flow forth into the land. Thus rivers were formed. Good Brother wanted each stream to have a two-fold current, so that one side of the river would flow in one direction and the other side in the opposite direction.

"In this way, people can always float downstream," he explained.

"That would not be good for the people," said Evil Brother. "They should have to work one way."

So he made the rivers flow downstream only. And to make paddling a canoe harder and more dangerous, he created rapids and waterfalls and whirlpools in the rivers.

In a dream, Good Brother was warned by the spirit of his mother to be careful, lest Evil Brother destroy him by treachery. When the twin brothers saw that they would always disagree, they decided to have a duel. The one who was victorious would be the master of the world. They decided also that each of them should tell the other what weapon could destroy him.

" I can be destroyed," said Good Brother, "only if I am beaten to death by a bag full of corn or beans."

" I can be destroyed," said Evil Brother, "only if I am beaten to death with the antler of a deer or the horn of some other animal."

They set off a fighting ground, and Evil Brother started the combat.

He struck his brother with a bag of corn or beans, chased him over the fighting ground, and pounded him until he was nearly lifeless. His mother's spirit revived him and he recovered his strength.

Then Good Brother seized a deer's antler, pursued his brother, and beat him until he killed the evil one.

After his death, Evil Brother appeared to his brother and said, "I am going to the far west. Hereafter, all the men will go to the west after death."

The Creation of the Northern Rocky Mountains (Dogrib)
Indian Legends of Canada (Toronto: McClelland and Stewart, 1960)
by Ella Elizabeth Clark

The Big Man, Naba-Cha, was one of the very largest men who ever lived. The lodge which was his home was made of three hundred skins of the biggest caribou that could be killed on the plains that lie north of his river. The dish from which he ate his meals was made of the bark of six huge birch trees. And it took one whole moose, or two caribou, or fifty partridges to feed him every day.

Big Man was known throughout the whole North Country, for he had often made war against the tribes to the north, the east, and the south. Northward he had travelled to the mouth of the Big Water to fight the Snow Men, the Eskimos. Eastward, he had crossed Great Bear Lake to the country of the Yellow-knives. There he had seen the pure copper shining in the sands of the rivers that flow toward Great Bear Lake and Great Slave Lake and toward the icy ocean.

Southward, he had travelled a long distance to the great plains, the country of the Crees, where he had seen many large animals. But westward he had never gone, because there lived a giant man, a man bigger than Naba-Cha.

Naba-Cha was not only big; he was wicked and very cruel. He was especially cruel to a Cree boy he had brought back from the south one time when he was on the war-path. The boy was an orphan, without father or mother, sister or brother, to help him escape. His name was Caribou-footed.

The boy had one friend in the lodge of Big Man. That was Hottah, the two year old moose, the cleverest of all the northern animals. Swift he was, too. He had travelled, in one day, all the long distance from the mouth of Big Water to the home of Big Man.

Hottah liked Caribou-footed so much that he wanted to help him escape from Big Man. He knew that far to the westward, much farther west than Big Man had ever gone, flowed another river almost as long and as wide as Big Water. The Yukon, it is called. West of the Yukon, he knew, lay safety for Caribou-footed. There lived Nesnabi, the Good Man.

So one day Hottah said to the boy, "We will go away. You take a stone, a clod of earth, a piece of moss, and a branch of a tree. Together we shall escape from the cruel Big Man. I will carry you on my back."

Caribou-footed gathered the things he was told to get, and soon the two were ready to leave. Hottah took the boy upon his back and carried him out to the great plains west of the Big Water. But before long they saw Big Man coming behind them, riding his great caribou.

"Fling out behind you your clod of earth," said Hottah to the boy.

Caribou-footed did so, and at once there rose behind them, between them and Big Man, great hills of earth. The hills were so high and wide that it was many days before Big Man came in sight again. During those days Hottah chewed the sweet grass that grew west of the hills, and Caribou-footed ate the ripe berries.

When Big Man came in sight a second time, Hottah called to the boy, "Fling out behind you your piece of moss."

Caribou-footed did so, and at once a vast muskeg-swamp lay behind them. For days the caribou and Big Man floundered in the muskeg, while Hottah and the boy moved on toward the setting sun. When Big Man appeared a third time, Hottah said to the boy, "Fling behind you your stone."

Caribou-footed did so, and at once there rose behind them, between them and Big Man, high rocky mountains. Up to the clouds they rose, white with snow, more magnificent than had ever been seen before. It was a long time before Big Man and his caribou had crossed the mountains and appeared again to Hottah and the boy. Then they were much nearer their goal, the great western river.

"Now fling out behind you your branch of tree."

Caribou-footed did so, and at once arose a mighty forest, with trees so thick that Big Man and his gigantic caribou could not pass between them. Big Man had to cut his way through. And because its horns had stuck in the branches, the caribou was left behind.

By the time Big Man came in sight again, Hottah had carried the boy safely across the great river, the Yukon. Away toward the west it wound, through high rocky hills, foaming as it flowed.

Big Man reached the bank of the river and, seeing Hottah on the other side, called to him, "Help me, Hottah. Help me cross this turbulent river. If you will assist me to the country that lies beyond, I will do no harm to the boy. I promise you."

Without a word Hottah went to get Big Man. But as they were crossing the great river, Hottah dropped the giant into the water. Down he was swept by the swirling rapids of the river, on and on toward the setting sun.

Thus the wicked and cruel Bad Man, Naba-Cha, was lost forever, and thus Caribou-footed was saved. And in the far Northwest, the foothills, the muskeg-swamp, the snow-capped Rocky Mountains, and the great forests remain where the Cree boy threw the clod of earth, the piece of moss, the stone, and the branch of a tree, long, long, long ago.

Ishka-Maatuk and the Thunderbird Boy

Windigo and other Tales of the Ojibway
(Toronto: McClelland and Stewart, 1969)
by Herbert T. Schwarz

Along the shores of Kashishibog Lake there lived a large settlement of Ojibways. Their Chief was a powerful Medicine Man, and he had a beautiful daughter named Ishka-Maatuk.

Ishka-Maatuk was very much alone, for her mother had died when she was very young, and she had no brothers or sisters. The Medicine Man was very jealous of his only daughter, and all the young men of the village were afraid of his powers.

One day a visitor appeared on the shores of Kashishibog Lake. This was the Limping Bear, a sorcerer of some repute, who came from the little Grand Rapids on the Barren River. Several weeks before, he had dreamed of Ishka-Maatuk, whom he had never seen. In his dream he was so much impressed by her beauty that he decided to take her as his wife.

So he travelled for many days to Kashishibog Village. He recognized Ishka-Maatuk immediately from his dream, and finding her even more beautiful than he had hoped, he wanted her more than ever.

At first the old Indian Chief would not give his consent to the Limping Bear. The sorcerer tried to induce him with numerous gifts, and finally tricked him into smoking some tobacco mixed with grey mushroom powder - a very potent and evil medicine when properly prepared. Soon an oblivious sense of well-being clouded his judgment, and he gave the Limping Bear his daughter's hand.

Ishka-Maatuk was surprised and dismayed at this turn of events. She did not want Limping Bear as a husband. He was cross-eyed, he limped badly and he had a violent temper. Not wanting to embarrass her father, she stole away in the middle of the night and paddled westward.

She travelled in her canoe for many weeks and many months, passing swift rivers and crossing lakes and portages until she reached a clear, deep, blue lake encircled by huge snow-capped mountains. Ishka-Maatuk pulled her canoe to the shore of the lake, ate some berries and went to sleep, for she was very tired.

She was awakened from her sleep by a loud clap of thunder and a flash of lightning. At first she could not understand what had wakened her, for the sky was blue and clear and no clouds were to be seen. But violent thunder and lightning continued briefly, then suddenly the storm ceased. And there, standing right in front of her, was a tall young Indian with the most brilliant and penetrating eyes she had ever seen.

Ishka-Maatuk was very startled at his sudden appearance, and she asked him who he was.

"I am the Thunderbird Man in the form of an Indian," he replied, "and I have come to take you as my wife."

He then took her by the hand. Out of nowhere there was a crash of thunder and lightning continued briefly, then suddenly the storm ceased.

Ishka-Maatuk found herself on top of the tallest mountain where the Thunderbird Man kept his wigwam and his medicine lodge.

For several years Ishka-Maatuk lived happily as wife of the Thunderbird Man, and soon they had a son named Paisk.

But as the years went by, Ishka-Maatuk began to miss her native land and the people she used to know. So she asked her husband for permission to take Paisk to visit them. He agreed, and led them to a cloud. There was a brilliant flash and a loud rumbling, and they found themselves at the bottom of the mountain.

Tied to a rock on the shore of the clear blue lake was the canoe in which Ishka-Maatuk made her journey so many years ago. As they were making ready to leave, the Thunderbird Man warned Paisk never to point his arm at any living thing. "If you do, you will become a Thunderbird forever."

For many months Ishka-Maatuk and Paisk travelled eastwards, until Ishka-Maatuk saw the familiar shores of Kashishibog Lake, lined with the wigwams of her people. She was welcomed by her friends. The Old Chief was very glad to see his daughter again, and was proud of his grandson Paisk.

He still felt ashamed for being so badly tricked by the Limping Bear so many years before. He told his daughter that he took his revenge by casting a powerful spell on the Limping Bear's canoe.

It turned to a stone just as he was nearing his village and sank to the bottom of little Grand Rapids with the evil sorcerer in it.

Young Paisk was very happy at his mother's village. He played with the other Indian children and he learned how to hunt and fish. He was very much respected by his friends.

One day, Paisk and three of his friends were picking berries in the bush when suddenly an enormous elk leapt from behind a tree and stormed past the startled boy.

"Look!" shouted Paisk to his companions, pointing his arm at the running elk. He had no sooner pointed than, with a deafening thunderclap, a bolt of lightning shot from his arm, instantly killing the great elk. Terrified, his three friends ran back to the village, leaving a very perplexed Paisk in the bush.

As soon as the village elders heard of what had happened, they realized that Paisk was no ordinary Indian boy, but that he possessed some evil power. They were afraid that he might destroy them all, so they decided to banish Ishka-Maatuk and Paisk from the village forever.

The next day, the old Indian Chief returned from hunting to find his daughter and grandson gone. He immediately demanded an explanation. When told of the strange events of the day before, he thought silently for a while, and then he addressed the elders in these words:

"My brave and trusted friends, you have committed a grave error in sending Paisk away from the village. It is obvious to all of us that he possessed the secret of thunder. Had he stayed with us, our enemies would have been afraid of us and the Ojibways would be the rulers of the earth. Let us make haste and bring them back to the village."

Upon hearing these words, the strongest paddlers in the swiftest canoes set out in pursuit of Paisk and Ishka-Maatuk. They travelled for several days until on the fifth day they spotted the canoe of Ishka-Maatuk tied to a tree at Eagle Rock Lake. A small fire was burning on the side of a rock and the voices of Ishka-Maatuk and Paisk could plainly be heard over the water. So they called to them.

Suddenly, out of the clear blue sky there was a tremendous crash of thunder, and when they ran to the rock for cover, Ishka-Maatuk and Paisk were no longer there.

High in the sky, they heard the loud, piercing cries of Thunderbirds. When they looked up, they saw three Thunderbirds with wild flashing eyes flying westward.

Very much afraid, the Indians returned to their village. That was the last they heard of Ishka-Maatuk and Paisk, the Thunderbird Boy.

Trickster Cycles

The trickster-figure is found in all world mythologies though he may be interpreted in a wide variety of ways. Every Native culture also has a trickster figure, and the stories are very similar. He goes by many different names - Raven, Mink, Napi, Old Man, Coyote, Bluejay, Badger, Ishimiki, Manabozo, Nanabush, Wee-sak-a-chak, Iktomi, Cahkapes and Wichikapache, just to name some. The trickster was responsible for the changes that took place in the world. He could create, change and destroy, and though his motives were usually self-centered, the results were beneficial to humanity. The figure still exists in oral narrative today and his character has not changed over the years. He does not plan, he is impulsive, he is jealous and he imitates others without thinking of the consequences. The consequences are usually disastrous for him, but he must suffer alone; no one comes to his rescue. He is neither good nor bad, but is responsible for both because the reader can learn from the trickster's actions what is good or bad. It is not so much that he plays tricks on others as that he "sets them up" and his ploys invariably fail, much to his own grief.

Trickster stories are funny; irony is found in almost every one. It is hard to know whether the readers are laughing at the trickster or because the trickster reminds them so much of themselves, their friends, and family.

The trickster is male, but he can change his shape at will and many stories tell how he moved from an inchoate shape to the shape of a human male and how he learned about his sexuality. He seems to have no moral values and is always looking for women.

He is superior to human beings because of his ability to choose his form, but he is inferior because he does not think his actions through. Often he changes into the shape of an animal and then forgets that he cannot, while in that form, act like a human being. He does not possess animal instincts and is incredibly clumsy, so he is inferior to animals as well. The reader who takes everything literally may have some difficulty with this shape-shifting, but once the phenomenal possibility is understood the stories are coherent and entertaining.

The trickster is also the first of the picaresque heroes, the loveable rogues of fiction who travel from place to place, largely ignoring the rules of society. Popular throughout history, they continue as characters in modern television programming.

The following myth tells about the trickster's origins.

Nanabush, Kitchi Manitou's Emissary

Ojibway Heritage (Toronto: McLelland and Stewart, 1976)
by Basil Johnston

Basil Johnston is a teacher of Ojibway language, history, and mythology. He attended university in Montreal and has written numerous books about Ojibway culture.

> Nanabush was born of a human mother, sired by a spirit, Epingishmook, (The West). Like his older brothers, Mudjeekawis, Papeekawis, and Chibiabos, Nanabush possessed supernatural powers and was a spirit in nature.
>
> By the time that Nanabush was born, his older brothers had left home. He knew them only by name. Not long after his birth Nanabush's mother died, although some said she had been destroyed. Nor did Nanabush know his father. Without parents Nanabush was raised and nurtured by his grandmother.
>
> During his early years, Nanabush was like any other boy. He had much to learn. What learning and wisdom he acquired came from his grandmother.
>
> As he grew older, he often questioned his grandmother about his origin and about his father and his mother. Nanabush did not get any explanation. "Later," said Nokomis. "When you are older," she promised.
>
> By the time he grew into manhood, Nanabush came to realize that he possessed powers not possessed by others. It was at this point that his grandmother told him about his mother and her death. She also disclosed to Nanbush that his father was still alive and living in the west.
>
> Angry, Nanabush set out to find his father and avenge his mother. He decided to test his own powers and those of his

father in spite of his grandmother's objections. Nanabush made his way westward toward the Land of the Great Mountains, carrying only his bows and arrows and a small medicine bundle which an old man had given him.

At last, after many months, he came to mountainous country. Tired, and not certain how to find or recognize his father when he met him, Nanabush encamped under a great tree.

As he sat, pondering how he might find and meet his father, Nanabush heard someone call his name.

"Nanabush, beware of Epingishmook. He has great powers. He knows that you are here, and he means to come to destroy you. Go to the place of flint. Gather the pieces. Collect them and put them into the bag. Sharpen them; give them another force. They, in turn, will give you another power. They have within them the element of fire. Carry them with you always. Use flint. It is the only substance your father fears. It will injure him, but it cannot destroy him."

Nanabush looked up into the tree and saw only a woodpecker chipping away at the tree. Nanabush knew that it was woodpecker who had delivered the warning and given the advice. Grateful, he thanked the bird.

Immediately Nanabush went to the place of flint, gathered as many fragments as he could carry, and bundled them up. On his return to camp Nanabush sharpened the pieces.

While Nanabush was busy sharpening and polishing the flint, his father arrived. Nanabush greeted his father with respect but, at the same time, with fear and suspicion. Nanabush's father was massive, and appeared still young and unafraid.

Together they talked all afternoon and far into the night. When the east was begining to show the dawn, Nanabush told his father the purpose of his journey. "Father, I have come to avenge my mother's death. I have come to punish you for killing my mother, whereby I have been denied a mother's love."

Epingishmook looked at his son sadly and warned him, "My son, you may harm me, but you cannot destroy me. Neither my injury nor my death will restore your mother or allow you to know a mother's love. You are more spirit than man. Beware, your own powers are limited and may betray you."

Nanabush, though fearful, was not cowed. Rising up, he answered, "What you say may be true, but tomorrow I will fight you."

The next day, as agreed, Nanabush met his father on the great plain. The battle began. Epingishmook fired arrows that sizzled like bees; Nanabush hurled flints that whistled. All day the battle raged, with no advantage gained on either side. The missiles darkened the sky like clouds. That evening, the contestants, having exhausted their arrows and flints (although Nanabush, mindful of woodpecker's warning kept one small piece tied around his neck with a thong), met in hand-to-hand combat. Such was the violence of the fight that great clouds of dust rose into the skies and the earth trembled. When it seemed that the fight was going against him, Nanabush took out the flint he had concealed and slashed his father's head with it, cutting him deeply. As soon as the blood began to flow, Epingishmook conceded. Nanabush ceased fighting.

Epingishmook addressed his son, "My son, you have great powers. You are my equal, not more, not less. For all your powers you cannot vanquish me, nor I, you. Let us make peace. I shall remain in my place. Return to the Land of the Anishnabeg. Teach them until they are strong. In this way you and your purpose will be fulfilled and you will know love. As a remembrance of our contest and peace, take this pipe; carry it with you always. It is the emblem of peace and goodwill. Give it to the Anishnabeg."

Nanabush took the pipe and thanked his father. Together they smoked the Pipe of Peace, and composed their hearts and minds. After smoking, Nanabush returned to the Great Lakes to serve the Anishnabeg and carry out his purpose.

Nanabush had much to learn about the nature, extent, and limitations of his powers. Not only had he to learn what they were, he had to develop them, and foster their growth.

Nanabush was a supernatural being. As such he possessed supernatural powers. Of all the powers he possessed, none was more singular than his power of transformation. As a tadpole changes into a new being with a new form, as a caterpillar becomes a butterfly of dazzling beauty, so could Nanabush assume at will, and in an instant, a new form, shape, and existence. Nanabush could be a man, and change to a pebble in the next instant. He could be a puff of wind, a cloud fragment, a flower, a toad. And though Nanabush could become a physical being, essentially he was a supernatural being.

It was the only way that Nanabush could accomplish his purpose. As pure incorporeal being he would be neither accepted nor understood. He learned this early in his association with the Anishnabeg. Beings accept and understand only their own kind. A man understands and accepts another man, an eagle, another eagle. Whatever form or shape he assumed, Nanabush had also to accept and endure the limitations of that form and nature.

If he were to become an eagle, Nanabush could soar among the clouds, but he could not swim or dive as a duck. He could become a pine, stately and enduring, but then, he could not sing or run. A pine he was in form and nature. Were he to become a man or woman he could be as courageous or fearful as a man or woman could be; he could be generous or miserly; he could be true or he could be false; loving or hating. As an Anishnabe, Nanabush was human, noble and strong, or ignoble and weak.

For his attributes, strong and weak, the Anishnabeg came to love and understand Nanabush. They saw in him, themselves. In his conduct was reflected the character of men and women, young and old. From Nanabush, although he was a paradox, physical and spirit being, doing good and unable to attain it, the Anishnabeg learned. For his teachings, they honoured Nanabush.

Trickster stories were traditionally told in cycles; that is, the trickster went from one adventure to another. The stories were always told in the same order, and listeners could predict what would happen next. Unfortunately, few of these cycles have been preserved in their entirety. Trickster stories are parts of these cycles, and this likely explains why the stories do not have definite endings — another adventure lies ahead.

The following four trickster tales tell the same episode from the cycle. Style and events vary because each comes from a different culture area; each was told by a master storyteller in his own way.

Excerpt from: ***The Wish Bone Cycle*** (Swampy Cree)
The Wishing Bone Cycle (Santa Barbara: Ross-Erikson, 1970)
re-told by Howard Norman

Howard Norman attended the telling of this trickster cycle by Jacob Nibenegenesabe on July 26, 1969, near Kiskito Lake in Manitoba. The way the tale is printed suggests the emphasis of the storyteller. Words spoken loudly are written in capital letters, those spoken softly are in italics. The ends of the lines represent normal pauses in speech. Three heavy dots . . . represent a much longer pause.

While walking
he came upon a lake.
Ducks
were in it.
"Elder Brother," one called,
"What is that
you have on your back?"

Wichikapache said,
"The shut-eye dance."

"Show us then,"
the duck said.

"It's very difficult,"
Wichikapache said.

"Let us try it at least,"
the duck said.

"All right."
All right
Wichikapache said.
Then
Wichikapache built a dance lodge.
He gathered
many ducks

to dance.
They were ready.

"You must shut your eyes
for this dance,"
Wichikapache said.
"You must,"
is what he said.

Then
he began to sing.

The ducks danced
with their eyes closed.

Then, THEN And some say it was because
he thought the ducks had taken his clothes.
He began
killing the ducks.
I say
he was hungry too.

That was another thing here.
He killed a lot of them.
But a few had only one eye closed
because they had heard of Wichikapache's tricks
as they danced
these few had only one eye closed.
One of these shouted,"He's killing us!"
Some got away,
the diver duck
and one with a mask on.

WICHIKAPACHE
Wichikapache said,"I didn't have any dance!"
He said
he was hungry
and angry.

But
there was no one left to listen to him.

He began
to cook the ducks.
They were cooking on a fire.
So
he went walking.

• • •

Outside
he ran into a fox
"Ho! Little Brother,
let's race.
Let's race
and whoever wins
gets to eat all the ducks.
What do you say?"

The fox said,"No, I have
a bad leg.
And
the wind put a knot in my tail,
so I am unbalanced."

"O.K. then," Wichikapache said,
"I'll tie some rocks
to my leg."

"That's fair enough," the fox said.
Fair enough
he said.

WICHIKAPACHE
tied rocks to his leg.
They began racing.
Wichikapache was going slow
because of the rocks.

The fox was limping along
and his tail was flopping from one side
over
to the other,
flopping.
They ran toward a hill,
and each of them
went a different way around it.
As soon as the fox is out of sight,
out of Wichikapache's sight,
he untied the knot in his tail
and ran well again.
He ran straight back to the ducks
racing with his nose
the way there
and quickly ate them.

He ate everything
except for the feet and bills.

Except
for those.

• • •

That night,
it took him until night

Wichikapache arrived there.

He pulled one duck
out of the ashes.
"I cooked him too long," he said.
He pulled
ALL the duck feet and bills
out of the ashes.
"I COOKED THEM ALL TOO LONG!"

THEN, *then*
he understood.
He called out loud, "I MADE THIS WORLD
FOX,
I'LL FIND YOU!"

He went walking.

Looking.

• • •

And
he found the fox sleeping
and fat.
Wichikapache tried to think what to do.
He thought to himself,
"If I club him
I'll bruise the fur.
And I want it for a carrying pouch.
Well,
I'd better build a fire,
and let smoke go into his nose and mouth."

So
he set fire to sticks
around the fox.
The fox leaped awake!
He was encircled by fire.

"Ha!
You can't escape, fox!
You who ate all my ducks.
You who tricked me
and snuck back
to do some duck eating!"

Then
smoke went up all around.
When it subsided
there was no fox.
He had escaped.

"Where did you go
duck-breath thief?"
Wichikapache shouted.
"WHO DO YOU THINK MADE THIS WORLD?"

He went walking.

Wesakachak and the Geese (Cree)

Kent Gooderham, *I Am an Indian* (Toronto: Dent, 1969)
by Jackson Beardy

Jackson Beardy was a Cree artist and storyteller from Island Lake, Manitoba. He is best known for his art, much of which illustrates the myths and legends of his people.

"I think I'll go for a walk," thought Wesakachak one day.

As he was walking by a lake, he spied a flock of geese feeding in the marshes.

"I'm hungry and I would love a goose for a meal. But I wonder how can I be able to get them over?" he thought to himself.

Finally, he produced a large leatherhide and went to the forest. Coming to a swamp, he picked up some moss and bundled it. Then he walked along the shoreline with his head down pretending he did not see the geese.

It did not take any time for the geese to notice him.

"Look at Wesakachak with the bundle on his back. Let's ask him what he's got in his bundle," one of them said.

"Wesakachak, what are you carrying?" they shouted to him.

Still Wesakachak did not seem to hear.

"Wesakachak, what are you carrying?" they shouted a little louder.

This time Wesakachak pretended to look around for the voices.

"What did you say?" Wesakachak shouted back.

"What are you carrying?"

"I am carrying my song-bag," Wesakachak said.

"Let's hear you sing then."

"Oh, I have to build a lodge in which to sing, my friends. Perhaps you would be kind enough to help me build it since you want to hear my songs that bad?"

After they had finished the lodge, Wesakachak started to sing, making up songs as he went along. He gave instructions in song form as the geese danced them out. The loon danced in one spot by the doorway.

Soon Wesakachak began to run out of words. "Now we shall put our heads together," he sang.

And the geese danced with their heads together.

"I bring you the Shut-Eye Dance," he sang again. "Shut your eyes with your heads together and dance."

As the geese danced with their heads together, eyes closed, Wesakachak kept howling as he proceeded to lasso the flock of geese.

Just as he threw the leather rope, the loon by the door took a peek with one eye and howled at the top of his lungs, "Wesakachak is killing us all!" Some geese managed to escape, but as the loon was rushing out the doorway, Wesakachak gave him the biggest kick in his life on his rear end. To this day, the loon has a flat hip and cannot walk on land. The loon howls in the stillness of the wilderness, holding his rear end.

Wee-sa-kay-jac and the Ducks

Sacred Legends of the Sandy Lake Cree
(Toronto: McClelland and Stewart, 1971)
by James Stevens and Carl Ray

Wee-sa-kay-jac was walking on the shore of the lake. Over his shoulder he carried a bag of songs.

"What do you have in the bag, Wee-sa-kay-jac?" one of the ducks who was swimming on the lake asked.

"I keep my songs in this leather bag," Wee-sa-kay-jac answered politely.

"What kind of songs do you have?" another duck asked him.

"Ducks, I have many new songs for dancing," he replied. Then he added, "I am having a pow-wow and all of you are invited."

Now, everyone knows that of all the creatures, none enjoy dancing more than the ducks and water fowl. They happily accepted his invitation to the pow-wow, which was to be held in Wee-sa-kay-jac's longhouse. This big longhouse was built so well that there were no cracks to peek in to see what was going on inside. All of the ducks and water fowl in the forest went to the longhouse, singing and dancing to the drums and the new songs of Wee-sa-kay-jac. Into the darkness the merry birds kept dancing. Late that night Wee-sa-kay-jac locked the door of his longhouse to prevent intruders from coming to their party.

Then as the fire began to burn low and darkness grew in the longhouse, Wee-sa-kay-jac started wringing the necks of his feathery guests. Many of the birds had already been killed when a loon saw what was occurring. He screamed a warning to the other birds and he and his wife slipped under the wall of the longhouse, but Wee-sa-kay-jac stepped on their backs, breaking their legs before they escaped. The same thing happened to the water hens. Wee-sa-kay-jac crushed their back legs as they wiggled under the wall of his lodge. Some of the other birds managed to get the door of the big lodge opened and they escaped into the night. Wee-sa-kay-jac kicked one of the ducks in the backside as it went out the door and its shit flew sticking on the birch trees.

Our people say that because of the pow-wow Wee-sa-kay-jac held for the ducks, the loons and water hens now have broken legs and the birch trees have black markings.

The Race

Blackfoot Lodge Tales (Lincoln: University of Nebraska Press, 1962)
by George Bird Grinell

Once Old Man was travelling around, when he heard some very queer singing. He had never heard anything like this before, and looked all around to see who it was. At last he saw it was the cottontail rabbits, singing and making medicine. They had built a fire, and got a lot of hot ashes, and they would lie down in these ashes and sing while one covered them up. They would stay there only a short time though, for the ashes were very hot.

"Little Brothers," said Old Man, "that is very wonderful, how you lie in those hot ashes and coals without burning. I wish you would teach me how to do it."

"Come on, Old Man," said the rabbits, "we will show you how to do it. You must sing our song, and only stay in the ashes a short time." So Old Man began to sing, and he lay down, and they covered him with coals and ashes, and they did not burn him at all.

"That is very nice," he said. "You have powerful medicine. Now I want to know it all, so you lie down and let me cover you up."

So the rabbits all lay down in the ashes, and Old Man covered them up, and then he put the whole fire over them. One old rabbit got out, and Old Man was about to put her back when she said, "Pity me, my children are about to be born."

"All right," replied Old Man. "I will let you go, so there will be some more rabbits; but I will roast these nicely and have a feast." And he put more wood on the fire. When the rabbits were cooked, he cut some red willow brush and laid them on it to cool. The grease soaked into these branches, so, even to-day if you hold red willow over a fire, you will see the grease on the bark. You can see, too, that ever since, the rabbits have a burnt place on their backs, where the one that got away was singed.

Old Man sat down, and was waiting for the rabbits to cool a little, when a coyote came along, limping very badly. "Pity me, Old Man," he said, "you have lots of cooked rabbits; give me one of them."

"Go away," exclaimed Old Man. "If you are too lazy to catch your food, I will not help you."

"My leg is broken," said the coyote. "I can't catch anything, and I am starving. Just give me half a rabbit."

"I don't care if you die," replied Old Man. "I worked hard to cook all these rabbits, and I will not give any away. But I will tell you what we will do. We will run a race to that butte, way out there, and if you beat me you can have a rabbit."

"All right," said the coyote. So they started. Old Man ran very fast, and the coyote limped along behind, but close to him, until they got near the butte. Then the coyote turned round and ran back very fast, for he was not lame at all. It took Old Man a long time to go back, and just before he got to the fire, the coyote swallowed the last rabbit, and trotted off over the prairie.

Stories about the trickster continue to thrive, but the stories told in contemporary times would better fit the "legend" category. They develop in human society and reflect cultural settings, occupations, and interests of contemporary people. A story about the trickster in contempory times is usually told for pleasure and entertainment and incorporates activities involving this technological age. A story about the trickster trying to fly like Santa Claus is clearly not a sacred myth. Many of the trickster stories have been re-told as simple aetiological tales which are especially popular with childern. ***How the World Was Made Again*** and ***Why the Moose's Skin is Loose*** are stories such as these. They were told to Charles Clay by a Swampy Cree called Kuskapatchees, the Smoky One.

How the World Was Made Again
Swampy Cree Legends (Bewdley: Pine Ridge, 1978)
by Charles Clay

For many days and for many nights the animals drifted about on Wesukechak's raft, and in those long-ago times the nights were very dark since there was no moon. But the animals were brave, because Wesukechak was with them. Only Maheekun, the grey Wolf, who is a great coward, grumbled.

The raft drifted for so long that all the food gave out, and even Wesukechak despaired, for he thought the waters would not go down and the land reappear in time and thus all would starve. The days and nights dragged by as slowly as the snail walks, and still the waters did not go down. And Wesukechak cried out aloud in his distress, and said:

"O little brothers, have I only saved you from drowning to let you die from hunger? If I had some dirt, even a little mud, I would make you another world."

When Wesukechak spoke thus, Maheekun, the grey Wolf, howled. But Wuchusk, the Muskrat, said:

"O brother Wesukechak, let me help. Tie a thong around my leg and I will dive down for some mud."

So a thong was tied around Wuchusk's leg and down he dove - down, down, down. But he could find no bottom, and he came back gasping, half-drowned, and very unhappy because he had not succeeded. And then spoke Amisk, the Beaver:

"O good my brother Wesukechak, I can swim somewhat better than Wuchusk. Let me try."

So a thong was tied around Amisk's leg and he too dove down, down, far into the water; and he was away a long time; and at last he came back, but he had no mud. When Maheekun saw that Amisk failed, he howled louder than ever. But Nehkik, the Otter, spoke:

"O my brothers, let us not despair yet. I am an old and tried swimmer, and stronger than Wuchusk or Amisk. Tie the thong to my leg, brother Wesukechak, and let me try."

So the thong was tied around Nehkik's leg, and he dove into the water; down, down, he went, swimming his best, and Wesukechak let out the thong quickly. Many feet of it followed

Nehkik. And then it disappeared more slowly, and still more slowly, and finally it stopped, and was very slack.

The animals waited. It seemed a long time. But Nehkik did not reappear, and Wesukechak got anxious lest Nehkik drown. So he pulled on the thong, and he could feel something on the other end. And he pulled and pulled. And finally Nehkik was pulled to the top. He was limp and nearly dead, but under one of his paws was a little piece of mud which he had succeeded in scratching from the bottom before he lost his senses.

And Wesukechak took this piece of mud quickly, and he rolled it between his hands, and he blew on it four times, and the piece of mud grew into a ball, and Wesukechak rolled faster and blew louder, and the ball grew bigger and bigger. And finally when it grew too big for Wesukechak he blew a very loud blast and sent it spinning into the air, where it expanded into an enormous ball too big to see over.

And all the animals went ashore. And Wesukechak said to Kehkawwahkeen, the Wolverine:

"Run and see how big the world is now."

And Kehkawwahkeen ran around the world in a week, and he said:

"The world is too small, Wesukechak."

So Wesukechak blew some more. And the Wolverine was twenty days in going around the world.

"It is too small yet," said the Wolverine, and the other animals agreed.

Then Wesukechak blew and blew a great deal. And Kehkawwahkeen said as he ran off once more:

"If I do not return in forty days you may quit blowing."

The Wolverine did not come back, for the world was big enough. And these experiences made Kehkawwahkeen a great wanderer.

Then Wesukechak told the snakes to make rivers. And Maheekun, the grey Wolf, jumped about with his big feet in the soft earth and made hollows that formed lakes. And he pushed up big piles of mud with his nose, and mountains were made.

And Wesukechak ordered trees and grass to appear, and they appeared, for he had the power.

And that is how the world was made again.

Why the Moose's Skin is Loose

Long, long ago, when the rivers were young, the animals of the world had neither fur coats nor horns. They were all the same color, grey; and being without vanity they lived much together, as one big family. Nehkik, the Otter, was a good friend of Pisseu, the Lynx; Wapoos, the Rabbit, and Sakwaseu, the Mink, were often seen together; even Atik, the Deer, and Maheekun, the grey Wolf, were on speaking terms.

But all the animals suffered during the cold winter months; and after one especially long and chilling winter, Muskwa, the Bear, called a great council. Thus he spoke:

"O my brothers of the wilderness, this has been a hard winter. We have all suffered greatly. Our coats are not warm enough. Let us ask the Keche Manitoo to give us warmer ones."

The animals thought this to be a very good idea indeed, and wanted it acted on at once. Kakwa, the Porcupine, who is a very vain fellow, said:

"Muskwa has spoken well. I should like to add that we also ask for horns while we are at it. I think horns would be a good thing."

So Muskwa, and Kakwa, and Atik were chosen by the council to see what could be done, and they went at once to see Wesukechak. And Wesukechak said he would take the matter up with the Keche Manitoo.

Now the Keche Manitoo had seen what a hard winter all the animals had had, and he was quite agreeable. So Wesukechak called Muskwa, Kakwa and Atik to him and said that the Keche Manitoo thought it good to give them warmer coats, and Wesukechak asked if they had any ideas about what kind of coats.

And Muskwa said he thought there should be a variety to choose from, of different colours. And Atik said that he for one would like horns. And Kakwa said that he wanted a special coat made, of which there should be none like it. So Wesukechak appointed a day in the coming autumn when all the animals should search out a certain cave and choose their new coats.

This was very satisfactory. Muskwa and Atik and Kakwa returned with this message, and Wesukechak set about at once to make the new coats. He worked hard all summer, and by autumn had a great store of them all ready, of many shapes and colours. He also made a small number of horns. And for Kakwa he made a special coat.

The appointed day slowly drew near, and the animals began to collect near the cave. They came from many parts of the country, and they all wondered what their new coats would be like. Only one animal was not in a flutter, and that was Mooswa, the bull Moose, and he was very greedily eating water-lily roots in a nearby stream. Even when the animals all went to the cave he was not worrying much, but continued eating.

At the cave, however, there was a great excitement. The animals were very busy selecting their coats. Wapoos, the Rabbit, picked out a creamy white one, saying no one would be able to see him in the snow with such a coat. Pisseu, the Lynx, chose a handsome yellow coat, with little tufts on the ears. Atik, the Deer, liked a pretty fawn coat, and picked a pair of fine horns to go with it. Kakwa, the Porcupine, found a special package for him, and when he put on his quill coat, and heard it click when he walked, he was so proud he would talk to no one.

And as the animals chose their coats they went away. And Mooswa, who was busily eating all this while, saw them, and he left his precious water-lily roots and hurried to the cave. But, alas! when he got there, for he had to stop twice to eat some succulent twigs, only a great loose coat was left. Mooswa put it on, and it hung in floppy folds, and did not fit at the neck at all. It was far too big, but there was no other coat. The cave was bare, except for one pair of horns, a large flat pair, and not at all beautiful. Mooswa put those on, too, and sadly left the cave. But he was soon hungry, and he forgot all about his loose coat in a little while, because he was busy pulling up water-lily roots.

And that, Nosesim, is the story of the Moose's loose skin. The other animals, in their new coats, became so vain they wouldn't speak to each other for a long time, and some of them don't speak yet.

Legends

Legends have more individuality than myths because they reflect the culture of a specific people. There is more description of scenery and of individuals though the individuals and their emotions are not described in any depth. The events involve everyday activities but there is usually some supernatural element. Historical events may be included. The trickster, little people, monsters, and giants are all found in the legends, and the real and supernatural blend to provide entertainment and learning for the readers.

The Legend of the Qu'Appelle River (Plains Cree)
Indian Legends of Canada
(Toronto: McClelland and Stewart, 1960)
by Ella Elizabeth Clark

> Many summers ago, a young man came up the river alone in his birch-bark canoe. He was on the way to the village of his sweetheart, to claim her as his bride. In the darkness of the twilight and of the wooded slopes, he heard a voice speak his name. A strange fear came over his spirit.
>
> "Who calls?" the young man asked.
>
> No one answered. He heard only the ripple of the water, the wind in the trees, and then the echo of his voice asking "Who calls?"
>
> In a few seconds he heard the voice speak his name again, clearly and near by. It seemed to him to be the voice of his sweetheart, though it sounded more like the voice of a spirit than of a mortal.
>
> "Who calls?" he asked again.
>
> Again there was no answer except the ripple, the breeze, and the echo of his own question.
>
> Lonely and fearful, he continued his journey all the night. At sunrise he drew his canoe up on the bank and went toward the lodges of his friends. As he neared the camp, he saw a number of people around the home of his sweetheart. They were singing the songs of death. Without being told, he knew that his loved one had gone to the Land of Souls.

"When did she die?" the young man asked.

"Last evening," was the reply. "Twice last evening she called your name. And then her spirit departed from this world."

The young man remembered the voice in the woods. Silently he returned to the river, launched his canoe, and was never seen again. Ever since, travellers on the river have heard a voice ask, "Who calls?"

The Little People (Micmac)
Indian Legends of Canada
(Toronto: McClelland and Stewart, 1960)
by Ella Elizabeth Clark

The Little People are human beings, but very small. They live in caves, or they burrow in the ground. You may sometimes hear their footsteps in the forest on a still day, though they themselves are rarely seen. They generally remain quiet during the day but come out at night to revel and dance, to do mischief and perform wonderful deeds. If you should happen to offend them and they give chase, you must run for the nearest brook; if you succeed in reaching the further bank, you are safe. The Little People do not like to wet their feet.

One of them seems to be rather fond of fun, and he enjoys a joke at the expense of other people. Invisible, he comes prying around when you are busy, snatches up something that you are continually in need of, and slips it away. After he has enjoyed your embarrassment for a while, he slips the object back. Then lo! To your astonishment, it is before you, in plain sight.

Once in a while, in the forest, you will come upon stones piled together so as to make a little house. If you move them and go away, when you return later you will find them placed just as they were before you touched them. You will also observe many tiny footprints; if you follow them, they will lead you to a hole in some rock. If you really see these little people and associate with them, they will make you small like themselves. But you will not notice the change, and you will return to your normal size as soon as you leave them.

One day, long ago, when a girl was bathing in a river, she noticed a curious object floating down on the current. As it came closer, she saw that it was a tiny canoe paddled by an equally tiny man. Curious about him, she took the canoe in her hand and carried it home with her.

Her parents, when they saw the little man, were alarmed.

"Take him back at once!" they exclaimed. "Take him back where you found him, and let him go."

Crying with disappointment, the girl left the wigwam, but she played with the little man for some time before she carried him back to the stream. She set the canoe adrift at the very spot where she had picked it up, and then stood watching it. Coming to a rapid, it seemed to be in great danger of being swamped. Very much alarmed, the girl ran toward the rapid, but the little man guided the canoe skillfully through the white water and into the smooth stream beyond.

Before passing out of sight, the dwarf promised her that he would come back again. So every day she went down to the river to look for him.

One day when picking berries with some other girls, she saw a dozen tiny canoes coming up the river. In the first one was the little man she had played with on his earlier visit. He proved to be the head chief of a band of Little People. The dwarfs landed on the bank of the stream, and cooked a meal there. When they had finished eating, they said to the Micmac girls, "We will take you across the river in our canoes if you wish to go."

The girls laughed. "How can we go in canoes so small that we can pick them up in our hands?"

The Little People coaxed, but the girls only laughed again. At last the head chief asked his former captor to step into his canoe. Willing to humour him, she did so. To her astonishment, the moment she put her foot into it both canoe and chief grew as large as any canoe and chief of the Micmacs. But to her companions on the shore, she appeared very small.

At last she persuaded the girls to step into the other canoes. The instant they did so, she saw them have the same experience she had had: the boat and the paddler seemed to grow large, each girl seemed to become small. The Little People took the whole group across the river. As soon as the girls stepped ashore, the canoes and the crew shrank to their former size and floated on downstream.

Dan Kennedy's Story
Recollections of an Assiniboine Chief
(Toronto: McClelland and Stewart, 1972)
by Dan Kennedy

Chief Kennedy's Assiniboine name was Ochankugahe. He lived to be a hundred years old and remembered many of the old stories which were published shortly before he died.

In a large tribal encampment, two handsome youths lived with their parents. They were brothers, but their resemblance was so similar that everyone thought they were twins. They both had dark brown mounts that looked alike, and each had a dog that resembled the other.

It was a very unusual combination: two handsome young braves that looked so much alike one could not differentiate between them, two saddle horses resembling each other, and two dogs that looked alike.

One day the younger brave told his brother that he was thinking of going over to visit a tribe that was living towards the mid-day sun. So the next day he packed his personal belongings and left on horseback with his dog following. He had to travel four days before he reached his destination. As he reached the outskirts of the camp circle, he reined his horse up and from a knoll, watched the panorama of the camp activities.

The tribesmen, always on the alert, saw the stranger and speculated on his identity. Of course, they knew he was not an enemy, otherwise he would not expose himself openly. The Chief, who had two pretty daughters, called the younger one and told her to invite the visitor to his lodge. She walked over and told the visitor that he was invited down to the camp by the Chief. The girl accompanied him to the Chief's teepee.

Soon the Chief's daughter became infatuated with the handsome stranger, and pleaded with her father to let her marry their guest, to which the Chief readily agreed. Thus, willing hands put up a new lodge for the young couple.

A few days later the Chief told his son-in-law that the camp had no food and the people were hungry. Then he told him that half of the camp's hunters had disappeared. Whenever any of them went hunting they never returned and the rest became afraid to venture out for game.

Although the young brave was now apprehensive, hunger drove him to take the risk. He told his bride that he had no choice but to go out and hunt to feed her and her parents. Early the following morning he mounted his horse and went out hunting. His dog followed him. As he rode near the edge of the forest he saw a moose grazing in the open. He made a charge on the moose, but as he got near, it lifted its head, turned around and disappeared into the woods. He put on speed and followed the moose into the forest. When he got to the thickest part of the forest, it suddenly turned pitch dark. It was so dark that he was afraid to move either way, consequently he had no choice but to dismount and secure his horse to a nearby tree and make a fire. He decided to pass the night and wait for daylight. He fell asleep and that was the end of him.

One moon later, the older brother decided to find the whereabouts of his missing brother. He got on his horse and rode off toward the distant encampment with his trusty dog. He arrived at the camp and made inquiries about his brother. They told him that he had gone hunting and had not returned. The Chief also told him about the mysterious disappearance of their hunters. There and then he decided to locate his brother, cost what it may.

Then his brother's wife saw him and mistook him for her missing husband because of their identical appearance. She took him to her teepee and fed him. When it was bed time she coaxed him to come to his bed, but he refused to share the bed with her and sat up all night. Early next morning he mounted his horse and rode in the direction his brother went.

He rode a good part of the day when he saw the forest. And there, out in the open, close to the forest, stood the moose grazing. He followed it to the dense part of the forest, when suddenly it became dark. He secured his horse and made a fire and laid down, when an old woman appeared and came over and sat by the fire and spoke: "My grandson, I am frozen and had no way to warm myself and when I saw the fire I hastened over. You can sleep and I'll tend the fire for you."

Suspicious of the visitor, he punched a hole in his robe, in order to watch her machinations. The old woman kept talking while the hunter pretended to fall sound asleep. She kept telling him that a spark had landed on his robe, but he kept on snoring. However, he was wide awake and through the hole in the robe he kept a sharp eye on her movements. When she thought he was sound asleep, she took a stick and from her medicine bag pulled out two magic herbs. She talked to herself in the preparation of the magic herbs. "This herb is death and that one is life," she said softly.

She chewed the magic herb of death and spit on one end of the stick. She reached over to touch him with the magic herb of death when he grabbed the stick, took it away from her and poked her with it. She turned into a scraggy tree, and then he threw the stick and the magic herb of death into the fire. After this act, he carved another stick and chewed the magic herb of life and spat it out on the stick.

With the stick he went and touched the tree nearest the fire and it became alive - it was his missing brother. The next tree he poked with his magic stick was his brother's horse and the next was his dog. He kept touching all the trees until all the victims of the old woman came back to life.

Thus, after resuscitation, all the hunters returned to their families and only the old woman was left standing, a solitary emblem of evil.

Ack-koo's Song (Kwakewlth)
by Ethel Gardner

Ethel Gardner, a Sto:lo, studied creative writing at the University of British Columbia. She is presently working for the First Nations House of Learning, a program which works toward making university resources more accessible to First Nations People.

Once, long ago, in a Kwakewlth village, there lived a little girl named Ack-koo who had a harelip. She lived with her aunts, uncles, cousins, grandmothers, grandfathers, and parents in a Big House. Although she was very happy living with her whole family, she wanted most of all to be friends with the village children. But the children avoided her because of her harelip.

One evening, when Ack-koo was feeling lonely, she asked her Mother if she could visit her animal friends, Deer, Squirrel, and Frog, who lived in the woods.

"No, Ack-koo," her Mother said. "You must stay in the village when Sun greets Moon. The Other Ones in the woods awaken at this time. If they catch you, you will never see the village again."

"But Mother," said Ack-koo, "I have no one to play with. The village children laugh at me and make fun of me. I am so lonesome."

"E-ey, Ack-koo, you are too young to be so unhappy. Talk to old Kloksum who lives at the edge of the village. He is a wise man and understands the troubles of people. He can help you."

Ack-koo wondered what old Kloksum could do about her problem. He was so old. His hair was white as goat's hair; his face had many folds and the skin hung from his arms. He must have seen Bakus, the first part of the Kwakewlth year, and Tsetseka, the second part of their year, a thousand times. Ack-koo had only seen several. Ack-koo had never seen any other child enter old Kloksum's Ma-Gwiss, the small cabin where he lived by himself. The thought of being alone with him made her stomach feel like it had a burning rock in it. But Ack-koo obeyed her Mother and went to visit Kloksum.

She walked along a trail at the back of the Big Houses so the other children wouldn't see her and throw stones at her. But two young boys, Gah-ma-gee and Bob-bee-dee, spotted her.

"Yooh! There's Ack-koo! Ha, ha, ha! Let's chase her and beat her! She is so ugly!" said Bob-bee-dee.

"Whoo-ee, here we come, Ack-koo!" both boys yelled. They picked up some branches to beat her with and ran after Ack-koo, jumping and hollering. They were going to have lots of fun!

Ack-koo ran into the woods to hide. She hid behind some bushes, and there was Squirrel.

"Squirrel, you must help me," said Ack-koo. "Bob-bee-dee and Gah-ma-gee are after me to beat me with some sticks. Go in the other direction and make some noises in the bushes to confuse them."

Squirrel scurried away.

"Where are you, Ack-koo? We're going to get you!" Bob-bee-dee sang.

When Squirrel was far enough away from Ack-koo, he jumped into the bushes here and there. Krish-krish, krish-krish. He sounded like a person pushing away branches.

"Ah-ha, there you are, Ack-koo. We can hear you!" said Bob-bee-dee. "We're going to get you!"

When Ack-koo saw them running to find her, she darted toward Kloksum's Ma-Gwiss.

She stood in front of his house and yelled, "Yooh! Kloksum. I wish to talk to you."

"Whose child are you?" he asked. He did not wish to speak with certain families who were of a different clan and were his enemies.

"I am Ack-koo, child of Dee-ta and Numus," she called.

Kloksum appeared at the doorway of his Ma-Gwiss to greet Ack-koo. He had a blanket made of goat's wool draped around him.

"Ah, come in, Child," he said. "Come in and sit on the mat and have some tea."

Ack-koo entered Kloksum's Ma-Gwiss and sat down on the mat. Kloksum poured her some tea in a clay mug and sat down on the mat facing her. He lit a candle made from dried oolichan fish, for darkness was setting in. As Ack-koo watched the old man silently moving around she began to feel calm. Her unhappiness lifted. She did not notice anymore how old he was, nor did she feel afraid. Her eyes met his. His eyes were deep brown and reflected the flame of the candle. She bowed her head, looking at her little brown hands folded in her lap.

"Speak, child," said Kloksum.

"My Mother sent me to talk to you. She said you are wise and can help me," said Ack-koo.

"And what is your trouble?" asked Kloksum.

"I am ugly. Because I was born with a harelip, all the children in the village make fun of me and won't play with me. Just before I came here, Gah-ma-gee and Bob-bee-dee were chasing me with sticks to beat me. How can I have friends?" asked Ack-koo bitterly.

"Ack-koo, you are feeling hurt and angry, and I can feel your sadness. I cannot make the children play with you, but I can show you something." Kloksum reached out a hand and from a nearby wooden bowl, took a black seed. Holding it in the palm of his hand, he continued, "Look at this seed and tell me what will happen if you plant it."

"Why, it will probably grow into a beautiful flower," said Ack-koo, feeling confused because Kloksum was not talking about her problem. "What does this have to do with getting the village children to play with me?"

"You will not understand right away. The plant will grow to be beautiful, as you say. But before it does, it will have to turn inside out. And when you learn to turn yourself inside out, you will be able to show how beautiful you really are." Kloksum spoke softly and this made Ack-koo feel calm. "Have faith in what I say and you will learn what you need to know." He handed the seed to Ack-koo.

Ack-koo held it in her hand thoughtfully and then she remembered Gah-ma-gee and Bob-bee-dee who had been searching for her in the woods.

"Tell me about the Other Ones who live in the woods, Kloksum. Mother forbad me to play with my animal friends at the time Moon greets Sun. She said if I did this, I would never see the village again." Ack-koo was forgetting her sadness for the time being.

Kloksum responded, "Ah, Ack-koo, your mother was talking about the giant, Dzonagua. She is a wicked being who steals children, blinds them with pitch and carries them away in a basket made of cedar roots, which she carries on her back. Then she eats them."

"Ah-ee!" cried Ack-koo. "Bob-bee-dee and Gah-ma-gee might be caught tonight. Noo-la-gah and Oh-Dun will have no sons. Oh, poor Bob-bee-dee and Gah-ma-gee!"

Seeing that Ack-koo was troubled, Kloksum spoke to her again with his soft voice. "Be calm, little Ack-koo. If Bob-bee-dee and Gah-ma-gee do not return to the village, they will be taken care of by their guardian spirits. Do not worry."

Ack-koo replied, "Oh, Kloksum, I don't understand about spirits and Other Ones. But I must go home. Mother Dee-ta will be worried about me. It is late. Good-bye, old Kloksum." She ran back the same way she had come, behind the Big Houses and though she heard "krish-krish, krish" in the bushes, it was only Squirrel.

Once inside her home she crept through the Big House, past the fire in the middle, past her uncles and aunts and cousins, to the farthest corner where the poor people lived. She found her mat, reached for her woollen blanket, pulled it over herself, and fell asleep, thinking of old Kloksum's words.

In a dream, she saw a very pretty woman rooted to the floor up to her waist in the corner of a cabin. The pretty woman called herself Zoh-la. Zoh-la sang a song, a gentle and mysterious song that made Ack-koo sleep, deeper and deeper.

Then day came. All the people were awake and gone from the Big House when Ack-koo awoke. She prepared to go bathe and do her daily chores. When she went outside she was surprised to see only a few people.

"Where is everyone?" she asked her uncle Da-geek, who was preparing a fire for cooking.

"Bob-bee-dee and Gah-ma-gee could not be found in the village. The people are looking for them. Maybe they went into the woods and lost their way," he said.

"No," said Ack-koo, knowing that Bob-bee-dee and Gah-ma-gee knew how to find their way in the woods. "The giant Dzonagua, caught them. They will never return to our village again." Da-geek only nodded his head in agreement.

Ack-koo went to find Squirrel after her chores were done. She told him how sad she was for Bob-bee-dee and Gah-ma-gee. And she told him about old Kloksum's words about the seed and about Zoh-la in her dream. Then they heard singing. It was the mourning song, coming faintly from a distance. The people were returning from their search.

Time passed and Ack-koo did the usual things to help in the village. She picked berries, dug cedar roots and prepared food for the winter. These goods were well guarded by strong men for it was known that Dzonaqua stole furs and food from all the villages.

Every day, Ack-koo watched the village children play on the beach. How she longed to be with them! One day, as she was watching the children eating mussels, she wondered if she dared approach them. She thought about it for a long time and then decided to give it a try.

"Yooh," she greeted them. "Let me join you. I want to play with you." The children, upon seeing her, picked up small rocks and threw them at her.

"Go away. Ack-koo," they yelled. "We don't want you here. Go to the animals in the woods. You are too strange to be with us." Ack-koo ran away with tears streaming from her eyes. She went to look for Squirrel behind the Big Houses.

Ta-dut, ta-dut, ta-dut. Squirrel came from the bushes and Ack-koo bent over so Squirrel could jump on her shoulder. Squirrel wiped the tears from Ack-koo's eyes with his tiny paws. She pressed his little body against her moist face. "The village children think I'm strange because I have this harelip. I can do nothing about it. I was born this way," said Ack-koo. Then she thought about what old Kloksum said to her. "I wonder what old Kloksum meant about turning inside out. What did he mean, Squirrel?"

Squirrel jumped down from her shoulder and made a motion for her to follow him. Together they went into the woods. "Yooh Deer, Yooh Frog," she said as they passed by the animals. Deer nodded and Frog jumped up and down. Ack-koo felt happy being with the animals. But, oh, how she wished the village children would be friends!

Squirrel stopped when they came to a beautiful flower, the most beautiful one Ack-koo had ever seen. "Ah, Squirrel, you remembered Kloksum's words about the seed. And do you think that I can ever be as beautiful as this wonderful flower?" Ack-koo picked the lovely flower, and sat down on a stump. She thought about Kloksum's calmness and how his gentle ways made her forget her fear of him. She thought maybe the village children were afraid her strange looks would bring them bad luck.

Suddenly she realized that nightfall, the time of danger, was near. Squirrel was jumping up and down and pointing to the sky. "Come, Squirrel, let's go quickly back to the village." Ack-koo stooped and held her palm out. Squirrel leaped on her hand and ran up to his usual place on her shoulder. Together they fled through the woods. Ack-koo tripped on a rock and fell. Squirrel went flying onto the ground, tumbling over in a somersault.

As she raised her head Ack-koo saw, right before her very eyes, two huge hairy feet. She lifted her head until she saw the terrible face of Dzonaqua with the huge hollow eyes. With her lips stuck out, red and rounded, Dzonaqua grunted horribly, "Uh! Uh!" Dzonaqua swooped Ack-koo up with a big, furry hand and flung her into the basket she carried on her back. There, Ack-koo saw two other children who were weeping, a boy and a girl. Ack-koo told them not to be afraid, that she knew how to make a trail to find their way back to the village when they could escape. While Dzonaqua went tramping through the woods, Ack-koo broke off hemlock branches and dropped them on the ground.

The children stopped weeping when they understood what Ack-koo was doing. They had not understood her words, for they were of another tribe and spoke a different language. Ack-koo remembered that she had a mussel shell in the pouch she had tied around her waist. She used it to slit open the bottom of the basket and she let herself fall to the ground, followed by the two other children. Too late! They had reached Dzonaqua's Ma-Gwiss.

There she saw Gah-ma-gee and Bob-bee-dee eating tallow. Their eyes were covered with pitch. The smell in the cabin made

Ack-koo feel sick. There were no mats on the dirt floor and spider webs hung in the corners of the Ma-Gwiss. From the light of the fire, Ack-koo could see all the goods that Dzonaqua had stolen from the villages - baskets of crab apples, dried berries, dried meat and piles of skins of beaver, fox and bear. Then she saw, rooted to the floor up to her waist, Zoh-la, the pretty woman in her dream. Zoh-la smiled at Ack-koo and nodded her head. Ack-koo knew what she had to do.

Just as Dzonaqua was coming toward her to blind her with some pitch, Ack-koo began to sing the beautiful song Zoh-la had sung to her. Softly, surely, the other children joined in. Dzonaqua stopped in her tracks. Her eyes became heavy and her arms fell to her sides. Thump! She fell on the dirt floor, fast asleep. The children stopped singing, looked at each other and sighed in relief.

Ack-koo removed the pitch from Bob-bee-dee's and Gah-ma-gee's eyes. "You must help us push Dzonaqua into the fire before she wakes up," said Ack-koo. Dzonaqua had been feeding the boys tallow to fatten them up. She had been ready to cook them in a roaring fire. Together, the five children pushed the giant into the fire that had been made to cook them!

They uprooted Zoh-la and headed back to the village following the trail of hemlock branches Ack-koo had made. They arrived behind the Big Houses and heard the people singing the mourning song for Ack-koo. When Dee-ta and Numus saw her, they fainted and fell to the ground. Then Da-geek took Ack-koo in his arms and questioned her.

"What happened to you?" he asked.

"Dzonaqua carried me away to her Ma-Gwiss deep in the woods."

"How did you come back?"

"We sang a magic song to make Dzonaqua sleep. Then we pushed her into the fire."

"Who are the others? Where are they?" asked Da-geek. Ack-koo motioned for the others to come forward. All came except Zoh-la, who had disappeared into the woods.

Noo-la-gah and Od-Dun were happy to see Gah-ma-gee and Bob-bee-dee, but scolded them for not listening to their warning about going into the woods when they should not. Ack-koo told the people about the trail she had made with hemlock branches and about Zoh-la, who had appeared in her dream. She told the people that the two children with her were from another tribe and spoke another language.

Day came and all the people went to Dzonaqua's Ma-Gwiss. A mask lay where Dzonaqua had burned. It was taken back to the village with the riches they found there.

Ack-koo's father, Numus, made a feast for the people and gave the goods to everyone in a potlatch. The strange girl child was given the name Kla-pa and the boy was given the name Sea-pa. Da-geek and his wife, Gah-na-oh, who had no children of their own adopted them. For this great potlatch, Numus was made chief of his tribe.

All day long, the children of the village asked Ack-koo to tell them the story of how she tricked Dzonaqua. At night, Ack-koo sang the magic song to make the babies sleep through the night. Everyone spoke of the brave and clever Ack-koo who sang beautifully.

The next day, Ack-koo and Squirrel went to visit old Kloksum. She told him of her adventure with Dzonaqua and thanked him for his kind words.

"No one sees my harelip anymore," she said. "They only see who I really am. I understand now, Kloksum, about the beautiful flower that came from a seed."

Myths and Legends With Historical Content

The West Wind

Tales of the Mohawks (Toronto: Dent, 1975)
by Alma Greene

Alma Greene, also known as "Forbidden Voice", was a Clan Mother on the Six Nations Reserve near Brantford, Ontario. She worked tirelessly at keeping the ancient stories of the Mohawks alive.

An Indian maiden, close to marriageable age, was reminded by her parents of the traditions of her ancestors. The parents would look for a suitable husband, and when they found one they would purchase five yards of the finest cotton and present it to the future husband's parents. If it was kept by them, the daughter was accepted, and the two families could begin marriage preparations at once.

The Indian maiden was not happy with her parents' choice and asked them for a little time. She knew she would have to obey them in this matter, but she did not love the man and did not want to marry him.

The girl went for a walk to think about her situation. Suddenly she heard a voice, but looking around could not see anyone. It could only be the wind. But again she heard a voice saying: "Choose; take me. I love you very much."

The voice grew louder, calling, "Take me - I love you." This time she called back, "Who are you? I cannot see you; how can I marry you?" The wind wailed again, "Marry me, marry me. I am the West Wind, and I will die if you do not marry me."

Slowly the West Wind sighed to a halt. Suddenly the birds stopped singing; the sun darkened, the waters stopped flowing and the trees whispered, "Oh, Indian maiden, marry him." And the hills and bushes echoed, "Marry him."

The maiden's heart was touched, and she cried out: "Oh, West Wind, do not die; I love you; I will marry you."

The West Wind and the Indian maiden were married by the Great Thunder, who was wise and knew what was happening all over the world. There was a great feast, and everyone danced with happiness for the married couple.

Then the Thunder spoke in a loud voice to all the people attending the wedding. "Listen to me," he said. "There is one more thing left for us to do. We have witnessed a fine marriage. The maiden has been a loving daughter; her heart is sincere and pure and she is full of compassion."

The Thunder gave three loud claps. The third clap caused beautiful fireworks. When the clouds drifted away, a handsome Indian brave was standing in front of the maiden.

A wicked witch had turned this young man into the West Wind, and it was the maiden's love which had broken the curse. The Indian brave kissed his beautiful bride and told her he had watched over and loved her for many years. There was great rejoicing, and the couple was showered with gifts.

In the second year of their marriage, the Indian brave and his lovely wife became the parents of a little boy called Hiawatha.

Long before the coming of the white man, the ancient tribes had fallen into a savage state and warred continually one against another. Then the Creator-who-sees-all-things sent the Good Message to his people. He wanted them to know there was a Hereafter but they could not expect to go there if they continued to behave as they were doing.

This is how the message came to the people: A sentry going his rounds saw a man by a fire. The man told the sentry he was the One-that-always-was and had been sent from above. His face glowed with light. The warrior did not understand what he saw and heard, but he carried the tale to the Mohawk settlement.

Around the Council Fire it was decided that if the stranger could prove himself, the people would listen to his message. The stranger, who was called Daganawida, agreed to the conditions.

The people had Daganawida climb a tree, then they cut it down, and he fell into a deep chasm with a wild stream at the bottom. Daganawida made a stone canoe and by his divine power was able to float to safety in it. The Native people again saw the smoke of his fire and knew he had survived the ordeal.

The chiefs accepted the message of peace and goodwill and agreed that the fighting between tribes should stop. Daganawida planted a tree, then he knocked it over. Under the tree was a great hole filled with gushing waters, and the Native warriors threw all their weapons into the hole.

The Mohawk chief Hiawatha became Daganawida's helper, and the two together ordained the Chiefs of the Confederacy, even including Atotarho, the wizard and chief of the Onondagas. The Five Nations of the Confederacy (and a sixth which was admitted later) remain joined in brotherhood to this day.

Shaking Tents (Ojibway)

James Redsky, an Ojibway medicine man, remembers the stories originally told by Mis-quona-queb, one of the great leaders of the Ojibway. He also tells of his own experience in a book called *Great Leader of the Ojibway: Mis-quona-queb.* (Toronto: McLelland and Stewart, 1972)

The young Ojibway go out into the forest for several days. During fasting a spirit visits each man and tells him something he wants to learn about. The spirit may tell him that he will be the head man of his band; or the leader of the Mide-wi-win; or that he will be a great leader of his people. It is during fasting that some of the Ojibways learn the secrets of the mysterious and powerful jeesekum or shaking tent ceremony.

A spirit from the heavens - maybe it is a spirit from some other place such as the east, west, north or south - will tell this man how to operate the shaking tent. The fasting Anishinabi learns of the placement of the poles, the hoops and the birch bark coverings. He is told of the songs he must sing so they, the spirits of the world, can listen to him.

When the spirits talk to the Ojibway, he might not be able to understand their language. If this is the case, mikikinuk, the sacred turtle, is called in to interpret the spirit language into Ojibway. Mikikinuk is not a real turtle; it is actually the soul of some god that has become embodied in the turtle.

When the spirits begin to talk to the fasting Ojibway he is told exactly how to build the tent. Then he is instructed to enter the tent and hold one of the poles right at the bottom to start the tent shaking. The tent won't shake unless he does this and the spirits will not enter the tent until it begins to jerk back and forth. Sometimes little bells are placed in the tent so the observers know when the tent starts to shake. The tent does not move far, only four or five inches.

Inside the man must sing his songs, calling the spirits to visit him and to give him their words of wisdom and guidance. Sometimes four or five spirits will enter the tent, but they do not stay long. They are only allowed to stay for a few minutes. This ceremony is very interesting and very sacred; many of the

Ojibways will not even talk about it lest they anger the spirits of the shaking tent.

If an Indian wants to know how his friend is feeling and his friend is two or three hundred miles away - maybe he heard his brother was sick and he wants to find out how he is - he can use the shaking tent to find out the answer to his thoughts.

The sorcerer who works the tent won't use it unless there is something wrong - if someone is sick; if someone is attacking him; if someone is trying to kill him. If you want a sorcerer to use his powers just for hellery he won't do it because it would anger the spirits of the world.

I have a daughter who lives at Regina Bay over at the Whitefish Reserve and a few years ago she was very sick; she was getting tuberculosis. I was worrying a lot about her and my father said, "Why don't you go and see Kee-ghe-gu, or Little Heaven, who lives at Mackenzie Portage and ask him to put up a shaking tent? If you want, I'll go and ask him for you."

"Okay."

My father came back and told me, "He is going to do it tonight."

Little Heaven put up his shaking tent at Shoal Lake and he went in there and started the ritual. He asked me what I wanted to have this tent put up for because he would not use it unless it was something serious. I told him,

"My daughter at Whitefish is getting pretty sick."

"What do you think she has?"

"I think she has tuberculosis," I said.

So the tent started to move and the spirits entered the tent. Mikikinuk was there too and we could hear him say;

"Your daughter will be all right in two years, maybe three. They will come and take her away and when she returns she will be cured. She may live for another fifty years after this."

I was very glad to hear this news.

"I'll go down there and see her," mikikinuk said. "I'll see how she is right now."

In about four or five minutes, mikikinuk returned. He had travelled about one hundred and eighty miles across the Lake of the Woods to see her.

"She's pretty sick all right, but don't you worry, she will recover. The spirits have told you the truth."

Well, they took her away for about five years and she has good health now. She is living at Whitefish and she now has four children.

Not everyone knew how to work the shaking tents. The turtle, mikikinuk, was used to interpret the language of the gods that came into the shaking tent because these gods did not speak the Ojibway language.

Fred Cody from Camperville, Manitoba, used to be very good with the shaking tent. This story about Fred Cody took place in the 1930's at Camperville, so they tell me. An Indian fellow lost a pair of horses and could not find them. So they got the police to see if they could find them and the police could not find these horses anywhere. One of the man's friends suggested that they get the shaking tent to see if the spirits could help find the lost horses. The man who lost the horses said, "Shaking tent, aw, it can't do any good."

"Well, let's try Fred Cody anyway."

"All right."

A shaking tent is just big enough for a man to go in and lie down. They use six poles spread around with two hoops around the tent. One hoop is half way up and the other smaller hoop is at the top. They cover the shaking tent with birch bark or cloth.

Fred Cody came up to the tent and started smoking his pipe, talking to his gods to help him help these people find the horses. When he was ready to start they tied Freddy up, his hands and his legs were bound and then they put him in the shaking tent. Inside the tent Freddy started talking to his gods.

"Help me get these bonds off so I can work the shaking tent." All of a sudden he had the power to take off the ropes and the tent started to shake. Out came the ropes, he was free. Then a strange language filled the tent as the gods began to talk but no one could understand what they were saying so they went and got mikikinuk to interpret for them. Then Fred Cody said to mikikinuk, "Now there is a pair of horses lost from here. Maybe someone stole them. If they walked away they would have been back already."

Mikikinuk started to talk.

"Well everybody tried to find these horses, I shall try too. Down here about five miles north there is a man there and he has a little dust shed big enough for two horses. You go and look at that shed in the morning, or go right now if you want, and you will find the horses in the shed."

Early in the morning they walked down to that fellow's place.

"Have you got a pair of horses here?"

"No horses, no horses. I haven't got any horses here."

The two fellows looked at the little shed that mikikinuk had been talking about. They walked over and opened the door and discovered the two lost horses. They took the horses back home with them.

Stories of the Windigo

The Windigo or other cannibalistic figures are found in the harsh climates of northern territories. The stories usually deal with cold, hunger, and starvation for it is in times of hunger and sickness that these spirits most often make their appearances. A windigo can take many forms - those of a giant, a wolverine or other animal, but the most fearsome is when he is in the midst of a band, disguised as a human being. Windigo must be killed before the evil spirit destroys the tribe, and there is only one way to kill a windigo. His heart of ice must be pierced. The following Sandy Lake Cree story describes what a windigo is. The Ojibway and Swampy Cree stories tell of the dreadful effects windigos can have on people.

The Windigo Spirit

Sacred Legends of the Sandy Lake Cree
(Toronto: McClelland and Stewart, 1971)
by Carl Ray and James Stevens

The dreaded windigo is the most horrible creature in the lands of the Cree and Ojibwa Indians. Nothing strikes more terror in the hearts of the Anishinabek than the thoughts of windigo.

The cannibalistic windigos strike from the north during the five moons of winter and restlessly haunt our lands searching for food as far to the south as the snow belt extends. Windigos have been known to attack during the summer but this is very rare.

The windigo was once a normal human being but has been possessed by a savage cannibalistic spirit. When a human is possessed by windigo, ice forms inside the human body, hair grows profusely from the face, arms and legs and an insatiable craving for human flesh develops.

When the ugly creature attacks, it shows no mercy. This monster will kill and devour its own family to try and satisfy its lust for human flesh. The windigo is inhuman because of the powerful spirit of cannibalism and destruction residing in its body. When a windigo has destroyed its own people it will travel in a straight line across the forest until it finds the next group of victims. Usually high winds and blizzards accompany the windigo in its travels. It is said that the scream of a windigo will paralyze a man, preventing him from protecting himself. Sometimes an attack by a windigo can be turned away by a powerful medicine man and this has occurred.

There is a place at Sandy Lake called Ghost Point that was marauded and destroyed by a windigo in the old days. The remains of the village are still there today.

Windigo

Windigo and Other Tales of the Ojibway
(Toronto: McClelland and Stewart, 1969)
by Herbert T. Schwarz

On the northern shores of Lake Nipigon there lived an Indian trapper by the name of Windigo.

There came a particularly cruel winter, cruel both for Windigo and for all the living creatures around him. It was so cold that the air crackled and the game vanished. Windigo had to go further and further from his cabin in search for food, and he became hungrier and hungrier as he tracked wearily back each day empty-handed.

Eventually, for his mere subsistence, he was forced to drink a brew made from the bark of a tree. When even this was depleted, he was weak, hungry, cold and crazed with fear. In desperation, he prayed to an evil spirit for help.

His call was not unanswered. He had a dream, and in his dream an evil spirit promised to help him by bestowing him with supernatural powers.

When Windigo awoke from his dream, he saw that it was a clear, cold night with a full moon. He was still suffering biting pangs of hunger, but he was suddenly no longer weak or tired.

With enormous swift strides he walked south and soon approached a distant Ojibway village about a hundred miles from his home. His eyes blazed as he gave three blood-curdling yells, which so terrified all the Ojibways in the village that they fell down in a faint. No sooner had they fainted than they were all turned into beavers by Windigo's evil sorcery.

At last Windigo had enough food to eat, so he began to devour the beavers one by one. As he was eating them, he began to grow taller and taller; first as tall as a wigwam, then bigger than the trees, then taller than the highest mountains, until his head was high above the clouds. The bigger he grew, the hungrier he became. So, when he had eaten all the beavers in the village, Windigo went away in search of more food.

Meanwhile, Big Goose had been away hunting in the forest and did not know that his village had been destroyed by Windigo. As he was returning from the hunt, he was surprised not to see smoke rising from the camp-fires, and when he came nearer, he found his whole village in ruins and all its inhabitants gone.

At first he thought that a war party of some unfriendly tribe must have carried off all his friends. But when he saw the huge footprints of Windigo in the snow, he realized that something very strange had taken place. As brave as he was, he knew he could never defeat such a monstrous giant.

So Big Goose sat on the ground feeling very afraid and unhappy, and he prayed to the Great Manitou for help.

Suddenly he was startled by a noise close behind him. Then there emerged from the bushes a great Bear Medicine Man, carrying a very large medicine bag. The Bear Medicine Man put his arms around Big Goose and blew his supernatural powers into him. Immediately, Big Goose grew and grew until he became a huge and mighty giant called Missahba.

With giant strides, Missahba caught up with Windigo near Hudson Bay, and there they had a violent fight, hurling great rocks, mountains and glaciers at each other. All across the land, people trembled in their wigwams as the earth quaked around them. After two weeks Missahba killed Windigo, and the evil spell was broken.

Big Goose shrank from his giant size and became once more an ordinary Ojibway. And all the beavers devoured by Windigo were set free and again assumed their human form. The arduous journey home from Hudson Bay took them many months, but they were all very happy to reach their village once more.

The Wrong Chill Windigo (Swampy Cree)
Where the Chill Came From(San Francisco: North Point, 1982)
by Howard Norman

Howard Norman heard the following story when he lived with the Swampy Cree in northern Manitoba. This story was told by Andrew Nikumoon near Cormorant.

In a village lived a man named Upichisik ("Teal Duck"). There was much illness from hunger in his village at that time. Many fevers, in children and others. Upichisik went out hunting to try to find food to eat. He went out by himself. It was when the first ice was breaking up on streams and lakes. "Maybe some ducks will arrive soon," Upichisik said. It had been a hard winter, with little food.

Some days before, Upichisik had found a wide stream that was mostly clear of ice. He set out for that stream. It wasn't too far from his village. But when he arrived, the stream was frozen over again! Just then Upichisik saw an owl fly down. "Why did you freeze this stream back up?" Upichisik called at the owl.

"Get out on the ice and shiver, then I'll thaw this stream open again!" answered the owl.

With that, Upichisik walked out on the stream. He sat down on the ice. He held himself tightly with his arms. Then he began shivering.

But the owl said, "No! That's the wrong kind of shivering! You've got the wrong chill in you! That's a chill from a childhood fever!" Then the owl flew away.

Upichisik stood up. That's when he heard, in the distance, another ice breakup! He said out loud, "Maybe that's where the ducks are!" Upichisik walked toward that sound. When he arrived at the distant stream, he saw that it too had frozen over! Again Upichisik saw the owl! The owl was sitting in a tree. Upichisik shouted, "Why are you doing this to me?"

Again the owl said, "Get out on that ice!"

Upichisik, further away from his village now, and starving, walked out on the ice. He sat down. He shivered.

But the owl said, "No, that's not it! That's the shivering from a nightmare dream, when it sits you up in fear... awake! That's the wrong chill. That's the wrong shivering." Then the owl flew away.

So Upichisik had shivered up the memory of a childhood fever, and he had shivered up that other thing... a nightmare. "That is enough for one day!" he called out at the flying owl. But just then ice was cracking in the distance, further yet from his village.

Again Upichisik walked in hunger toward cracking ice. Again he arrived at a frozen stream!

Again, the owl was there! The owl said, "The right chill will thaw this ice for ducks to arrive. Then you can get food. Then you won't starve!"

So Upichisik went out on the ice to shiver. He sat down. With his fever he sat. With his nightmare he sat. Upichisik shivered. He shivered past those two things ... past those days. He was very hungry.

Then a Windigo arrived.

Upichisik knew where the chill came from. The Windigo sent a chill into him. The Windigo did that.

Upichisik called at the owl, "You've been working for this Windigo, now you'll do so for me!" With that, Upichisik conjured all the fevers from his village into that owl! The owl began burning up! Then Upichisik shouted, "Strike your talons into it!" The owl did so. The owl struck its talons into the Windigo's chest. That melted its heart. The Windigo was dying. It howled loud in a tremendously fearful way. Then it died.

That howl brought the others all the way from Upichisik's village. They arrived. Upichisik said to them, "As the owl is now working for me, I'll make it thaw more ice!"

Upichisik said, "Owl, get to work!"

With that, the owl thawed more ice open. It had such powers. It cracked open the ice on many lakes and streams. Upichisik and the others could hear the owl on the ice in the distance, thawing it. The owl, full of those fevers that Upichisik had conjured into it, was hissing in the water.

So that is what happened.

After that, there were ducks to eat.

Individuals can benefit from myths and legends because they teach so much about humanity. Students who gain an appreciation of them can transfer their understandings back and forth between the world of spirit and imagination and their everyday reality. Mythology can become a guide to the complexities and crises of life and can serve as a model to help people create poetry, fiction, and other art forms.

Native children who are raised in homes where stories are told orally are able to learn the myths and legends from their parents and grandparents. Some older Native people are also willing to talk to school classes. In these ways the oral mythology remains strong because it is passed on by a person who understands all the nuances and meanings of a story.

It cannot be overemphasized that Native myths and legends are much more than one-dimensional tales about animals and people. They have the same psychological power as a good play or novel in Western society. In re-telling a story a skilled narrator elaborates the dramatic episodes which have personal appeal. Just as the best literature can be read at more than one level, so also can myths. As an expression of the thoughts and feelings of the people they continue to have meaning long after their origins. For these reasons, an understanding of contemporary literature, modern social and political structures, and individual psychology depends on at least a passing acquaintance with the themes of mythology.

CHAPTER 2

Traditional Poetry

Introduction

Types of Traditional Poetry

Long before the arrival of the Europeans, North American Native people had a magnificent body of poetry. Though there were differences among the various culture groups there were still many similarities. Europeans believed it was their duty to Christianize the aboriginal people as quickly as possible so traditional literature, song, dance, music, and art were discouraged, ridiculed and in some cases destroyed or outlawed. It is not surprising that aboriginal people ceased to tell their myths and legends or sing their songs publicly. Much of the literature was lost, but fortunately there were some Native elders who held on to stories, songs and dances and these were passed on to succeeding generations. As well there were always some priests and folklorists who were interested in preserving certain forms of traditional literature. Today, the work of recording and translating it is still going on, with the result that many volumes of traditional poetry are in existence.

Traditional poetry was not poetry as we think of it today, but songs. Songs were part of everyday life; every tribe member composed and sang songs. Most of the songs had spiritual significance but some of them were purely for enjoyment and entertainment. There were also officials who were chosen for their good voices and memories to perform sacred rituals and ceremonies. These rituals were long and had to be performed accurately, so it could take the singer a lifetime to learn them.

The role or function these songs played in traditional cultures was much greater than the role songs and poetry play today. It can, perhaps, be compared to the position prayer holds today, but much of it did not appeal to a divine power for help. Rather, it was directed at the invisible life forces all around. It was believed that proper songs and rituals would harness the power of the forces of nature which would then help tribal members survive. The songs and rituals would keep the forces around them positive; to forget to show proper respect or to neglect to perform a ritual could mean unleashing negative forces which would lead to danger and hardship. It was believed that by singing about favourable events it would help them come to pass.

Various attempts have been made to categorize songs - old, new, mythical, historical, sacred, secular, occasional, ceremonial, private, or communal. Because none of these categories serves to describe all the recorded poetry, most collectors categorize poems according to occasion or use, and by the culture group. This greatly assists the reader, unfamiliar with Native poetry, in its interpretation. The list of occasions is virtually endless if all poetry is considered.

Stylistic Features of the Poetry

Some of the stylistic features commonly used in Western poetry are not found in traditional Native poetry. Through translation, however, some of these forms appear which likely were not present in the original. They include rhyme, regular rhythmic verses, similes, metaphors, synonyms, and personification. Lyrical poetry about nature and poetry expressing strong personal emotion was uncommon in Native poetry.

There are, however, specific stylistic devices that are found in the poetry. Some of the more common ones are as follows:

Repetition is included for its own sake. Great pleasure was derived from repeating words and phrases. This repetition does not always appear in translation.

The *number four* is significant. There were four repetitions and things were composed in fours. The number four was used for ceremonial purposes because it was analogous to the four planes of the human body - left, right, front, and back - and placed human beings at the centre of the universe, at the centre of the four directions. Thus they remained in harmony with nature. Four repetitions of a complete line or stanza are frequently not recorded by the translator. It is fairly easy to identify lines in many poems that would have been repeated.

Rhythm was the most important aspect of the poetry and meaningless linguistic vocables were often used to maintain the rhythm; unfortunately they do not often appear in translations.

The *present* tense is used most often.

A close relationship with nature is implied by the imagery.

Strong visual images are used.

Various senses are often synthesized and used for a dual purpose. The poem may appeal to several senses simultaneously.

The following Ojibway poem presents not only the panoramic view but also the actual experience of a spring day on the prairie. At the same time it suggests impending changes which can be sensed by a reader familiar with a hot summer day on the prairie.

A SONG OF SPRING[1]

As my eyes
search
the prairie
I feel
the summer
in spring.

(Colombo I, p. 42)

Dualism is found in pairing, as in earth and sky, sun and moon. The following Malecite poem serves as an example. The poem would not be complete unless the passage on the sun is followed by the passage on the moon. It makes for "closure" just as rhyming words make for completeness in a ballad.

1 Most of the songs in this anthology have been taken from
John Robert Colombo, *Songs of the Indians I* and
John Robert Colombo, *Songs of the Indians II* (Ottawa: Oberon, 1983).

INVOCATIONS OF THE SUN AND THE MOON

1

The father of the day can never fail us, he who makes every thing vegetate, and without whom cold, darkness and horror would everywhere prevail.

Beautiful, all-seeing, all penetrating luminary! Without whose influence the mind of man has neither efficacy nor vigour.

Sun! Be thou favourable to us in this point, as thou are in that of our hunting, when we beseech thee to guide us in quest of our daily support.

2

Beautiful spouse of the sun! Give us to discover the tracks of elks, moose-deer, martins, lynxes and bears, when urged by our wants, we pursue by night the hunt after these beasts. Give to our women the strength to support the pains of childbirth, render their wombs prolific, and their breasts inexhaustible fountains.

(Colombo I, p. 27)

Coercive lines and phrases are evident in many poems; for example,"Invocation of the Sun and the Moon" is a direct appeal to the sun to make favourable events happen. Another example is found in the following Ojibway hunter's song. The statement of facts is intended to make the events happen.

HUNTER'S SONG

The fattest of the bucks I'll take,
The choicest of all animals I'll take.

(Colombo I, p. 41)

Cultural References

All literature comes from within a culture; it is only by understanding something about the culture itself that the poetry can be appreciated. For example, the following poem from the Haida culture requires some explanation for those readers unfamiliar with West Coast cultures.

SONG OF RIDICULE

Laugh at the chief,
for, although he is a chief,
he has no rattle in his hand.

(Colombo II, p. 63)

The rattle can have all kinds of meanings; it can be used for music but also has many other purposes. To accurately interpret this poem it is important to understand that traditionally the rattle was found in many Native cultures and was used to accompany ceremonial singing and dancing. Among the Haida, a culture that practiced the potlatch, the display of possessions was a very important part of the ceremony, as were the songs which had to be performed in a certain way. A Haida chief without a rattle would certainly not be a very important chief!

Poetry is based not only on ceremonial customs and religious beliefs but also on the everyday life which is strongly influenced by geographic surroundings. West Coast Natives depended largely on the sea for survival; therefore, their songs emphasize the weather, the ocean, and the sea animals. Their poetry is quite different from that of, for example, the Montagnais-Naskapi who are a woodland tribe in what is now Quebec. Compare the West Coast Clayoquat poem with the Montagnais-Naskapi poem which follows it.

LOOK DOWN AND MAKE IT CALM (Clayoquat)

Look down, you,
Whose day it is,
And make it calm.

(Colombo II, p. 27)

WE WILL GO (Montagnais-Naskapi)

We will go to the bush,
you and I.
Maybe you will catch something,
Maybe I will catch something.
I will sing.
You will sing.
Tomorrow maybe you will catch something,
maybe I will catch something.
I will catch something
Because I am a man.

(Colombo I, p. 31)

The task of selecting songs for this anthology was extremely difficult as so many songs exist and the temptation to add "just one more" was strong. Culture groups from across the country are represented but these songs are only a small fraction of the poetry that has been preserved.

Poems

Songs of the Hunt and Animal Songs

Hunting was always vital to the survival of tribal groups in what is now Canada. Thus, hunters sang to invoke the assistance of unseen powers to lure game into range and guarantee a successful hunt. Sometimes the songs came to hunters in dreams or visions and they felt the powers could be recaptured at a later time if they sang the songs. Nowhere are coercive words and phrases more evident than in the hunting songs.

SONGS OF THE HUNT (Montagnais-Naskapi)

1. TRAVELLING ALONG

Happy am I
To have slain something
Along the way.

2. OTTER

Happy am I even now,
Tightening the pack on my back.
And an otter going in and out of snowdrifts!

3. OTTER

I am waiting, waiting, waiting,
For the otter, otter, otter,
To come out, out, out.

4. CARIBOU

Because there's a caribou coming,
Everything's just fine!

5. ESKIMO COMRADE

My first time for food
In Eskimo country, Tcunaga,
And you're here to play and dance with me!

6. BEAR'S SONG

The hunter's a singer and a jerk.

(Colombo I, p. 30)

BUFFALO SONG NO. 1 (Ojibway)

I hear the tread of the buffalo
in the distance;
I wait for him in ambush.

BUFFALO SONG NO. 2

I have found the tracks;
all are going around this way;
we will go around, too,
and head them off.

BUFFALO SONG NO. 3

I've followed him so far
that his tongue is hanging out;
he will have to go
to the river to drink,
and there I will kill him.

(Colombo I, p. 33)

BUFFALO CHANT (Blackfoot)

When summer comes,
He will come down
From the Mountains.

(Colombo I, p. 58)

WALRUS HUNTING (Inuit)

The walrus, I harpoon it,
Stroking its cheek.
You have become quiet and meek.
The walrus, I harpoon it,
Patting its tusks.
You have become quiet and meek.

(A. Grove Day, *The Sky Clears*, Lincoln:
University of Nebraska Press, 1951, p. 40)

COMPLAINT OVER BAD HUNTING (Inuit)

How is it with you?
Are you, I wonder, a man? Are you, I wonder, a real male?-
My throw [with the weapon] is not smooth and firm,
I cannot get hold of the seals.
How is it with you?
Are you, I wonder, a man? Are you a real male?-
These whales and walruses I cannot get hold of.

(Day, p. 45)

HUNTER'S SONG (Micmac)

For the little animal which they seek
I will sing.
For the little animal which they seek
I will sing.
After all had flown aloft,
then those ones danced.
Then the old man sang it thus:

iiko ellilo kuko aio ellile aueiiaaa.
Were they beasts, those I sang for?
Nay, no beasts are they; only
hunters of wild beasts.

(Colombo I, p. 25)

A PRAYER BEFORE WHALING (Clayoquat)

Whale, I want you to come near me,
O that I will get hold of your heart and
deceive it,
so that I will have strong legs and not be
trembling and excited when the whale
comes and I spear him.
Whale, you must not run out to sea when I
spear you.
Whale, if I spear you, I want my spear to
strike your heart.
Harpoon, when I use you, I want you to go to
the heart of the whale.
Whale, when I spear at you and miss you, I
want you to take hold of my spear with
your hands.
Whale, do not break my canoe, for I am going
to do good to you.
I am going to put eagle-down and cedar-bark
on your back.
Whale, if I use only one canoe to kill you, I
want to kill you dead.

(Colombo II, p. 27)

Prayers were said and rituals were performed for slain animals. It was believed that punishment would follow if anyone killed an animal not needed for food or even if disrespect were shown for the bones.

Animals were thought to possess special powers because they adapted more easily and were more at home in the environment than were human beings. Because people learned from them and depended on them, they were thought of with reverence and called "elder brothers." Native people believed that the power of the animals could be captured through songs and that animals would willingly give themselves as food for their "younger brothers." The careful observation and description of animals in the poetry shows the depth of respect Native people had for them.

PRAYER TO THE SPIRIT OF THE SLAIN BEAR (Lillooet)

You died first, greatest of animals.
We respect you, and will treat you
accordingly.
No woman shall eat your flesh;
no dogs shall insult you.
May the lesser animals all follow you,
and die by our traps, snares and arrows!
May we now kill much game,
and may the goods of those we gamble with
follow us,
and come into our possession!
May the goods of those we play lehal with
become completely ours,
even as an animal slain by us!

(Colombo II, p. 10)

ANIMALS (Ojibway)

1.

I should have known this!
Turtle
was here all along
splashing us,
and we thought it was waves.

2.

Noise
at the centre of the lake.
I knew otter
would keep his promise.

3.

I know he's fat,
he who left it --
even his tracks make noise!

(Colombo I, p. 39)

THE HARE AND THE LYNX (Ojibway)

Lynx:

Oh where,
Oh where,
Little White One,
Little White One,
Are you going?

Hare:

To the point of land
In my native country,
I go.

Lynx:

What,
What
Causes it?
Why like strips of leather
Are your ears?

Hare:

My uncles,
When from the south
They came,
They did fix me so.

Lynx:

Oh where,
Oh where,
Little White One,
Little White One,
Are you going?
Why?
Look they so,
Like dry bits of leather,
Your feet -- ha!

(Colombo I, p. 40)

BEAR SONG (Quileute)

I am hungry
For salmonberries.

(Colombo II, p. 29)

Songs of the Seasons and the Weather

Songs marked every season of the year and weather played a crucial role in the success or failure of hunts. Severe winters could create extreme hardships for wandering woodland tribes. A slow spring could lead to near starvation as winter supplies were depleted. Storms and winds influenced West Coast Natives who depended largely on the sea for survival. Agriculture was not practiced in most areas of what is now Canada, but for the Iroquois who farmed in the eastern lowlands, rain was vital for crops of corn, squash, and beans. As in hunting songs, coercive words and phrases were used to call upon unseen powers in positive ways.

SONG OF THE SNOW (Ojibway)

See how the white spirit presses us —
Presses us — presses us, heavy and long;
Presses us down to the frost-bitten earth.
Alas! you are heavy, ye spirits so white,
Alas! you are cold — you are cold — you are
cold.
Ah! cease, shining spirits that fell from the
skies,
Ah! cease, so to crush us, and keep us in dread;
Ah! when will ye vanish, and seegwun return?

(Colombo I, p. 39)

WINTER SONG (Ojibway)

Warm
is my door
in winter.

(Colombo I, p. 32)

FOR RELIEF FROM RAIN (Bella Coola)

Wipe your face, Father!
that it may be fair weather!

(Colombo II, p. 18)

SEND US A RAINBOW (Clayoquat)

You, whose day it is,
Make it beautiful.
Get out your rainbow colours
So it will be beautiful.

(Colombo II, p. 27)

WEATHER CHANT (Tsimshian)

Hold in your breath, Chief,
  that it may be calm.

(Colombo II, p. 58)

THE BIRDS ARE BEGINNING (Nootka)

The birds are beginning to sound merrily
  talking in the spring.
the birds are beginning to sound merrily in
  the spring,
The river duck is talking.
When growing things start pushing through,
The wrens raise their peculiar sound,
Doubling their voices.
One knows it when the tide comes in and
  leaves its mark
At Village Island. Wait! I mean at Yasayis.

(Colombo II, p. 24)

RAINMAKING (Iroquois)

I want you to take care
of the Indians,
your own people.
My family here,
I want rain.
Things won't grow,
too dry,
we must have corn,
so here is some tobacco
for you
do you know we are here
and want rain.

(Colombo I, p. 77)

Prayers to a Divine Being

The Christian religion and the concept of "God" as we know it today did not exist before the coming of the Europeans. The Native people, however, were very spiritual and recognized powers greater than man. The day was greeted with a morning prayer, usually sung by an older "singer" or a medicine man. Sacred songs were sung to petition for specific favourable events or to praise the unseen powers. Sacred songs were also sung as parts of ceremonies such as the Sun Dances of the Plains or the West Coast potlatches.

PRAYERS TO THE FOUR QUARTERS (Blackfoot)

Over there are the mountains
May you see them as long as you live,
For from them you must receive your sweet
pine as incense.

Strength will come from the North.
May you look for many years upon "the star
that never moves."

Old age will come from below, from the East,
Where lies the light of the sun.

May the warm winds of the South
Bring you success in securing food.

(Colombo I, p. 56)

SONG OF THE GREAT SPIRIT (Blackfoot)

Great Spirit,
Bless us all,
Man, woman and children.
Sacred Medicine Bundle,
Help us to live a straight life.
Sacred Medicine Pipe,
Bless us, also the rivers,
Mountains, prairies,
Animals and birds.
Mother Earth,
provide for us
Until we die.

(Colombo I, p. 59)

FOR ABUNDANCE OF FOOD (Bella Coola)

Father! You make me happy.
You give me what I desire.
Thus I find what I wished for.

(Colombo II, p. 18)

PRAYER FOR FOOD (Micmac)

Our Sun,
or our God,
give us something to eat.

(Colombo I, p. 25)

PETITION (Iroquois)

We ask that the sun will continue to shine on us and make all things grow.

We ask that the moon may always give us light by night.

We ask that the clouds may never cease to give
us rain and snow.

We ask that the winds may always blow.

We ask that the trees and plants may always grow.

We ask that Thou wouldst send all sorts of
animals for food and clothing, and make the
birds increase in number.

(Colombo I, p. 79)

INVOCATION TO THE SUN DANCE (Cree)

Our father, master of us all,
of course I have to name you first.
Look at this dancing.
All Spirit Powers,
I beg a good life for the people
that are coming here to fast.
Last fall when my children were having bad luck
I promised you this lodge.
Now I am glad and happy
that it is being completed for me.
I am satisfied
and I think manitou is satisfied.
Now I give us good health
for all the people.
I cannot say more
for I shall take up too much time.

(Colombo I, p. 62)

HAMATSA SONG (Kwakiutl)

I went all around the world to find food
I went all around the world to find human
flesh.
I went all around the world to find human
heads.
I went all around the world to find corpses.

(Colombo II, p. 50)

Medicine and Dream Songs

Songs which served as tribal conductors of dreams and vision powers are found in all cultures and are often referred to as "medicine" songs. In dreams and visions, special powers spoke to the tribal members, giving their lives a sacred dimension. Supernatural elements could be dealt with through dreams; together with visions, incantations and sacred rituals they all worked toward securing well-being and power through forces thought to be beyond human limitations.

In the following section, the first three songs appeared to fasting youth in search of spiritual guidance for their futures. Though it might take a lifetime to fully understand the visions, the songs were one of the most precious possessions of the individual. The obligations of the dream were as binding as the necessity to fulfill a vow. The nature of the dream allied the man or woman with others who had similar dreams. In later years it was believed that by singing the dream song the singer could recall the condition under which it came to him — a condition of direct communication with the supernatural.

VISION SONG (Ojibway)

Blue-bird I feel his legs
Blue-bird I feel his legs
Oh, Yes, Of course, I feel his legs
Oh, Yes, Of course, I feel his legs

(Colombo I, p. 50)

HAWK DREAM SONG (Iroquois)

I dreamed
I saw as I walked along
that beautiful hawk

he stopped
beautiful hawk
he stopped oh he stopped

(Colombo I, p. 78)

CROW SONG (Blackfoot)

I fly high in the air.
My power is very strong.
The wind is my medicine.

(Colombo I, p. 58)

In every culture there were people, both male and female, who were unusually sensitive to supernatural influences. These were known as medicine men and women, also referred to as "shamen." Their role was two-fold -- they provided spiritual guidance for the tribe and also practiced healing rituals. A part of the training was to learn the uses of healing herbs and roots and the songs to sing while administering them, but equally important were the other rituals and ceremonies of the people.

The Ojibway had an association called the **Midewewin** (Mide) which was committed to the belief that a long life was the product of good upright living. The medicine men and women of the Mide undertook rigorous training for many years to become fully participating members. Plains cultures had medicine bundles made up of sacred objects which varied according to the tribe. These bundles were handled with careful ritual and ceremony. Like other tribes, Plains tribes practiced the vision quests, but it was also possible to purchase medicine bundles and the songs which went along with them. These bundles became more valuable as they were transferred in this fashion from one individual to another, from generation to generation.

THE SKY CLEARS (Ojibway)

Verily
The sky clears
When my Mide drum
Sounds
For me
Verily
The waters are smooth
When my Mide drum
Sounds for me

(Colombo I, p. 50)

CANADIAN MEDICINE SONG (Ojibway)

Look, and see me! You see me on top of the ground.
My brother, I ask you about the gods. My brother, I ask you about the gods of the clear sky.
A-ia-ia. I want you to see the middle of the sky.
I give you a medicine dance in the middle of the land area of the earth; I give you a dance in the zenith above.
Walking in the night, in the door, smoke walking in the night.
I, too, am keeping a medicine lodge for the gods.
It was said to me: "Sometimes I see a chief; sometimes I see a god."
It looks like billows on Lake Superior. What is waving in billows on Lake Superior?
Somebody tells me about somebody getting old. I see a pretty old man.

(Colombo I, p. 51)

COYOTE MEDICINE SONG (Blackfoot)

I want the eagles
To eat my body.

(Colombo I, p. 57)

CHARMING SONGS (Blackfoot)

1. MEDICINE BUNDLE

Untie me,
I am powerful.

2. OTTERSKIN CHARM

The lake is my lodge.

3. OWL CHARM

The night is my medicine;
I hoot.

4. JAY BIRD CHARM

The mountains are my lodge;
The woods are my medicine.

5. SWAN CHARM

The daystar,
He hears me;
He is my medicine.

6. EARTH CHARM

The earth is my medicine.
It is powerful.

7. MEDICINE BUNDLE

You stand up; you take me.
You untie me; I am powerful.

(Colombo I, p. 60)

Organized ceremonies like those of the Ojibway, Iroquois, West Coast tribes, and Plains tribes did not exist in the sparsely populated northern areas. The following Kutchin song, however, shows that shamen played a very important role as spiritual leaders and healers for their people.

SHAMAN'S SONG (Kutchin)

Animals teach by dreams -
song this way to heal people.

(Colombo I, p. 88)

War songs

Much of history and literature slanderously portrays Native people as "blood-thirsty savages," giving the impression that they were continually on the warpath. Inter-tribal rivalries did exist as tribes encroached on each other's territories in search for food. Warfare was considered an honourable occupation but there was also grief and despair associated with war and a continuing desire for peace as people prepared for and returned from battle.

BATTLE SONG (Ojibway)

I bid farewell
to all my people
as I go forth
to battle.

(Colombo I, p. 33)

MEDICINE SONG FOR WAR (Ojibway)

I am rising.
I take the sky, I take.
I take the earth, I take.
I walk through the sky, I walk.
The eastern woman calls me.

(Colombo I, p. 52)

WARPATH SONG (Cree)

Because on yellow grass I stand
Supernatural is my eyesight.

(Colombo I, p. 62)

SONG OF THE RETURNING WARRIORS (Micmac)

I am returning from the hunt now.
We did well then.
What are we doing now?
We are all returning,
All who started out.
Now all are coming back.
Nobody, not one, was killed.

(Colombo I, p. 25)

WHERE THE FIGHT WAS (Ojibway)

In the place where the fight was
Across the river,
In the place where the fight was
Across the river:
A heavy load for a woman
To lift in her blanket,
A heavy load for a woman
To carry on her shoulder.
In the place where the fight was
Across the river,

In the place where the fight was
Across the river:
The women go wailing
To gather the wounded,
The women go wailing
To pick up the dead.

(Colombo I, p. 46)

SUNG AFTER BATTLE (Blackfoot)

What is the matter
with us?
We arrive,
we come here,
we are all crying.

(Colombo I, p. 59)

WAR SONG (Passamaquoddy)

I will arise with tomahawk in my hand, and I
must have revenge on that nation which
has slain my poor people.
I will arise with war club in my hand, and
follow the bloody track of that nation
which killed my people.
I will sacrifice my life and the lives of my
warriors.
I will arise with war club in my hand, and
follow the track of my enemy.
When I overtake him I will take his scalp and
string it on a long pole, and I will stick it in
the ground, and my warriors will dance
around it for many days; then I will sing
my song for the victory over my enemy.

(Colombo I, p. 28)

TREATY SONG (Micmac)

Now we are all dancing well.
We are taking one year.
We shall see how it will do.
The treaty.

(Colombo I, p. 25)

PEACE DANCE (Tahltan)

My brother was killed fighting.
And when word came to me,
My heart was sad and I wanted to die.
But now I am Kau-ah-kan,
And I love peace,
And I do not want to kill
Now any more.
Now I do not bear hatred
Toward the one who killed my brother.

(Colombo I, p. 87)

Love songs

An unusually large body of poetry has been collected from the Ojibway. Some folklorists believe that this is because they were the most musical of all Native people; others believe it is because more Ojibway songs were collected by ethnologists due to easier access to their territory. Perhaps the most widely known of all traditional Native poetry are the Ojibway love charms and songs, many of them composed by women. The Ojibway were by no means the only cultural group to preserve love songs. There was a great diversity of style and content from other cultures as well.

LOVE SONG (Ojibway)

It is my form and person that makes me great.
Hear the voice of my song -- it is my voice.
I shield myself with secret coverings.
All your thoughts are known to me -- blush!
I could draw you hence, were you on a distant island;
Though you were on the other hemisphere.
I speak to your naked heart.

(Colombo I, p. 34)

LOVE SONG (Ojibway)

A black-haired girl
I wanted to marry.

A black-haired girl
I wanted to marry.

(Colombo I, p. 35)

I WILL WALK (Ojibway)

I will walk into somebody's dwelling,
Into somebody's dwelling will I walk.

To thy dwelling, my dearly beloved.
Some night will I walk, will I walk.

Some night in the winter, my beloved,
to thy dwelling will I walk, will I walk.

This very night, my beloved,
To thy dwelling will I walk, will I walk.

(Colombo I, p. 34)

OH I AM THINKING (Ojibway)

Oh
I am thinking
Oh
I am thinking
I have found
My lover
Oh
I think it is so

(Colombo I, p. 35)

DAWN SONG (Ojibway)

Let us go home before daybreak or people will
find out what
we have been doing.

(Colombo I, p. 35)

MY LOVE HAS DEPARTED (Ojibway)

A loon
I thought it was
But it was
My love's
Splashing oar

To Sault Ste. Marie
He has departed
My love
Has gone on before me
Never again
Can I see him

(Colombo I, p. 37)

LOVER'S LAMENT (Ojibway)

Ah, me, when I think of him, my sweetheart.
Nindenaindum.
As he embarked to return, he put the white wampun
Round my neck, my sweetheart.
Nindenaindum.
I shall go with you to your native country,
My sweetheart.
Nindenaindum.
Alas, my native country is far,
Far away, my sweetheart.
Ninemoshain wee.
When I looked back to the spot where we parted,
He stood looking after me, my sweetheart.
Kewe naube, Ninemoshain.
Alas, when I think of him --
Alas, when I think of him!
Makow weyuh, nindenaindum wee.

(Columbo I, p.37)

LOVE SONG (Ojibway)

Here are four versions of the same song. It is possible for all four versions to be the same song because #1, 2 and 4 all have 9 beats. #3 has more beats.

#1, 2 and 4 could have been lengthened by adding vocables or prolonging vowel sounds. It is more likely, however, that an exact translation of #3 was impossible so the English rendition has more beats.

1
Do not weep, I am not going to die.

2
Do not weep, I am not going away.

3
Do not weep, I am going away but I
will return soon.

4
Do not weep, I will take care of you.

(Colombo I, p. 35)

LOVE SONG (Malecite)

Again you look up,
Up the river.
Again the spring ice
Breaks up.
Again you might see me
Coming down the river.
  Ku we nu de nu,
  Ku we nu de nu.

(Colombo I, p. 27)

SONG OF A MAIDEN DISAPPOINTED IN LOVE (Blackfoot)

My lover looked like an eagle from a distance,
but alas!
When he came nearer I saw that he was
nothing but a buzzard.

(Colombo I, p. 57)

SONG OF THE MOTHER OF A CERTAIN YOUNG GIRL (Blackfoot)

Though I was going to have him
for a son-in-law,
now I shall marry him myself.
I all at once admire him!

(Colombo I, p. 57)

LOVER'S SONG (Cree)

1
I wonder if she only looks out,
Near to weeping, my sweetheart,
And says,
"Ah me, me sweetheart,
I love him."

2
Hasten
Your walking,
My lover.

3
When my sweetheart said,
"Later surely again I will see you,"
"Indeed if I live,
I shall see you,"
I said to her.
Hi hi hi!

(Colombo I, p. 63)

THE BUDS OF SPRING (Tahltan)

Let the old leaves fall and new ones grow in
their stead.
The autumn of year must give way to the buds
of spring.
My yearning is great.
Pray, come to me, O my beloved!

(Colombo I, p. 87)

THEY SAY I LOVED HER (Bella Coola)

They say I loved her very dearly?
No!
The dimple in my left cheek
merely had a good opinion of her.

(Colombo II, p. 19)

Lullabies

The birth of children was a joyous event in every tribal society, for without the birth of new members, tribal life could not continue. Children were loved and indulged, and mothers quieted them by singing, just as all mothers do. Some lullabies were spontaneous compositions; others were passed down from generation to generation. No reader needs to be a specialist in the interpretation of poetry to be able to enjoy the cradle songs of North American Native people.

FIVE CRADLE SONGS (Haida)

1
Be careful,
be careful,
be careful.
This is going to be
a great man.

2
Be careful,
Is this you, grandfather?
Be careful.
Is this you, ancestor?
Take care.
This is perhaps the one
that touched the sky.

3
Whence have you fallen, have you fallen?
Whence have you fallen, have you fallen?
Did you fall, fall, fall, fall,
from the top of the salmonberry bushes?

4
Your grandfather's canoe
is looking for you, dear.
Go straight up to it.

5
Even dogs love their offspring:
So I love mine.

(Colombo II, p. 60)

CRADLE SONGS FOR GIRLS (Haida)

For this you are a woman,
you are a woman,
you are a woman,
you are a woman,
you are a woman.
For this you are a woman,
you are a woman,
you are a woman,
you are a woman,
you are a woman,
to command the sticks
of Skidegate Inlet,
you are a woman,
you are a woman.

2
You alone are fit to be a chief woman,
you alone are fit to be a chief woman.
For you they will beg for a long time.
You alone are fit to be a chief woman,
you alone are fit to be a chief woman.

3
Come, let her sit on my lap!
Come, let her sit on my lap!
Come, let her sit on my lap!
All the villages used to hand her to one
another.
Now only I take care of her,
now only I take care of her.
Come, let her sit on my lap!
Come, let her sit on my lap!
Come, let her sit on my lap!

4
You are not the only woman of our low-class
family,
you are not the only woman of our low-class
family.
There are plenty of women,
there are plenty of low-class women.

5
You came to me, you came to me, ye he he!
You came to me, you came to me.
You came walking to me, calling me
"mother,"
instead of to someone else.
To me, my child, who is a chief's child,
came walking, calling me "mother."
Mother of noble family,
mother of noble family, mother of noble
family,
mother of noble family, mother of noble
family.

6
For what do you cry, dear?
For clothing?
You shall wear it, dear.

7
Use your hands,
my dear,
to walk about
upon grandmother's land.

(Colombo II, p. 61)

CRADLE-SONG FOR A BOY (Tlingit)

Let me shoot a small bird for my younger brother.
Let me spear a small trout for my sister.

(Day, p. 57)

A HELPLESS BABE (Sekani)

Now my child is a helpless babe,
A son in need of his mother's care.
Soon he will grow to manhood and test his
strength,
Spearing the fish and hunting the bear.

Let him ever remember his mother Toultel!

(Colombo I, p. 85)

SONG (Tsimshian)

She will pick wild roses, the little girl.

That is why she was born.
She will dig up wild rice with her index
finger, the little girl.
That is why she was born.
She will gather the sap of young hemlock trees
in the early spring.
That is why she was born.
She will pick strawberries in the early spring.
That is why she was born.
She will, the women, pick up blueberries in
the early spring.

She will pick strawberries in the early spring.
She will pick elderberries in the early spring.
She will pick wild roses in the early spring.
That is why she was born.

That is why she was born.

(Colombo II, p. 57)

PETTING-SONG (MODERN) (Inuit)

How charming he is, that little pet there!
How charming he is -
How amazing he is, the dear little creature!

How bland he is and gentle, the great little one there!
How bland he is and gentle -
How amazing he is, the dear little creature!

How sound he looks and vigorous, the great little thing there!
How sound he looks and vigorous!
How amazing he is, the dear little creature!

(Day, p. 42)

Songs About Everyday Activities

The role of various songs for specific occasions should not be underestimated, but equally important to the life of the tribe were songs about everyday activities — to spread laughter, to ease the burden of work, to relieve monotony. These everyday poems give intimate glimpses of daily living rarely found in other kinds of literature.

DANCE SONG (Malecite)

How are you?
  Ya hi ye.
How are you?
  Ya hi ye,
  Ya hi ye.
Come dance, please!
  Ya hi ye,
  Ya hi ye.
Young girls, please!
  Ya hi ye.
Young boys, please!
  Ya hi ye.
How are you?
  Ya hi ye.
Come, come, come, come!

(Colombo I, p. 27)

GAMBLER'S SONG (Cree)

Nothing
you will have
for nothing.
You will compete
with me.

(Colombo I, p. 63)

ONG OF THE TREE (Blackfoot)

Oh tree! I ask that you fall easily.
I promise to plant you in a new place
And to give you many presents.
May you stand firmly in your new home.

(Colombo I, p. 58)

WOMAN'S SONG (Blackfoot)

Do not feel uneasy about me,
I shall be eating berries on my way home.

(Colombo I, p. 57)

PRAYER FOR THE FIELD (Lillooet)

O Zemuha!
know that we come
to dig roots.
May no lizards
harm us
or follow us!

(Colombo II, p. 10)

PRAYER OF THE STONE-CARVER (Thompson)

May I have the strength of arm;
may my arm never get tired --
from thee, O Stone!

(Colombo II, p. 14)

SONG OF AN OLD WOMAN (Tlingit)

Already I am going,
I am going to die:
I have dreamed of my son.

(Colombo II, p. 69)

COURTESY SONG (Clayoquat)

"It seems that my husband is scolding me all
the time."
"Perhaps he has a reason for scolding you."

(Colombo II, p. 28)

PRAYER OF A WOMAN IN LABOUR (Thompson)

May I have no trouble
and give birth
to my child easily!
. . . .
I rely on thee, Dawn
of the Day. Pity me!

(Colombo II, p. 14)

A WOMAN'S SONG (Ojibway)

You are walking around
Trying to remember
What you promised,
But you can't remember.

(Colombo I, p. 43)

PADDLE SONG (Ojibway)

Throughout the night
awake am I,
throughout the night
awake am I,
upon the river
awake am I.

(Colombo I, p. 32)

THE LONESOME YOUTH (Salish)

I am lonesome, travelling alone. There is none here.
I am lonely in this land, because there is none here.
My heart is to cry, because I am travelling alone.
Just when the sun is sinking, I am lonely as I go.

(Colombo II, p. 17)

SONG OF THE DEPARTED (Tlingit)

Perhaps my brother went
into the sun's trail
so that I can never
see him again.

(Colombo II, p. 70)

SONG OF MOURNING (Tlingit)

It is as if my grandfather's house
were turning over with me inside:
Where is the person who will save me?

(Colombo II, p. 70)

DIVORCE SONG (Wakashan)

I thought you were good at first.
I thought you were like silver
and I find you are lead.
You see me high up.
I walk through the sun.
I am like the sunlight myself.

(Colombo II, p. 33)

BOASTFULNESS (Kwakiutl)

I am too great to be bitten by those little
mosquitoes
That are flying about.

(Colombo II, p. 46)

CROSSING THE ICE (Iroquois)

My father told me how the Indians came here.
Long ago they didn't know there was land
here.
He said long ago they began to starve.
In the old world nothing would grow.
For many years they were starving.
They held a council.
Because they were starving they decided to go
and look for another land.
They made up their minds.
They thought elsewhere there was land.
They will try to eat.
As they were walking suddenly they knew
they were walking on ice.
For many days they walked on ice.
Then they chose seven of the best runners.
So the two groups started out.
One group didn't want to go.
One group went to the east.
They went where the sun rises.
They went in search of food.
Early in the morning several of the runners
went away to the east.
They continued a long time in the direction of
the east.
They rested when night came.
Suddenly they saw a black streak in front.
They thought a big snake lay there.
The seven of them stopped.

They started out.
They separated.
They spread out.
The first runner calls.
He will hear.
He will call.
The next will hear.
Until the message returns to the south.
When the seventh runner arrived he saw a big woods with abundant food.
There was so much food to eat here they decided to go back for the others.
Here they will also live.
They went back to find where they had come across.
They were not able to find it.
The ice had melted.
Then they were not able to go back for the others.

(Colombo I, p. 75)

Songs that Show European Influence

The content of the following song is likely authentic but it has been translated in a rhyming couplet. This was not a traditional song form.

CORN-HUSKING SONG (Ojibway)

Crooked ear, crooked ear,
Walker at night.

Stop, little old man,
And take not to flight.

Crooked ear, crooked ear,
Stand up strong;

Little old man,
I'll give you a song.

(Colombo I, p. 42)

Scalping is not thought to be a traditional Native practice in warfare. Of the many explanations about how it became identified with Native warfare, the most common one is that Native warriors were paid a bounty by Europeans for killing the enemies of the Europeans. The scalp was proof that someone had actually been killed. Gradually the practice spread.

VICTORY CELEBRATION (Sioux)

A scalp,
An Indian scalp
I have.
Dance!

(Colombo I, p. 94)

Native people in what is now Canada did not have alcoholic drinks before the coming of the Europeans. The effects of alcohol had a profound influence on all aspects of their lives for intoxication was new to them.

DRINKING SONG (Ojibway)

I don't suppose
I'll get drunk
if I take one drink;
if I should get drunk,
take care of me.

(Colombo I, p. 32)

CAUGHNAWAGA SONG (Iroquois)

Chorus:

I love him, I love him, father --
That young man!

Maiden:

Well, father, what is thy word?
My Spirit is now to marry.

Father:

Ashamed be thou, my child --
Thou whom I hold my little one --
Thou are yet too young;
Thou canst not get thee thy food.

Maiden (in the words of the chorus):

I love him, I love him, father --
That young man.

Father:

Hard drinks he, he thou lovest;
Great tears this would later make thee shed.

Chorus (Passionately):

I love him, I love him, father --
That young man.

Father:

Thou askest for food; he will show thee a
bottle.

Chorus (softly):

Yet I love him, I love him, father --
That young man.

(Colombo I, p. 77)

The following three songs show how the cultures gradually changed due to the trading of goods and influence of different social customs.

STOP ALL THIS IDLE CHATTER (Tlingit)

Stop all this idle chatter,
Let me hear no more gossip!
You drive me almost mad
With your idle and noisy chatter:

You old maids and old housewives,
Clean your fish, gather berries,
Mend your fires, boil the kettle;
Let me have peace and quiet!

Do not meddle with my business!
Why not mind all your small affairs,
And let me lead my own life?

You old maids and you housewives,
Stop all this idle chatter,
Let me hear no more gossip,
Let me have peace and quiet!

I could tell tales if I wished to,
I too could tell tales and gossip,
I have an eye on you women!
I have seen things most curious.

Stop all this idle chatter,
Mend your fires, boil the kettle,
Let me have peace and quiet!

My heart is filled full of sorrow.
I only want my own sweetheart:
I cannot see her among you.
My own sweetheart, my beautiful.

Stop all this noisy chatter:
Mend your fires, boil your kettles,
Let me have peace and quiet!

(Colombo II, p. 67)

GAMBLING SONG (Kutenai)

Gambling many are lost things.
Horses blankets shirts guns knives money.
Everything lost.

(Colombo I, p. 98)

WHITE MAN'S DANCES (Kutenai)

Approximately
  being about ten years ago
Precisely
  I started out to Cranbrook Mission.
Precisely
  people were dancing white man's
  dances.
Precisely
  I went like they did
precisely
  I danced white man's dance with Pete
  Andrew.
And then
  night being half over,
Precisely
  food was eaten.
And it being eaten
  then
Precisely
  people danced again.
So when we went
  I was two with Ignatius Bighead.
Then precisely
  we were going to white man's dances.

And then
   when we came back to Bonners Ferry
   Mission
Then the Indians
   precisely
laughed at us
   over us going there
To white man's dances.

(Colombo I, p. 98)

The Chinook people lived in what is now the State of Washington. With the coming of European goods, trade on the west coast was brisk and a common trade language evolved by the late 1800's. It was a jargon of French, English, Chinook and a few words of Nootka and Salish. The following songs were recorded in this Chinookian dialect. They show the changing life styles of the people and how cities, even then, did not seem to be very happy places for them.

1. Very unhappy I was
   With my wife,
   In Victoria.
   Nobody
   Said goodbye to us
   In Victoria.

2. Goodbye, oh my dear Charlie!
   When you take a wife,
   Don't forget me.

3. I don't know how I feel
   Toward Johnny.
   That young man makes a fool of me.
   Aya.

4. I am very glad
   When the steamboat comes here.
   I think I shall cry
   When the steamboat leaves.

5. I went to town,
   I saw my sister,
   My heart was glad.

(Colombo II, p. 72)

Members of Native tribes were much more preoccupied with composing and singing songs than members of European cultures were at the time of contact. Poetry was an integral part of everyday activity for tribal members; singing the songs was an important aspect of life.

Often the most emotionally honest statements of a culture are found in the poetry. The natural eloquence of the culture is revealed as needs, desires, passions, aspirations, and dreams are expressed. Traditional Native poetry reveals the people's capacity to hear the voice of a supreme being. It demonstrates their capacity for introspection, their relationship with others, their profound belief in the sacredness of nature and the importance of remaining in harmony with it. The traditional songs can, however, be studied and appreciated purely as literature. Even though they have passed through translation into another language, the soul of Native society is still preserved in the songs and the reading of traditional poetry can be a rewarding experience for members of all cultures.

CHAPTER 3
Memoirs

Introduction

A memoir is a recording of memories by a person who remembers the events that happened. They can be a form of history but usually there is little attempt to put the history in strict chronological order or to include all the important events. More often, a person recalling memoirs does so randomly; one idea leads to the next one. Not only the important things are mentioned but also the inconsequential everyday things. Some memoirs were recorded in diaries; for example, some trappers carefully recorded daily events on the trapline-- what the weather was like, the condition of the snow, the numbers of animals they caught and, later, the price they received for the furs. Others, of course, did not record events in writing because they had not learned to read and write.

Many memoirs are still passed on orally. To ensure that they are preserved as accurately as possible a recorder transcribes the story as the person is talking, or a tape recorder is used, and then the memoirs are written down in the exact words of the person who was talking.

Memoirs may vary widely, as is shown in this anthology. They range from Chief Thunderchild's experience of hunting buffalo on the plains to Augusta Tappage's memories of the gold rush days in the Caribou area of British Columbia. Whatever the content, they share certain similarities in style, including the following:

1. The stories were told orally, or written down as they would be told orally. There is no attempt to use sophisticated literary style.

2. The storyteller addresses the readers directly. In reading the stories it is important to keep in mind the facial expressions and gestures of the storyteller as the story was being told.

3. The storyteller assumes that the reader has certain information about the events mentioned, the environment, the beliefs, and the values of the time. There is little elaboration

and description so the reader may have to do some research or use imagination to fill in the gaps.

4. The storyteller is very concerned with accuracy. In cultures where reading was not a way of life, the people depended on storytellers to keep accurate records. This does not mean they could not use their imaginations to expand on ideas, but they were very careful to point out when they were not sure of their information.

5. The storyteller often goes into minute details about some aspects of the story or about some everyday event. The event may have had particular significance or it may have been very important at the time. Just what kind of a gun was used to kill a moose may not be of particular interest to contemporary readers but it was very important as the event was taking place.

6. There is little discussion of personal emotion. The events speak for themselves; the readers must use their imaginations to try to understand the emotions people were actually feeling.

7. Understatement is used. There is a tendency to say less rather than more than is needed to make a point.

8. Words are used sparingly; not many modifying adjectives and adverbs are used. There may have been long pauses in the story telling.

9. The speech is slow and measured as the storyteller recalls events. The contemporary reader should attempt to read the stories in the same manner, especially when they are read aloud.

10. Incomplete or fragmentary stories may be recorded. The reader may be left with some unanswered questions about the story.

11. Non-standard English may be found in the stories. This adds a special dimension to the stories because more of the original story is retained. The storyteller was likely thinking in a different language and was translating the ideas into English before telling them or writing them down.

A wide variety of styles are evident in the memoirs included in this anthology. They have been arranged in chronological order giving glimpses of what life was like for Métis and Native people at various periods of Canadian history. The memoirs span a period of approximately one hundred years, and each writer shows intimate glimpses of the sorrows and joys of that era.

Excerpts from Memoirs

Voices of the Plains Cree
(Toronto: McClelland and Steward, 1973)
by Edward Ahenakew

Edward Ahenakew (1849-1927) wrote his memoirs in 1923 but they were not published until after his death. The book, *Voices of the Plains Cree*, was published after his niece found the manuscript in a tattered state among his personal effects. The stories were printed just as Ahenakew had written them. His style is fluent; his grammer and sentence structure is correct since he was an ordained Anglican priest who had received his university education in Toronto and Saskatoon.

Ahenakew recorded stories told to him by Plains Cree storytellers, particularly Chief Thunderchild. Ahenakew also wrote of his own experiences and expressed opinions on the life of Native people on reserves in 1923. The following two stories were told to him by Chief Thunderchild. Thunderchild experienced the changes from a life of buffalo hunting on unlimited prairie territory to the restrictions of reserve life. He was a Cree storyteller recounting Cree legends, traditions, and tales about a lifestyle when aboriginal people were still lords of the plains. Ahenakew took notes as Thunderchild spoke, and translated the stories into English. The original style and imagery of Thunderchild's versions have been retained as much as translation allows.

The Foot-race

When I was young, I was a good runner; but, in his time, my father was the swiftest on the plains. He ran against many others and was never left behind; but anyone who is good at something always has those who think that they can beat him. This is the way my father told the story:

"There was a time when Stoneys and Crees were camping near one another, and we had games in the clear space between the two encampments. I was playing a game when Ta-te-pa-wa-ty came to me and said, 'Ne-se-say (Uncle), the Stoneys want to race against the Crees, four runners to each side. You are chosen as one of our runners.'

" 'Who are the other Crees?' I asked him, and he named two who always thought that they could leave me behind. 'Let them run,' I said, but he came back with a short pipe-stem for me. 'Nes-chas (cousin), you are the one who is wanted and I have come for you. I will give you a new gun.'

"I sat with the other Cree runners, and a young Stoney came past us, dressed in strange clothes. It was said that no one in the country to the east could leave him behind in a race, and the Stoneys were excited and put up more bets. To help me run against him, my friends chose a good runner to stay beside me at the start of the race and sing a spirit song.

"There was a hill in the distance that was called the blue hill. We were to run to that, and then around it, and back to the starting place. I said that I would wait until the others had started, and I let the one who was to run with me go on, and then I caught up to him and we ran together.

"As we came near the hill, one of the Stoneys passed us, tall and straight and springy. I was good-looking too, and my hair was long. I had it tied on the top of my head in a tuft. Stoneys on horseback raced around us, calling their bets. My brother and Ta-te-pa-wa-ty came on horseback too, and my brother said, 'Is that all you can do, grandfather?' teasing me. I said, 'I'm waiting for those two Crees who always say that they can run faster than I can. Let them win for us.' Then O-ho-sis (Little Owl) rode up to one of them and pulled his hair and neighed four times to make him run faster but it made no difference. First one of them and then the other said, 'A-a-hay, I am left behind.'

"My brother rode close to me, and pulled the fringe from my waist-band. I ran faster, and I said, 'I know there is no man with two legs who can leave me behind - a bird told me that.' The Stoney was still ahead, and I lengthened my step. I felt free. I left my partner behind. The tall Stoney ahead seemed to be standing still. I overtook him; I passed him on the right; I called to him, 'Run, namesake. This is a race.'

"The Stoney they were betting on was close behind me and then we were nearing the end of the race. Stoneys who were riding ahead tried to block my way, and my brother was really fighting them off. He called to me, 'He's going to overtake you.' Then I ran my best - I ran so fast and got so excited that I didn't know until the race was over that I had dropped my breech-cloth."

The Buffalo Chase

Buffalo would attack people only during the mating season. When we chased them, we always let the horses have their heads free, or there could be accidents. The closer one raced to the buffalo, the better it was, because of the dust. Some men were afraid to go close up to a buffalo, but I - we all boast when we talk of the chase - I raced close up and my pony was well trained.

The bulls had great agility in turning to fight. Up would go the tail first. I saw one hunter chasing a bull when it turned on him like that. The horse swerved aside, but the bull's horn caught the man's belt just enough to pull him off. Then it was like a ball - toss, catch, toss, catch - twice before he fell to the ground. The second time, the horn caught him back of the thigh, and it was as if a knife had cut him. I was ahead and I had to go on, but the riders behind me stopped to help him, and they killed the bull.

Our powder horns were small, holding just enough for one shot. We kept the bullets in our mouths, so that they were wet with saliva and needed no wadding when we dropped them into the muzzles of our guns after the powder was poured in.

Once when we had finished chasing buffalo near a coulee (not far from the place that is now called Wilkie), some of the men decided to go back to the hunt. Lightfoot's father was one of them, and he was a good man in the chase. That time he did not return to the camp when it was night, but in the morning his horse was there, and the saddle was twisted under its belly. We went to look for him. Many of us looked. He was never found. Much later, hunters came on a wounded bull, and the buckle of his belt was round the bull's horn.

Vanishing Spaces: Memoirs of Louis Goulet
(Winnipeg: Éditions Bois-Brulés, 1976)
by Guillaume Charette

Louis Goulet (1859 - 1936) told his stories to Guillaume Charette in French and they were translated into English by Ray Ellenwood.

Goulet's stories were sprinkled with quaint original expressions and words from aboriginal languages; many of these have been retained because no translation can quite catch the flavour of the original.

Louis Goulet was remembered as a very handsome, dashing man who worked as a voyageur. He was born where the town of Morris, Manitoba now stands and grew up with seven brothers and two sisters. Not only was he a gifted storyteller but he was also a living legend as a boxer.

Goulet has a reputation for having been a very objective storyteller. His stories were true, the facts he gave were authentic, and the people he told about were real. He told stories of Métis life in settlements and of their adventures as they hunted buffalo on the prairies, often roaming as far west as Alberta and as far south as the United States.

The Buffalo Hunt

As soon as the snow melted in the spring, we would leave our winter camp as we always did and head for another location, either farther south or farther north, around Fort Layusse (Edmonton), or St. Albert and beyond. Finally we'd return to the Red River, where the buffalo were getting scarce. They would disappear completely in 1868, after the devastation that went along with the grasshoppers.

I'd turned nine years old the autumn before and my father had decided to return to St. Norbert. We'd been gone for two years. Our return journey was uneventful except for three or four buffalo chases first in the Cypress Hills and later at Wood Mountain. In both places we'd come upon what we called a *foule,* an enormous herd. Our caravan had stayed in contact with them, giving the hunters travelling with us time to kill around four thousand animals.

There were about five hundred carts in the caravan and it took us three weeks to strip the meat and make pemmican of it.

Once they were claimed, the killed animals would be skinned as soon as possible and dressed on the spot. The hides were hung on stretchers, which were a kind of frame made of straight poles, to be dried in the sun and smoked until they were stiff as a shingle. Then they were scraped with a sharp tool, on one side to remove the hair and on the other to clean off any fat, meat or other impurities that might be left sticking to the skin. That last process was called *enlever la maque.*

The hair and the *maque* were removed with sharp scrapers handmade from a piece of knife blade, a bit of metal hoop or a wood chisel solidly attached to some kind of convenient handle or grip.

Scraping hides was men's work, but the women helped when they had time, and they were very good at it because they were so painstakingly patient. But usually, while the men were stripping the hides of hair and *maque,* the women cut up the carcasses, cutting the meat into very thin strips so that it would dry quickly in the sun lying on grids of branches over smoking fires of buffalo chips which drove away the flies and hastened the drying.

The meat took at least two days to dry perfectly, after which it was put in skin bags or baskets made of wicker, rushes or leather. When the skins had been thoroughly scraped, *plumées* as the Métis used to say, they were called *peaux de batterie* or drumskins, sheets of hide out of which we would cut our tents, leather bags, thongs, whips, drums, even shields that could stop an arrow.

The hunting expedition did not stop until carts were all full, that is if the weather was favourable. We never killed more animals than we could dress quickly, otherwise there was a danger the meat might "go off" as we said, become tainted or spoil completely. Without the prairie tradition of helping one another to get the butchering done before the sun got too hot or it started to rain, there would have been a lot more spoilage. Everybody had a job to do after the kill, whether or not he'd joined in the hunt. In those days there was none of this everybody out for himself like we see now. There were still some practising Catholics among the Métis. We hadn't all been spoiled by civilization!

We stopped hunting when it was time to make pemmican. When the meat was dry enough to be brittle, it was pounded as fine as possible with a stick, a bar, the head of a hammer, or a small stone. The powdered meat was put into big cast iron pots full of boiling fat or, more often, marrow got by breaking buffalo bones and letting them boil.

As it cooked, this mixture of pulverised dry meat and fat or marrow turned into a paste. The thickness could be easily regulated. To this paste we would add dry or crushed berries when they were in season: saskatoons, wild grapes and chokecherries, a kind of small berry with a pit which grew in bunches and had to be pounded before it was used as an ingredient in pemmican.

Still boiling hot, the paste would then be poured into bags made of *peau de batterie* sewn up with tendon or rawhide to form an air-tight seal. The bags would be left to dry as hard as tallow, either in the sun as we travelled or over a patient forty, fifty, sixty years. The older pemmican got, the better it was. It was eaten in different ways; either straight from the bag with no preparation, or else roasted in its grease or boiled. Many people liked it boiled in dumplings, as a kind of stew called *rababout*. A bag of pemmican, called a *taureau*, was supposed to weigh exactly one hundred pounds. People who tried it for the first time said it tasted of suet, but after a while they'd get used to it and not notice, which just goes to show that anything tastes good if you're hungry enough.

The strips of dried meat left unpowdered were delicious. We used to carry them in our pockets to nibble on while we were travelling, like biscuits or candy.

There were several products the Métis knew how to extract from the buffalo. First, we did business in skins as hides or as leather, raw or cured. The meat was sold dry, salted, smoked and especially in the form of pemmican. We supplied the whole country with buffalo tongue prepared in the same way, and we also exported some. In addition, the skins gave us material to make our tents, clothes, shoes, ropes and the *babiche* we used to strengthen our carts and sleds. *Babiche* was rawhide cut into strips thin as laces, very useful as cord for binding things.

The main market for distributing our products of the hunt was the Hudson's Bay Company, which sent them to posts farther west or in the north, even to England. Finally, there was the United States, with St. Paul being the main outlet.

Our journey from St. Norbert to the highlands of the Missouri River had taken us almost two years. We'd left when autumn was coming on in 1865 and returned in July 1867. A plague of grasshoppers had swept over the entire country destroying the crops. I remember seeing the devastation, the woods and fields stripped bare, every last leaf and head of grain devoured.

People were completely destitute, waiting for help from the outside: the States, Canada and England. The Hudson's Bay Company had already distributed all kinds of supplies among the population.

It was obvious that the buffalo were disappearing before our eyes. Ordinarily, when we were coming back from the open prairies, all we had to do was climb a hillock or any height of land and we could see them here and there, grazing in twos, threes and fours. And there would be larger groups, closer together, as we looked farther away on all sides.

We noticed this time that we hadn't spotted a single buffalo since coming down from the highlands on the western edge of the Red River Valley. The grass was high, showing it hadn't been grazed as it normally was.

Heavy rains during the last two springs had filled all the little lakes, sloughs and lowlands, so there were plenty of ducks and small game birds, but also clouds of mosquitoes.

The Days of Augusta
(Vancouver: J.J.Douglas, 1973)
by Jean E. Speare

Augusta Tappage (1888 - 1982) was a Shuswap from the Williams Lake area of British Columbia. As a child of four she was sent to a residential school where she spent ten years of her life, not even going home in the summers. At the age of fifteen she married a non-status Native, George Evans, so she and her children lost their treaty rights.

She had four children but two died in infancy; one son was killed when he fell from a bucking horse. Augusta was forty-three years old when her husband died. She supported herself by doing housework for others and she provided a home for many foster children, so many she could not remember all their names in her old age.

She told her memoirs to Jean Speare who edited the book *The Days of Augusta*. In it, Augusta tells legends, comments on her everyday life, and recalls events like the Cariboo gold rush. Speare did not change Augusta's style; readers feel as though Augusta is talking directly to them.

Augusta is very concerned with the accuracy of her stories but at the same time she also displays a lively imagination. She brings the past alive with her attention to detail. Though life was hard for her she shows little bitterness. Helping others was uppermost in her mind, whether it was as a midwife or housekeeper, telling legends to children or leading the hymn singing in church, teaching her readers how to make baskets or dessert from soapallalie berries. She met every aspect of life with enthusiasm which is reflected strongly in her memoirs, making her one of the most memorable women in Native literature.

The Holdup

My aunt told us. We were excited.

It was at Three-Mile Creek
there at the Hundred-and-Fifty-Mile on the old trail;
well the same way you go to Ashcroft now;
well here is this creek,
they call it Three-Mile.

It was all bushy
right to the edge of the trail it was bush;
the government didn't cut right-of-ways
in those days, no -
so it was all bush.

The date I don't know how long ago it was.
I must have been out of school,
married and out of school.
We were in mountain meadows
my husband and I, cutting hay.

When we came back my aunt told us.

Anyhow this place was bushy
and here the robbers must have waited
till the stage went by. "Stop!"
They told the driver to stop
but he was hard-of-hearing.

Many people were on the stage
some inside, some out, riding on top
by the driver, all from Barkerville, yes,
going to Ashcroft from Barkerville -
every week, up and down, up and down.

The driver, he didn't stop, no,
when they told him. They shot at him
above his horses. They didn't kill a soul.
They scared the horses.
I think they scared everyone.

My aunt told us everyone was scared.

But the driver was strong, I guess,
and the man who rode beside him;
together they controlled the horses,
together they made the horses stop
by Three-Mile Creek.

They took the mailbags, the robbers did,
the bags, some has money, some has mail;
I couldn't tell you what all they had,
but they took them
and ransacked them.

They didn't hurt anyone
but they emptied the bags, took the money.
It doesn't say gold; I never heard gold.
But they came from Barkerville
and maybe there was gold.

But my aunt didn't say 'gold'.

There were some of us suspicious
who they were, yes, we thought local maybe,
but we couldn't tell; we couldn't say
who robbed the stage,
who took the money.

But when we came from making hay, my husband and I,
this is what my aunt told us.

Christmas at the Mission

I remember Christmas at the Mission.
Always we used to have midnight mass.

But we didn't know about Christmas and holidays
Until the Sisters came.
The Sisters came from France, you know,
And they brought Christmas with them.

They were the Sisters of Infant Jesus,
Those who came.

The teachers who had been teaching us before,
They didn't bother or care
Or hold Christmas. When the Sisters came
Was when we first knew Christmas!

The Sisters made us a Christmas concert, taught us
To sing hymns and songs,
Say recitations to everybody, helped us
Decorate our first Christmas tree.

I can't tell you how beautiful that first Christmas tree!
Everything was changed!

And our shoe, our right shoe, had to be polished
And put up on a bench
On Christmas Eve for holding candies, yes,
And whatever present you were going to get.

And then we all went to chapel through the snow
That first Christmas for midnight mass.

Doctor's Book

I bought a doctor's book from Eaton's.
It was down at Regina then.
It cost me three dollars, yes.

But I read that book from end to end.
I learned it by heart.
At night in my kitchen by candlelight.

It was this thick and it had pictures
About everything - mother, baby, boils, breaks,
Yes, I learned it by heart.

I said, "I'm not scared to help them."
No doctors, nobody; so I learned that book
And I helped them.

An Indian Remembers
(Winnipeg: Peguis Publishers, 1971)
by Tom Boulanger

Tom Boulanger (1901 - 1973) was a Saulteaux from Berens River, Manitoba. This book is about his life as a trapper and about events at Berens River. He had little formal education so his writing is truly oral narrative -- except that he wrote it down. He kept a record of his life's experiences and took the manuscript, tied into a bundle with fish cord, to Winnipeg where friends helped him get it published. Adam Cuthand, who wrote the Foreword says,

"His writing lacks fluency and correct sentence structure, but the weaknesses disappear as you begin to read this fascinating tale."

It is not possible to read Boulanger's writing as rapidly as one would read fluent English but for the reader who takes time, it is an interesting story. Reading it aloud brings out the true flavour of Boulanger's style and Saulteaux speakers will readily relate to the style of an elder struggling to express ideas in an unfamiliar language.

Now I have another news about my friend and myself in 1927. My friend's name was the old chief of Berens River, Old Billy Berens. He was a very smart and good chief. I was with him a lot of times while trapping and met him a lot of times. He was trapping and fishing too sometime. A lot of times I have been out camping with him making open fire place anywhere. When I would lie down he start telling me stories of long ago. How to do more experience in trapping outside in cold weather. I told him our experience in trapping in cold weathers, how to start a fire with cold hands and in the cold weather. The best way to start a fire is with a birch bark and dry jack pine. That's the best way to start a fire when it's cold weather in the north. Before registered trapping-lines, he was trapping the same place for nine years and he was with two sons trapping. One name was Billy Berens (his nickname is Lapoo) and the other one's name was Jacob Berens and sometimes the other one that was usually with him was Joe Berens. Sometimes we were all talking together about trapping and fishing.

Long ago when you kill one fur such as fisher, mink and otter, it was a great thing because it was a good price that time (the fur). Another thing when you buy food from stores there was very low price that time.

The meaning of "trapping line" it is not the same when you have a job and get paid five or ten dollars a day and sometime you work for nothing a few days. Sometimes you get fifteen to one hundred dollars a day. We believed this day it's not hard to get something "good luck" because we are sure God Bless us to get something. That's what we were talking about together. Sometimes we had a praying meeting when we were at the camp.

All the work I have done since forty-three years I never worked for a boss much. I mostly worked myself. Sometimes I work at nights and tried to finish the job to reach some place to sleep. I am real sure a lot of times God help me. Any place wherever you are, it's wonderful how the bless when there's a man working. That's what Billy Berens and I mentioned about, and Billy Berens when he was a very old man he changed his trapping ground at Head Leaf Lake. It's not far from the north side of Berens River. When there was registered trapping lines, his trapping ground was made at Head Leaf Lake. When he died he left the trapping ground for his boy. Head Leaf Lake, young Billy Berens to be senior trapper now. Old Billy Berens was eighty years old when he was still trapping at Head Leaf Lake. He was married for fifty years to Mrs. Nancy Berens and the old lady is still living. She is about ninety years old.

Old Billy Berens died in the age of 85 years old and in August 22nd, 1967. He died in his own house right in the treaty grounds. When the body was took out of his place a whole of Berens River people were there outside. That very same time the **S.S. Keenora** came in Berens River. That's the time a Johnny Okinson was the captain and Tom Beers was a purser (clerking in the boat on books). It was a good day. When the body was took to the church the people were walking. They started singing the song that says:

> I am going home, I am going home
> Not to die again
> Our father gone far away to heaven
> I am going home over there.

That's the song the people sang as the body was moved. Everybody in the **S.S. Keenora** stopped and listened to the beautiful song. Johnny Okinson and Tom Beers and myself were standing together. Johnny Okinson told me that the song the people sang was a beautiful song when the old chief died. I was feeling in my heart that it's very kind. I think that what they felt, too. That was the last of Old Billy Berens. I knew he was a very honest man and he was a nice speaking man when he lived in this world.

When they made a new chief, it was young Billy Berens now. He was also so many years a chief too. One time they voted to get a new chief again and the second chief was Stanley Ross; the next vote in a couple of years was Willie Swain for the chief. The next voting was Young Billy Berens the chief again. The next chief was Erveyen Flex the chief in Berens River 1967. The councillors are Gordon Berens Jr., John J. George, Sandy Berens, Sandy Patrick and Fred Baptiste. That's all the new gang of 1967.

Trapping is My Life
(Toronto: Peter Martin Associates, 1976)
by John Tetso

John Tetso (1920 - 1964) was a Slavey who lived and trapped near Fort Simpson in the Northwest Territories. In the early 1960's he wrote short articles for a newspaper called *Catholic Voice*. After his death the stories were collected and published in this book.

Tetso attended residential school for only four years. He does not give the sources of his vast store of knowledge but he was obviously well read. He likely read books and magazines, listened to the radio, and attended movies in Fort Simpson. This adds a unique quality to his writing because his vocabulary is extensive and he uses figures of speech freely. This leads to unexpected combinations of traditional Native expressions and contemporary speech which are often humourous. At the same time, his stories retain the flavour of oral narrative; he addresses the readers directly and carries on intimate conversations with them.

John Tetso has many profound ideas about life and living which he passes on to his readers. He remains a humble man, saying that elders helped him learn about life and it is his responsibility now to pass the learning on to the next generation. He felt that integration of races was important and hoped that his stories would help bridge the gap between cultures.

Inviting a Moose for a Picture

Well, I wonder what you think about my experiences that I have been telling you about? Maybe you think I made them up, maybe you think I'm bragging too much. No! These were my actual experiences, that I had lived through. Sure, I had some unpleasant experiences, too, some close shaves. But a guy could always profit by learning from these bad experiences too. Life in the bush is not easy, but nothing in life is easy. Many times I have gone to bed without supper in weather thirty below, not because I was bad, but I made mistakes. So you see, this is not the life of

Riley, but I have gone thus far, learned a few things through understanding, acquired a fair amount of knowledge about this kind of life, and I have the scorched pants to prove it. Scorched from being too close to campfires of the bush trails. . .

Enough of this for now. Let's look into the diary.

September, 1957 and we were back at our winter camp at Sibbeston Lake. We wanted to put up some fresh fish for the winter, so we got our canoes loaded and left home. My brother Henry and I in one canoe, George Cli, a brother-in-law, in the other canoe. About an hour from home, while crossing a bay, we saw a moose wading out in the lake. George had a camera loaded with colour film, so we decided to take a picture of the moose. We all paddled that way. We did not go far and saw two more moose come out of the bush.

We were still a little way when they all walked back into the bush. We landed there on the shore and pulled up our canoes and walked from there. When we got within hearing distance of them, we decided to make the bull come to us for his picture. I had a piece of flat bone, shaped like a short paddle with a handle, and I was going to use that to make him come. George had the camera, so he came next to me.

The bush was so thick, but we found a little clearing where the sunshine filtered in and we selected the spot for our shot. I rubbed my bone hard against a tree. A little way in the thicket a tree started swinging hard, back and forth, and we heard his horns being rubbed against a tree. After a minute, he stopped. I called him and he called me too. I used the bone again and he used his horns. I called and he called. On and on we called each other, I and the bull moose. Between calls I used the bone and he used his horns. Every time he rubbed a tree, it was a different one. We could see it swinging and noted that the moose was coming our way all the time, though we couldn't see him yet.

Soon, he was near our clearing, which was about twenty feet across, and I kept on calling him till he came into the clearing and stood there for his picture. For a second or two I had a funny, topsy-turvy feeling inside of me as I stood there facing the bull moose. He was standing only yards away, with his big, wicked-looking horns and no sign of friendship in his eyes. What a ticklish situation I got myself into, just to satisfy a fisherman turned photographer.

After a while, I looked at the cameraman out of the corner of my eyes, and saw him put the camera down to pick up the rifle. Soon, he fired and the bull went down. We passed the bull, went after the cow and calf. I still had my flat bone and was going to use it on the cow too, but I guess she heard the shot. I saw them running away, but I couldn't shoot, bush being too thick. With the speed that they went, I figured they could be south of the border that same day.

Well, we got one moose and one picture, which did not turn out too good, but the meat was good. We cut up all the meat, cached it good, and went to our fishery.

Memoirs by aboriginal writers tell of experiences and offer points of view that are not present in most other literature. The authors of these memoirs lived before aboriginal people were writing literature to any large extent so the insights they provide are invaluable. All the memoirs speak of everyday events but they reveal a beauty and richness in the lives of the people. In a physical sense their daily existence was harder than it is today, but it was also a life of satisfaction and excitement. The stories were told as the memories were recalled by the storytellers. The readers are drawn into the life of the past; sharing, mutual support, helpfulness, respect for and appreciation of others characterized their daily lives. But their lives also had laughter, competition, beauty, impulsiveness, playfulness, humour, and fun. From Thunderchild to Tetso, these storytellers have left an invaluable legacy for contemporary readers.

CHAPTER 4

Biography and Autobiography

Introduction

Although biographies and autobiographies are similar to memoirs they are usually organized along a chronological time line and include more information. Some tell about a person's life from birth to death, whereas others tell about only a portion of the subject's life. Biographers often interview their subjects if they are still alive, or they rely on written sources — letters, newspaper accounts, church records, or whatever information can be acquired.

Autobiographies may have many of the characteristics of memoirs. The oral narrative style of intimate interaction with the readers, the lack of background detail, little description of emotions, understatement, and imperfect English may all be found. They often show a strong sense of community and the subject's attachment to a specific "home" location. Community rituals, ceremonies, and customs are lovingly recalled and described. The uniqueness of the lifestyle is portrayed by the language the writer uses and the content that has been selected.

Authenticity of biographies and autobiographies is enhanced by careful descriptions of physical surroundings, descriptions of how people look, act, and feel, and a careful rendering of their speech. The writer has to be objective; that is, personal opinion must not interfere with the accuracy of the book. The characters must be presented as real people with faults as well as virtues. There is a tendency for biographers to overemphasize the positive aspects of a person's character. This is to be expected because biographers choose to write about people they find particularly interesting or people with special accomplishments. If the person is made to appear super-human, however, the readers will become skeptical.

Biographies and autobiographies are written about the past. People's actions, speech, dress, and even values and beliefs change over time. The readers must be prepared to enter a time period where daily life was different than it is today. The reader must be aware that today's explanations may not clarify people's actions in the past. Some knowledge of history may be necessary in order to fully understand the time period in which the subject lived, since historical events often have a profound influence on human behavior.

How these historical events are interpreted will depend on the subject of the biography and the point of view of the biographer. Much of Canada's history is written from the point of view of the conquering Europeans and almost all of it is written from the male perspective. Biographies and autobiographies can be a valuable source of information not found in other kinds of writing. Three of the biographies included in this anthology are of historical figures: Chief Peguis, James McKay, and Marie Rose Smith. Seven are from the female perspective, giving insights into what the women were doing and thinking during the various time periods.

Excerpts From Biographies And Autobiographies

Forty Years a Chief
(Winnipeg: Peguis Publishers, 1979)
by George Barker

George Barker (1896 - 1981), lived at Wanipigow or "Hole River" in Manitoba. This place is more commonly known as the Hollow Water Reserve. He was the son of an Irish sailor, who worked on a tug boat on Lake Winnipeg, and a Saulteaux mother. Because his mother died a few days after his birth George was raised by his grandparents.

George Barker remembered happy childhood days living in a wigwam, helping his grandfather build a birch bark canoe, making moose pemmican, and harvesting and processing wild rice. These carefree days came to an abrupt end when his grandfather drowned by falling through the ice. As a result George, then seven, and his grandmother had to fend for themselves.

By the time he was fifteen George thought of himself as a man, and he and four friends decided to find work off the reserve.

They cut hay, worked for farmers, and hired on as sailors on the boats and barges that plied Lake Winnipeg. George then got a job as a forest ranger, a job he held for thirty-two years from the beginning of May to the end of October of every year. When he was twenty he started to take a serious interest in trapping in the winter time, which he continued to do for forty-eight years. At the age of twenty-two he got married and moved into a house he had built for his grandmother on the Hollow Water Reserve. He and his wife, Ida, had eighteen children, of whom six died in infancy. George was rarely at home so the responsibility for caring for the family rested largely with his wife. She supplemented their food supply with vegetables from the garden and she made money by sewing moccasins and leather jackets which she sold to travellers.

George became involved in working for registered traplines for Native people. Later he became chief of Hollow Water Reserve, a position he held for forty years. In 1950 he became president of the Manitoba Indian Brotherhood. In 1968, at the age of 72, he resigned both his positions because he had difficulty getting around. He retired to his comfortable home and at the age of 83 he wrote his life story, an honoured person not only on his reserve but across Canada. He died in 1981 at the age of 85.

The following excerpt tells about his early life, his school years, and the life of the community in the early part of this century.

> Before I started school, grandma still was in the habit of moving up the Bloodvein River to spend the winter. The supply of rabbits and fish was good there, and we badly needed the food to stay alive. We still were living in a wigwam.
>
> When I reached the age of seven word was received from the teacher at the Bloodvein Reserve - I think his name was John Reynolds - that the time had come for me to go to school. I would be able to visit my grandmother only on weekends. My first school was a large tent.
>
> One weekend when I wanted to visit my grandmother, Uncle John, with whom I was staying, asked three boys to take me to her. They were Gabriel Green and his brother, and Jack Spence.

On the way we stopped at an island, later known as Potvin's Island, to have a feed of gooseberries. The boys pulled a fast one and left me alone on that island, telling no one what they had done. I soon found that they meant business because they did not return. All my yelling and crying did no good.

I was on the island for three days, with only a few berries to eat. It was the most frightening experience of my early life. On the third night as I lay shivering and crying I heard a voice say, "Don't cry, I will sleep with you." That night I slept comfortably, and I awoke in the morning to find I was huddled close to a large black dog.

On the fourth day a young councillor from the reserve paddled past the island on his way to my grandma's to see why I had not returned to school. While passing, he was certain he had heard a faint cry. He stopped to investigate and found me under a windfall. I slept there for shelter. He took me to my relatives. The teacher instructed them to give me soup as I had not eaten for three days. Grandma came down the river, and was mad as a hatter at those boys for what they did.

It was soon after this that we moved to Rice River, not far from where I now belong at Hollow Water Indian Reserve, because grandma was frightened to let me go to school after my experience. We lived in our teepee for about four years. The few families who lived there were very good to us. Jim Black built us a small cabin and also helped by giving us food. This was the first time I had lived in anything but a wigwam. I was twelve years old now. At first I found it hard to sleep in our cabin because I thought it would fall on top of us. Grandma didn't get any rations living there, and I did not attend school since there was none near. The next time I attended school was two years later at Hollow Water. We moved to Hollow Water in the summers but returned to Rice River in the fall because hunting was better there.

It was during those years that she told me many stories of the early days. I really didn't know grandfather very well because he drowned before I was old enough to work and hunt with him. The times I can remember being with him I'm sure I was not very helpful, but he didn't seem to mind.

One of the things grandma told me was how strong the women

were in her time. Once, she and my grandfather were travelling from Bloodvein Reserve to Sasaginnigak. It was winter. She was almost ready to give birth but they started out anyway. She carried the birchbark for the teepee since the trip would take five days. Grandfather carried the rest of the necessities, food, gun and other supplies.

When they arrived at Shining Lake, about halfway, grandmother began to feel the pains. They decided to make camp and grandfather went searching for poles to put up the teepee. While he was gone, grandmother made a fire to keep warm. The pains were coming more frequently now. While she was alone, the baby came, and she managed to be her own midwife. She used snow to wash the baby and then laid it down on a blanket near the fire. The baby was very cold and shivering, but kept its health. After this incident, grandmother believed strongly that this baby adapted to the cold and was able to stand the winter weather. When grandfather returned, he could hardly believe what he was seeing. The baby had been born! It was a boy and they named him John.

The next day they continued the journey to Sasaginnigak where grandpa's brother lived. Grandmother couldn't carry the birchbark, but she did carry the baby about fifteen miles on snowshoes.

This is a difficult story to believe but other women have had similar experiences. Mrs. Whitesand, for instance, was even stronger than grandmother. Mr. Whitesand was so afraid of water he would not travel by canoe. He would walk on the shore and hunt while his wife paddled. If he killed a moose they would camp to dry the meat and tan the hide to make the load lighter.

On a trip down the Bloodvein River, en route to the reserve, Mrs. Whitesand was almost ready to give birth. She travelled until it was almost time for the baby to be born. She told her husband it was time to stop, but he became very scared and refused to stay with her. He went hunting rabbits. When he returned sometime later he found his wife lying on the river bank and beside her lay two babies. She had had twins! They stayed there about three days before continuing the journey, and by the time they arrived at Bloodvein, Mrs. Whitesand had regained her strength and was as strong and healthy as ever.

Another story my grandmother told me was about when someone would die. She said the soul of the dead person was believed to wander around in an attempt to find someone else to go to heaven with. So the people would find protection by rolling birchbark in the form of a snake and hanging it on their wigwam. This would frighten the soul away and the person would be saved.

Grandma was full of advice too. A great thing she told me was to keep my religion, which was called *Me-tah*. The white men called it the Medicine Dance. Later I will tell you more about this.

Another bit of advice was not to have bad friends. "Try to have good friends," she would say. "A person could live a much better life in this world. Everybody will like you." So said my grandmother, and I can now see what she meant, since I have many friends.

"When you are old enough, go hunting. Some day you will have a wife and children and you can feed them that way. You will never have to go hungry," she said. "If you work somewhere for money do not spend it on drink." She never drank alcohol in her life. "If you start drinking, you are not a man any more." These and many other things my grandmother told me.

Jim Black and his wife Agnes, who was a sister to my grandmother, had a son named Joe. He was about my own age. This made me feel much better. I now had a friend for the first time.

Joe and I decided to go trapping one time. We were very inexperienced and did not know what difficulties we might encounter. We took very little grub; there wasn't very much to take. I remember leaving half of our bannock at a place called the Long Dam with the intention of using it on our return journey. We knew enough to plan this way, as we heard stories of trapping by the men in the community. On we went to a place called Three Rivers, north of the Bloodvein River. We trapped here for a day or two, but before long we were running out of food and ammunition. This was all we needed to return home. Our packs were light - we didn't catch much fur and our food was so little. We were really counting on the half bannock at Long Dam.

When we got there we found only a few crumbs left. Mice had

uncovered our cache. It was a disappointment because we were quite hungry by now. It was tough going from then on, and we still had about four days' travel ahead of us. I was never so glad to see home.

But this experience didn't stop us from trapping. Joe and I went back to look at our traps, and each time we went on the trapline we learned a little more.

Trapping only serves as winter and spring work. The money is hard to earn, and one never can tell how much will be made.

When I was fourteen a man named Chris Doll came to hire someone to fish for him. He was an Icelander. I asked him if he would take me. At first I think he was afraid to because I was so young. However, he did, and I was very proud to go on my first real job. My clothing wasn't very good so I had a tough time standing the cold. I had never owned a set of underwear before. When Mr. Doll found out how I was dressed he was amazed and he bought me my first pair of underwear. It was hard to get used to them; they seemed too warm. After a while, though, I sure appreciated what Mr. Doll had done.

The Icelanders had a fishing camp not too far away. That fall, I went with grandma to set rabbit snares. Rabbits were plentiful so there was no shortage of food that time. With the pelts grandma made robes. A robe took about 180 skins. When she was finished I would take the robes to the Icelanders' camp and sell them. Each one sold for about six dollars. This really helped us to buy more food.

When I was fifteen, grandma decided to move to the Hollow Water Reserve. I attended school for a short while but soon found myself wanting to go back on the trapline. I felt like a grown man now. I liked school and maybe would have continued, but my school friend, Arthur Quesnel, was about to leave to go to the Catholic boarding school in Fort Alexander. He wanted me to go with him, but grandmother wouldn't allow it. She wasn't too impressed with the white man's teachings. This pretty well ended my life as a school boy.

My dear grandma took sick in 1927. She was living with her son Peter and his wife at the time, near the mouth of Hole River. Grandma sent a message that she wanted to talk to me. When I arrived she was sitting on a chair, but looked quite ill. After a good visit I returned home for something to eat, and there was only a short while when someone came running to tell me Grandma had died. I was shocked. I returned to Uncle Peter's house but, sure enough, she was dead.

People were not buried in coffins in those days. So, as usual, a new Hudson's Bay blanket was wrapped around the body. Sticks were placed in the grave on which the body was laid to rest.

John Henry Skye, better known as "Whiskey Jack", performed the burial service. He was one of the head men on the reserve, and was a distant relative to Uncle Peter. He also led the singing in our language, Saulteaux, as all the adults on the reserve - about fifty - shared our sorrow by taking part in the burial.

I Walk in Two Worlds
(Calgary: Glenbow-Alberta Institute, 1987)
by Eleanor Brass,

Eleanor Brass (1905 -) tells of her life on the File Hills Colony at the Peepeekisis Reserve in southern Saskatchewan. Her father, who was Cree, and her mother, who was Saulteaux, met at the Indian industrial school in Regina. The File Hill colony was a farming settlement which was meant to be a model for Native progress in adapting to the European way of life. And indeed, the colony did open up an era for many Saskatchewan Native people as they turned from a life of hunting to farming. Only graduates of the industrial schools were allowed to settle in the colony.

When Eleanor was six she was sent to a boarding school where life was extremely harsh and staff members were incredibly insensitive and cruel. The children were, however, allowed to go home at Christmas, Easter, and during the summers, a privilege not allowed at all schools. Eleanor did very well in school but did not finish grade twelve, preferring to go to work instead. At the age of nineteen she married Hector Brass. They farmed on the reserve for a while and then decided to broaden their horizons by working in the outside world.

Living in an integrated world had its difficulties because there was much discrimination against Native people, so they devoted most of the rest of their lives to improving conditions for Native people in the cities. Eleanor told Cree legends on the radio, wrote newspaper articles, and published two books, *Medicine Boy and Other Cree Tales* and her autobiography. Her husband died in 1965 and Eleanor started a job as an information writer with the Department of Agriculture. She soon transferred to the Indian and Métis Branch to work as a placement officer and counsellor for Native women. She had to retire from her government job in 1971, but went on to a new career as Executive Director of the Friendship Centre in Peace River and news correspondent for the Alberta Native Communications Society. Finally, at the age of 80 she had to retire due to poor health. Today she lives in Regina and, though her eyesight is poor, she still takes a lively interest in the world around her. She said she was "real pleased" that excerpts of her writing would be included in this anthology.

My sister used to say that I came with the frogs and my mother said I came with the flowers. It was a typical day in spring on the first day of May, 1905; the buds on the trees were bursting forth, the frogs were singing lustily, and the birds were joyously chirping as if to welcome my entrance in to the world.

I was born in a log cabin on the Peepeekisis Indian Reserve near Balcarres, Saskatchewan. Our home was cosy and comfortable, with lovely curtains at the windows and colourful patchwork quilts on the beds. Mother was an excellent homemaker. My grandmother, who was the midwife at my birth, travelled two hundred miles especially for the occasion. There were no hospitals nearby and the doctor lived quite a distance away.

My sister Janet was fifteen months old at the time and still an infant. Mother was still breastfeeding her; she thought it was the proper thing to do. Because my sister was always the delicate child, she got all the attention. I didn't have any clothes at birth, so dad wrapped me up in one of his shirts, saying, "Poor little darling." Later on a lady who was a principal of the nearby Indian school brought me a layette so at least I had some clothes.

I was put on the bottle and received only passing notice. There was a small hammock suspended from the ceiling in the upstairs bedroom where I spent most of my infant days. They said that I was a very good baby; no wonder, I had no chance to know what it was like to be pampered. But I had a happy childhood; our parents were proud of us and gave us the best care. We were fortunate. . .

Our childhood days were interesting. Our parents took us to Indian feasts and sometimes to funerals. We liked the feasts but the funerals used to scare us. We didn't understand the rituals where the women seemed to do a lot of wailing. After attending them I would get nightmares, so my parents stopped taking us.

Instead, they would leave us with some elderly Indian woman to babysit us. They were our *kokooms* (grandmothers). They were so kind to us and would lovingly say, *"Nosisim, mitoni, kitamakasit nosisim."* ("My poor grandchild.") This was their way of petting and caressing us. We didn't speak Cree in our house as our parents spoke two different languages — mother was Saulteaux while father was Cree. Our parents thought we would be held back in school if they spoke nothing but Indian languages to us. I am sorry about this. When we went to school we learned some Cree from our schoolmates but we often found that what we learned wasn't in good taste when we repeated it to our parents. They told us never to say those words again and not to learn any more Cree from our schoolmates.

As we grew older we often accompanied our parents to town. While they were doing their shopping we would sometimes wait for them outside on the street and watch the people go by. Some of them would stop and speak to us while others would just smile. Once some boys came by and called us "little squaws" but we didn't realize then that we were Indians. We called back to them "little squaws yourselves." This marked the first of many episodes both good and bad that were to influence and affect my life.

It has never ceased to be interesting to be an Indian and to walk in two worlds, watching, learning and trying to understand the many cultures and the thinking of the various races of people. While I know that my Indian culture is one of the noblest in the world, I feel that other cultures have affected my life in various ways.

I remember in the early days, the farmers on the colony had to haul their grain quite a distance away to Indian Head. It meant having to stay over a night or two since they used horses and wagons. The women were left to do the chores and look after the stock. One day while father was away on one of these trips mother couldn't find me. I was about four years old and as usual had been snooping around where I shouldn't have been. Somehow I got into a manger in front of a team of colts that were being stable broke. I was terrified and crying while the frightened colts were stamping and snorting. Mother heard the racket and came down to see what was going on. When she saw me in the manger in front of the colts, she stood there for a minute not knowing what to do. Then she quietly spoke to me, telling me to come towards her slowly till she could get hold of me and drag me over to the other stall. Somehow she got me out without anyone being hurt. She was so frightened and relieved that she forgot to punish me. I think the experience itself was enough punishment for both of us.

I also remember when a great cyclone struck in 1914. We watched the black cloud coming towards us, looking like a huge snake dragging on the ground. Quickly father put us all down in the dirt cellar while he watched from the upstairs window. He saw our neighbour's house being lifted off the ground and blown to pieces. Father immediately went out to the barn, hooked up a team to a democrat and drove over to their place. He found Henry McLeod badly hurt and trying to crawl over to our place for help. Dad loaded him on the democrat then looked for his wife, Eliza; he found her lying under a portion of roof. He thought she was dead as she was pale and covered with blood but she eventually recovered.

Then dad looked for the baby, Jaky, who was about a year and a half old. He searched around the wreckage but couldn't find him until the dog came running out of the barn, barking as if trying to get dad's attention; he went over and found the baby in the stable. He thought the dog must have dragged him there for safety, as the mother said the last thing she remembered was hanging onto him. The baby wasn't hurt except for a small bruise on his forehead but he was soaking wet and cold. The dog should have been decorated for it must have been responsible for Jaky's safety.

This was a horrible experience for the McLeods. They were just recently married and Jaky was their first child. After the cyclone they stayed at our place for a while. Mother put up beds for them in our front room and the doctor came to treat them. Henry had a broken back and multiple bruises while Eliza had a broken leg and bruises.

My sister and I had the job of looking after Jaky. We changed him and fed him and babysat him. The neighbours also came over, taking turns to assist in any way they could. Then the grandparents came and took Jaky to look after him. As soon as the parents were in a condition to be moved, they were taken to Labret and put in the hospital wing of the school where they were nursed back to health. They built another house almost on the same spot as their old one and never had the same experience again.

Meanwhile, our family was growing. I had a little brother by the name of Charles but when he was fifteen months old he developed pneumonia and passed away. We were all so sad and for a long time mother hardly ever smiled. About two years later I had another brother, Harold. We girls were so happy and always wanted to hold him but we weren't allowed to do that for very long.

In the early years there were no churches on our reserve. The Presbyterians sent out a minister - or as they called them at that time, a missionary - to look after our spiritual needs. He boarded in the different homes in turn. When he lived in our home, it was extra work for mother and a certain amount of worry.

I was always a lively, curious and outspoken child which kept mother on edge wondering what I was going to say next when the minister was around. Apparently I embarrassed her a few times in spite of her constant cautioning me not to speak, especially at mealtimes.

The minister had his sleeping quarters in our living room and we had to go through it to reach the dining and kitchen areas. Once when I was passing through I caught the minister just getting up and as he pulled on his trousers, they fell to his ankles. I was shocked and in my childish way I ran into the kitchen to describe the incident to mother.

"Momma, Momma," I shouted, "I saw the minister's bum."

"Shh! Shh!" she said. "Don't ever say that to anyone and don't you say one word at the breakfast table."

That morning at the table, every time I was going to speak, mother would give such a look that I kept my mouth shut.

Church services were held in the various homes until a church was built. These services were always an ordeal for me. When I sat with mother, she pinched me if I didn't sit quietly and when I sat with dad, he only stood so much from me, then took me outside and gave me a spanking. When he brought me back into the building, I sat quietly even afraid to breath too loudly. There were no Sunday school classes for us and we were expected to sit with the grownups all during the service. I wondered why the minister had to talk so long and sometimes yell at the people.

While I was small, I noticed that mother had a large book that she guarded carefully from us children. This made me very curious and once when she forgot it on the table, I immediately grabbed it, put it on a chair, and started turning the pages. It was full of coloured pictures of the human body. As I slowly turned each page. I tried to figure out what the pictures were. My aunt was visiting at the time and they wondered why I was so quiet, so they began to watch me from the doorway. I was chattering away to myself, wondering what this was and that was. When I came to a picture of a naked man, I turned the book upside down and looked at it from every angle; some parts of the body were obviously different from a girl's. I kept saying to myself, "What's that? What's that?" Then I finally turned the page over and said, "A mouse, I guess."

Later, the twins, Edna and Edward, were born. Mother had her hands full but the neighbours were always ready to go over and do what they could for her. From there on the family grew to twelve children - nine boys and three girls. Wilfred, the last one, was born the year I was married and always thought that my husband was his real brother.

Geniesh: An Indian Girlhood
(Toronto: New Press, 1973)
by Jane Willis

Jane Willis (1940 -) tells of her childhood at Fort George on the eastern shores of James Bay in northern Quebec. She describes herself as a stubborn, strong-willed child. This often got her into trouble. The worst trouble she brought upon herself was insisting that she attend the Anglican Residential School as a boarding student. Though the school was right in the community, children were not allowed to see their families except for three hours every weekend. Only in summer were they allowed to go home. Treatment of the children was very harsh by today's standards and staff members were extremely cruel.

It was largely because of Jane's stubborness and strong willpower that she actually graduated from grade eight along with another girl, an event that had never happened before. She went on to high school in Sault Ste. Marie. She had great hopes for high school because she would be attending an integrated high school while living in the Indian residence. There was little change; rules at the residence were as strict as back home and the teachers' and supervisors' expectations of the Native students at the school were low as ever. Jane stayed in school until she completed grade eleven, always maintaining an *A* average. Then she chose to go to work. Her self-concept was very low and she was intensely aware of being a Native, which, she believed, automatically made her an inferior human being. She felt untrustworthy, inferior, incapable, and immoral.

In her adulthood she regained her early self-confidence and learned to be proud of the fact that she is Native. In the following excerpt she tells about her birth and her childhood before she started school.

"No white person employed by the Hudson Bay Company shall fraternize with the natives [Indians]." This was a rule of the "Bay" — as the company is more commonly known — which I, the daughter of a Cree Indian and a Scotsman, can attest is more often ignored than obeyed on the small island of "jisah-seebee" (Great River) where I was born.

The island was named "jisah-seebee" by the Cree Indians of northern Quebec because it is situated at the mouth of a great, swift river - the Fort George River. Fort George, as the river and the island were named by unimaginative fur traders, is located on the eastern shores of James Bay in northern Quebec, Canada, about eight hundred miles south of the Arctic Circle.

When I was born in 1940, the island was inhabited by approximately twenty white people, seven hundred Cree Indians - who came from their trapping grounds for two months each summer to trade with the Bay - and forty "white-status" Indians, descendants of Indian women who had married white men.

Our island was five miles long, one mile wide and covered with pine trees. In its centre, five distinct communities clustered together: the Catholic mission, the Coaster village with its huddle of teepees, the Hudson Bay Company compound, the Anglican mission, and the Inlander village. (Coasters are Indians who trap along the coast; Inlanders trap inland.) Scattered around the fringes of these communities were the tar-paper shacks and one-room log cabins of the permanent residents of the island, those who could no longer trap - the aged and the white-status Indians, who on losing their native status had, consequently, lost their trapping rights - and those who did not need to trap - the few Indians who were lucky enough to get the few menial positions available at the white settlements.

My grandfather was one of the lucky ones. As an employee of the Bay, he did everything from waiting on customers to collecting the garbage. It was through him that my mother acquired the coveted position of the Bay manager's maid, and it was there that she met my father, one of the company clerks. Falling in love had been simple, but getting married was more difficult.

Without the company's permission, it would have been impossible; but since my mother had proved herself to be a clean, trustworthy, hard-working girl, the manager and his wife, acting for the main office, gave their consent. My father's parents, thinking that my mother, whom they had never met, couldn't be a "dirty savage" if their son was willing to face the consequences of an inter-racial marriage, also gave their consent.

Only after he had gained the vitally important consent of these two parties did my father approach my maternal grandparents, and they, after holding several pow-wows with the whole family - aunts, uncles, cousins, in-laws, anyone even remotely connected with the family, which meant practically everyone on the island - consented to the union.

It was during these long, touchy, and occasionally stormy negotiations that I made my untimely presence known and all plans came to a grinding halt. My mother, who had been considering the consequences of such a marriage and who had more or less resigned herself to them, suddenly rejected the proposal when her suspicions of me were confirmed.

Why? Because, according to the over-zealous missionaries who had come to the island to save my people from eternal hell and damnation, all white men drank, robbed, raped, murdered, beat their wives and children, had countless extra-marital affairs, and eventually ran off with their mistresses, leaving their poor defenceless wives and children to starve. Only those on the island, those "chosen and sent by God," could be trusted. This type of preaching was meant to scare the young, curious Indian maidens and to keep the races pure - mainly the white race, I suspect.

My mother, who went to church every day and twice on Sundays, believed all this propaganda and decided that a few months, or possibly, years of happiness would not be worth the years of misery and deprivation that were to follow. While she had been willing to face the risks by herself, she could not subject an innocent baby to such a depraved society.

Her refusal, of course, created a scandal. Nobody could understand why a girl in her condition would turn down any marriage proposal. Even a white man was better than nothing.

When it became a glaring fact that I was on the way, my father was transferred to another store two thousand miles away to save the company further embarrassment. He left weeping and begging my obstinate mother to reconsider, but she was adamant. It was not the man that she was rejecting, but his society.

Shortly afterwards, he joined the Air Force and was sent

overseas. While he was stationed in Europe, I was born and given the grand old Indian name of Janie Margaret Matthews. Everyone, however, called me Geniesh, which means Little Janie.

Before my first birthday, my father was shot down on a bombing mission over Germany. My mother returned to work and left me in the care of my doting grandparents who had been waiting impatiently for this moment, this second chance at parenthood. The circumstances were not exactly what they had hoped for, but they did not care. Once their own children had reached their teens, they, like most Indian parents, were eager to push them into production so that they could be surrounded by grandchildren in their old age. They were a loving and over-indulgent couple.

My grandmother was a huge moose of a woman who weighed about three hundred pounds. Her face was typically Indian - dark brown, deeply furrowed with wrinkles, with the acquiline nose and high cheek-bones - but her hair was not; it was jet-black all right, but it was also naturally curly. A generous freak of nature had endowed her with this unIndian and enviable trait, a trait which was inherited by all four daughters and quite a number of her grandchildren, but which completely bypassed me.

My grandfather was exactly the opposite to my grandmother in size. He was a wizened-up old man, small and thin, probably weighing no more than 130 pounds. His skin was rough and leathery; his hands gnarled and misshapen like the weather-tortured branches of a tree. His brown wrinkled face was topped by a shock of white hair which stood out in all directions. He also had one non-Indian trait. He had blue eyes! Unlike my grandmother's ancestry - her parents were born before the first white men settled in the area - his was suspect. To me, though, the colour of his eyes was not unusual. I thought all Indian children had blue-eyed grandfathers.

Their backgrounds were also different. She had been raised in the old Indian tradition, learning from an early age all the skills - skinning game, tanning hides, weaving nets, treating various ailments - she needed to become a good wife and mother. She could not speak a word of English because she had never gone to school. She had been too old when the first regular day school was started in 1907. The school was mostly for religious instruction and the learning of Cree syllabics, however. Only the names of the days, months, and numbers were taught in English. Arithmetic - only the basics of addition and multiplication - was added to the curriculum about 1928. Even when the first boarding school opened in 1933 - when my mother was thirteen - the half-day sessions were still mostly on religion.

My grandfather, however, spoke English well. He had learned it in his youth, which was spent guiding the skippers of trading schooners and steamers through the unfamiliar and ever-changing waters of James and Hudsons Bays, and acting as interpreter for the traders as they bartered with flour, tea, sugar, blankets, and guns for the furs of the Indians.

In the mixture of English and Cree that he always used when speaking to me, he would spend hours, whittling as he did so, telling me about the things he had seen in his travels - strange instruments which carried your voice for miles, vehicles which did not need dogs to pull them; subjects much too alien to me to be believable.

My great-grandmother was about eighty, but she still spent her winters trapping in the bush, returning only for the summer months to live with us. I loved listening to her stories in the evenings as we squatted on the aromatic pine-covered tepee floor. Each spring we moved from our one-room cabin to our summer home by the seashore, a huge tepee only a few feet from our cabin. The extra space was needed to accommodate the numerous relatives who had returned from their trapping grounds.

My great-grandmother constantly told me how spoiled I was. When she was young, she said, she never had candies and chocolates. She had been ten when her parents made their first visit to the island, shortly after the first clergyman settled there in 1852. She told me their first gift upon arrival was a bag of flour from the other Indians, but after trying to eat it raw, her parents had decided it wasn't much of a gift. One of the other Indians showed them how to mix it with goose grease and water and then cook it on a stick over the fire. This early version of bannock had been so delicious that she and her parents, in spite of the Indians' warnings, had eaten it all while it was still hot.

That night they suffered terribly from violent cramps, their stomachs distended and hard as rocks. Apparently, it took some time before they could eat it without any ill effects.

I was a very healthy child. I had to be for self-preservation. When I was ill, my doting grandmother always took the precaution of dosing me with her own home-made remedies after I had been treated by the nurse. It was the dreaded combination of the white man's blunt hypodermics and marble-sized pills and my grandmother's sinus-clearing, eye-irritating and throat-searing remedies which forced me to keep many of my ailments to myself.

I was not always successful, however. I vividly remember waking up one sunny morning with every part of my body aching and my throat feeling as if I had swallowed a bottle of lye. I bounced out of bed as sprightly as I could, but my observant grandmother felt my burning forehead and gently pushed me back under the goose-down comforter. Then I heard her yell the dreaded words, "ndo-wabin mah ndi-queensquogh," to some child outside.

The nurse wasted no time on preliminaries, but thrust a thermometer in my mouth as soon as she entered. My grandmother was gesticulating wildly, clutching at her throat and pointing at mine. The nurse nodded and smiled at her. She took the thermometer out of my mouth and shook her head sadly. She came at me with a flashlight and a tongue depressor, stuck her tongue out and said, "Aaah."

I shook my head violently and clenched my teeth. My grandmother said sweetly, "wabtee mah. dahbah jig-ahk-heok."

I could not believe that it would not hurt. My grandmother had threatened me with the nurse much too often. I shook my head more violently.

"wabtee! yahgaw jig-oot-dumhoodin!" she said, a little less sweetly, but since she had hit me only twice in my life - once for using her favourite pipe to blow bubbles, and once for squeezing the chicken-pox pustules on a friend of mine - I knew she was bluffing.

Letting out a war whoop, I jumped out of bed and raced past them across the room. I made a dash for the door and darted outside around to the back of the cabin. I glanced back to see the nurse, clutching her flashlight and tongue depressor in one hand and hiking up her tight skirt with the other, breathing down my neck. My grandmother was nowhere in sight. I whizzed around the corner of the cabin hoping to lose them in the dense bushes behind the outhouse.

Suddenly, a fat brown hand grabbed me from the open window and jerked me back against the cabin. My sneaky grandmother, who had often chased me all over the island to force some of her home-remedies down my throat, had anticipated my usual escape route. She yanked me inside, muttering about all the terrible things she was going to do to me as soon as the nurse left, as I kicked and screamed. She threw me on the bed, and before I could jump up, she plunked all three hundred pounds of herself on my stomach.

The air exploded from my bursting lungs, and as I opened my mouth to take a breath, the nurse, who had come racing inside, laughing, rammed her tongue depressor down my throat. Again she shook her head sadly. She pulled out a monstrous hypodermic from her black bag and proceeded to fill it with white liquid right in front of me. My grandmother shifted her weight, rolled me over slightly, and the nurse jabbed the blunt needle into my rigid backside. Only after the nurse had yanked the needle out did my grandmother let me go.

The nurse, still laughing, reached into her bag and pulled out a container of pills which she handed to my beaming grandmother. They walked to the door, laughing and nodding, and shook hands.

By then my lungs were fully inflated once more, and I started shrieking. My grandmother put her arms around me and rocked me gently, telling me what a horrible person the nurse was and how much better I would feel as soon as she heated up some goose-grease and brewed one of her own cures for me.

She rubbed my throat, back, and front with warm goose-grease and forced a few spoonfuls down my throat for good measure. The vile-tasting concoction which she had brewed was also forced down my throat by squeezing my nostrils shut until I had drunk every drop.

I lay in bed for several days, pulling the chinking from between the logs to pass the time, smelling like a half-decayed body while the penicillin and my grandmother's obnoxious brews and salves did their work. Sheer will-power and a deep sense of self-preservation, I believe, cured me more than either the white man's medicine or my grandmother's.

My grandmother had a cure for everything - sips of warm goose-grease for coughs; goose or bear grease, sometimes rancid, rubbed on the chest and back for colds; weak tea or mother's milk for snow blindness; black bear bile for liniment; beaver castors for poultices, the oil from the castors for sores and rashes; liquid from boiled and strained beaver castors to prevent hemorrhaging after childbirth; and brews from certain plants for various aches and pains.

Sometimes I questioned her cures because all they did was substitute one form of pain or discomfort for another. For a headache, she tied a piece of cloth or a bandanna tightly around my head. All that was missing was the feather. On our island, an Indian wearing a headband was not necessarily reverting to the old ways; he could simply be trying to get rid of a headache.

Another of my grandmother's questionable remedies was wrapping beaver or muskrat fur around a sore or an ache. When the ache started to itch, she considered the cure effective.

Summer was the time for gathering medicinal herbs and my grandfather's clover-like tobacco, which he dried and saved for the times the Bay ran out of regular tobacco. This was done on fishing or berry-picking trips. My grandparents always took me along but invariably rejected my contributions: too many flowers, not enough flowers; leaves too dull, leaves too shiny; plant too big, plant not big enough.

The only thing I ever learned to recognize was a spicy shrub which when brewed with tea was my grandmother's favourite drink. If brewed for a short period, the tea is slightly spicy and not unpleasant, but she always brewed it until it was strong and pungent. Then she would take a sip, smack her lips appreciatively, and say, "ahk mac tea!" I preferred the store-bought variety myself.

This brew was also taken for upset stomachs, headaches and coughs. My grandmother, who believed strongly in taking every conceivable precaution, insisted I drink her gut-dissolvant tea each time she brewed it. I shuddered whenever I saw her taking out her precious leaves and throwing them into the teapot.

"min-gaw oo," she'd say when the brew had cooled down enough. "nastahbaw jig-weej-heegune."

When I complained that it did not make me strong and healthy, that I suffered violent cramps, a throbbing headache, and violent coughing fits from the bitter tonic, she would urge me to drink more of it. She told me I got this reaction because I did not drink enough of it, and I argued that I would probably die if I drank more than I did. She would insist, invariably adding, "wasa! mingawshj oo. oowhan jahminheesk gahdigh-anah?"

Not wishing to be responsible for her early demise, I would give in to her unreasonable demands, whining and complaining all the while.

"wasa! oowah-eejanhee naspit-what?" she constantly wondered, but I knew the answer. It was my white-tainted blood that made me so stubborn, so curious, so pesky, so contrary - all the traits a good, obedient and pliant little Indian was not supposed to have. I had heard people say it often enough. It was never explained to me why full-blooded Indian children behaved exactly as I did.

My Name is Masak
(Winnipeg: Peguis Publishers, 1976)
by Alice French

Alice French (1930 -) was born on Baillie Island in the Northwest Territories. Her father was an Alaskan Laplander who spoke both Inuit and English in their home. He worked as an interpreter for the police. Her mother was an Alaskan Inuit. The baby was given an Inuit name, Masak, after her father's mother and a Christian name, Alice, after her mother's mother.

Though life became hard and often lonely for Masak as she grew up, she had a happy early childhood with her younger brother and her travelling parents. This changed when Masak was seven. Her mother got tuberculosis and the children were sent to a boarding school. Here Masak became "Alice" and it was to be four years before she saw her father again. During this time her mother had died and her father had remarried. When Alice got home she had to get acquainted with a whole new set of relatives. She missed her mother's family but soon grew to love her new grandmother, who taught her all the skills she would need as an adult. Alice went back to school for another year, then accompanied her parents for a year in their travels. When she became ill she stayed in a boarding school in Aklavik until she finished her schooling.

Alice did well in school but she found many things that were very strange. In this excerpt she tells of her reactions to the material she learned and to the school routine.

> My teacher's name was Miss A. Farrow and after Christmas her job was much easier for we were all able to speak fairly well in English. I was luckier than some of my girl friends, because I had learned English from my father. We had not been allowed to speak our native tongue since coming to school and it was hard on some of my friends. If we were caught speaking in Eskimo we were punished. This was a frustrating but effective system.
>
> I really did not mind reading and writing but I sure did not like arithmetic. Some of the subjects we read about puzzled me. Dogs I already knew about, and cats. I had seen my first horse,

but what were sheep and cows and pigs? Chickens looked something like ptarmigan and the eggs were good to eat. We learned a nursery rhyme:

Humpty Dumpty sat on a wall
Humpty Dumpty had a great fall
And all the king's horses and all the king's men
Couldn't put Humpty Dumpty together again.

According to the picture book Humpty Dumpty was an egg, so how could he be dressed and sitting on a wall? I asked Miss Farrow about this and did not seem to get any answers. A rhyme that puzzled me even more was:

Hey diddle diddle, the cat and the fiddle
The cow jumped over the moon
The little dog laughed to see such sport
And the dish ran away with the spoon

Now, I knew cats could not play fiddles. I did not know whether cows could jump over the moon or not, but I was sure that dishes could not run and certainly not with spoons. I worried about my teacher sometimes. She did not seem to know the difference between what creatures could and could not do.

Each year, as my reading got better, I found that books held a vast store of information and could take me away to distant times and places. I learned that Ottawa was our capital city in Canada. That was where our Prime Minister lived. He was the one who told everyone else how to live. Besides Canada there were different countries with different kinds of people. England was the country where my teacher used to live. This was hard to feature but I told myself never mind; there were all my tomorrows ahead to learn something new.

Wintertime in the Mackenzie was cold and dark, quite depressing sometimes, especially from the end of November on when the sun no longer came up. Mid-day brought a little twilight and our walks were much shorter now, because of the cold weather. We went just around to The Bay store, about half a mile away, and back. My winter clothing was not as warm as my fur clothes used to be. My parka, mitts and mukluks were made from blanket cloth, covered with blue denim, and the wind blew right through them. Only the soles of my boots were made of skin - moose-hide. The only birds we saw on our walks were the ravens rooting in the garbage for food, and the occasional whiskey jack. On some nights the moon was full and shining; it transformed our dark world into a land of shimmering brightness. Looking out our dormitory window we could see the snow-covered trees and houses much better than we could during the day.

Quite frequently in the cold months we would wake up in the night shivering with cold and head for the hot-air radiator. Some nights I was lucky because no one else was up and I could have the radiator to myself for a while. I let the hot air billow out my nightgown and warm my body with heat. Then more girls woke up cold and I got off and sat on the floor, with just my feet on the radiator. Soon there would be ten or twelve girls shoving each other for a place on the radiator. Then I would crawl back into bed.

Fire drills were a nightmare for all of us. We never knew when they would be called. Sometimes they were a week apart; other times three or four weeks would go by before we would hear the alarm. Each evening, before bedtime, we collected our parkas, mitts, and mukluks from the playroom and took them up and laid them at the foot of our beds. Then as we undressed we placed our dresses, stockings, bloomers and longjohns on top of our outer clothing. Most of the time we were careless and did not bother. When the alarm went off in the middle of the night we had only three minutes to dress and that was just enough time to put on our parkas, boots, and mittens. In the fall and spring drills were not bad, but in winter it was cold. We lined up in front of the fire-escape window, which was located in our dorm, and waited for the signal. We were to start sliding down the chute every three seconds. Our supervisor, Miss Neville, counted - one, two, three - and the first girl started off. There was a small platform attached to the window with a slide leading to the ground floor below. Often one girl would stand on the platform and look down and be scared. She would hesitate for a second and that would throw the rest of us off. Miss Neville was not able to see what was happening at the bottom and would still keep sending girls on down. Soon we had a tangle of bodies in the snow below. After one of these drills we came back in with our teeth chattering. It would be a while before we went back to sleep and the next day it was a chore to stay awake in classes.

As we grew older we helped in the kitchen, dining-room and staff dining-room. We were taught the use of the washing machine and the mangle. We worked one day a week at each chore. I hated to work in the dining-room. We had to wash all the dishes by hand. When we worked in the staff dining-room we learned the correct way to set tables and serve the meals. I did not mind this job; we ate the same meals as the staff. Once a week, in the evenings, we helped to punch down the bread dough. Before breakfast we put this dough into breadpans, ready to bake.

The days were getting longer now that January was almost over. The sun started peeking up, just a sliver at first, but each day it got a little stronger and I was glad that the long darkness had ended. Now our afternoon walks were through the bush. This was to allow us to snare rabbits which we sold to the school for 25 cents each. If we were successful we could make quite a bit of pocket money. On Saturdays our walks were much longer and we took along a picnic. We would walk about three miles, stop, build a roaring fire and huddle around it trying to warm ourselves. The hot tea always tasted good and so did the wieners and buns that we toasted over the fire. After eating, we relaxed and sang campfire songs around the fire.

Sometimes we played hookey on our walks through the settlement. If our supervisor needed something from the Bay store and went in to buy it, we would run back to the school. If we were caught at this we would be sent to the principal's office, and sometimes we got the strap. At recess or on days we did not go for walks, we made our own entertainment. We had a swing in the yard and a slide made out of snow and ice. Our sleds were pieces of heavy cardboard that we soaked in water and left out to freeze overnight so they would go faster and farther down the slide. Even though we liked the slide we were usually glad to go back into the warm school.

Halfbreed
(Toronto: McClelland and Stewart, 1973)
by Maria Campbell

Maria Campbell (1940 -) is a Métis from northern Saskatchewan. Her ancestors on her father's side fought on the side of Riel in 1885. After their defeat their attempts at farming also failed, so they went back to a life of trapping, supplemented by illegal hunting and making illicit whiskey. On her mother's side her ancestors were Native; Maria's mother was educated in a residential school.

Maria's parents married when her father was eighteen, her mother fifteen. She describes her father as very good-looking with black, curly hair and blue-grey eyes. He was warm, happy, and always laughing and singing in his younger years. Her mother was auburn-haired and tiny, with blue eyes. She was soft-spoken and loved books and music. She was always busy cooking, sewing, and caring for the family and often read or sang to the children.

Much as Maria loved her parents, the most important person in her life was her great-grandmother, Cheechum. It was Cheechum who had the time to answer Maria's questions and teach her what she needed to know about living.

When her mother died, twelve-year-old Maria had to look after the family — seven younger brothers and sisters, one a newborn baby. Cheechum could only give advice because she was ninety-six years old. After struggling to keep the family together for three years Maria resorted to marriage to a non-Native man, hoping he would support them all. This ended in failure and the children were placed in foster homes.

After this Maria's life went downhill as she moved from city to city. She became an alcoholic, a dope addict and a prostitute. Finally she remembered her Cheechum's teachings and was able to regain control of her life. Today she lives at Gabriel's Crossing at Batoche, Saskatchewan. She conducts writing and drama workshops, and encourages young Native and Métis writers in their creative efforts.

I was born during a spring blizzard in April of 1940. Grannie Campbell, who had come to help my mother, made Dad stay outside the tent, and he chopped wood until his arms ached. At last I arrived, a daughter, much to Dad's disappointment. However this didn't dampen his desire to raise the best trapper and hunter in Saskatchewan. As far as I can remember Daddy taught me to set traps, shoot a rifle, and fight like a boy. Mom did her best to turn me into a lady, showing me how to cook, sew and knit, while Cheechum, my best friend and confidante, tried to teach me all she knew about living.

I should tell you about our home now before I go any further. We lived in a large two-roomed hewed log house that stood out from the others because it was too big to be called a shack. One room was used for sleeping and all of us children shared it with our parents. There were three big beds made from poles with rawhide interlacing. The mattresses were canvas bags filled with fresh hay twice a year. Over my parents' bed was a hammock where you could always find a baby. An air-tight heater warmed the room in winter. Our clothes hung from pegs or were folded and put on a row of shelves. There were braided rugs on the floor, and in one corner a special sleeping rug where Cheechum slept when she stayed with us, as she refused to sleep on a bed or eat off a table.

I loved that corner of the house and would find any excuse possible to sleep with her. There was a special smell that comforted me when I was hurt or afraid. Also, it was a great place to find all sorts of wonderful things that Cheechum had - little pouches, boxes, and cloth tied up containing pieces of bright cloth, beads, leather, jewelry, roots and herbs, candy, and whatever else a little girl's heart could desire.

The kitchen and living room were combined into one of the most beautiful rooms I have ever known. Our kitchen had a huge black wood stove for cooking and for heating the house. On the wall hung pots, pans and various roots and herbs used for cooking and making medicine. There was a large table, two chairs and two benches made from wide planks, which we scrubbed with homemade lye soap after each meal. On one wall were shelves for our good dishes and a cupboard for storing everyday tin plates, cups and food.

The living-room area had a homemade chesterfield and chair of carved wood and woven rawhide, a couple of rocking chairs painted red, and an old steamer trunk by the east window. The floor was made of wide planks which were scoured to an even whiteness all over. We made braided rugs during the winter months from old rags, although it often took us a full year to gather enough for even a small rug.

There were open beams on the ceiling and under these ran four long poles the length of the house. The poles served as racks where furs were hung to dry in winter. On a cold winter night the smell of moose stew simmering on the stove blended with the wild smell of the drying skins of mink, weasels and squirrels, and the spicy herbs and roots hanging from the walls. Daddy would be busy in the corner, brushing fur until it shone and glistened, while Mom bustled around the stove. Cheechum would be on the floor smoking her clay pipe and the small ones would roll and fight around her like puppies. I can see it all so vividly it seems only yesterday.

Our parents spent a great deal of time with us, and not just our parents but the other parents in our settlement. They taught us to dance and to make music on the guitars and fiddles. They played cards with us, they would take us on long walks and teach us how to use the different herbs, roots and barks. We were taught to weave baskets from the red willow, and while we did these things together we were told the stories of our people - who they were, where they came from, and what they had done. Many were legends handed down from father to son. Many of them had a lesson but mostly they were fun stories about funny people.

My Cheechum believed with heart and soul in the little people. She said they were so tiny that unless you are really looking for them you will never find them; not that it matters, because you usually only see them when they want you to.

The little people lived near the water and they travel mostly by leaf boats. They are a happy lot and also very shy. Cheechum saw them once when she was a young woman. She had gone to the river for water in the late afternoon and decided to sit and watch the sun go down. It was very quiet and even the birds were still. Then she heard a sound like many people laughing and talking at a party. The sounds kept coming closer and finally she saw a large leaf floating to shore with other leaves following behind. Standing on the leaves were tiny people dressed in beautiful colours.

They waved to her and smiled as they came ashore. They told her that they were going to rest for the evening, then leave early in the morning to go further downstream. They sat with her until the sun had gone down and then said good-bye and disappeared into the forest. She never saw them again; but all her life she would leave small pieces of food and tobacco near the water's edge for them which were always gone by morning. Mom said it was only a fairy tale but I would lie by the waters for hours hoping to see the little people.

Cheechum had the gift of second sight, although she refused to forecast anything for anyone. Once in a while if someone had lost something she would tell them where to find it and she was always right. But it was something over which she had no control.

Once, when we were all planting potatoes and she and I were cutting out the eyes, she stopped in the middle of a sentence and said, "Go get your father. Tell him your uncle is dead." I ran for Dad, and I can remember word for word what she told him. "Malcolm shot himself. He is lying at the bottom of the footpath behind your mother's house. I'll prepare the others. Go!" (Malcolm was Dad's brother-in-law.) Dad took off, with me right behind him. When we reached Grannie Campbell's no one was home. While Dad went to the door I sped down the footpath. Just as Cheechum had said, my uncle's body was lying there just as if he was sleeping.

Another time, late at night, Cheechum got up and told Dad that an aunt of ours was very sick and that he should go for Grannie Campbell as there was no time to waste. They arrived a few minutes before my aunt died.

She often had this kind of foresight and would tell Mom and Dad days before someone died or something happened. I wanted to be able to see things as she did, but she would reply that it was a sad thing to know that people who are close to you are going to die or have bad fortune - and to be unable to do anything to help them because it is their destiny. I am sure that she could see what was in store for me but because she believed life had to take its course she could only try to make me strong enough to get through my difficulties. . .

Sometimes in the evening when people were visiting, we children listened to them tell ghost stories, and because we lived beside the cemetery those stories would keep us awake long into the night. Daddy always seemed to run out of tobacco about eight o'clock in the evening and Jamie or I would have to go to the store. To get there we had to take a foot path down the hill, climb a barbed-wire fence into the graveyard, walk between rows of graves, climb over another fence, and go around the blacksmith shop to the store. We knew every single person buried in that graveyard for we had listened to so many stories about each one.

One grave in particular, right beside the fence, had a horrible story associated with it. Grannie Campbell used to tell us that the old man buried in it was called "Ke-qua-hawk-as," which means wolverine in Cree. He was just as mean and as ugly as the animal and never allowed anyone near his house, not even relatives. They all died before he did and because there was no family left, the Halfbreeds got together to build his coffin. They held a wake for him at Grannie's house. The men didn't finish digging his grave until quite late. Old Mrs. Vandal was outside, alone, when she heard someone talking. She listened and it was coming from the empty grave. The spirit of Wolverine was standing there complaining about the size of his grave and how useless those people were. So Mrs. Vandal got very angry and told him he should be happy that someone was kind enough to make him a grave after having always been so miserable. The men found her beside the hole shaking her fist. Grannie said every so often on certain nights you could still hear Wolverine complaining.

Whenever I had to go to the store in the evening I would jump the fence and run as fast as I could, feeling sure that Wolverine was behind me. I would jump the other fence and arrive at the store completely out of breath. And then going home through that graveyard again I would nearly die. It was worse climbing the hill as I couldn't see behind me. Daddy's youngest brother,

Robert, was a terrible tease and was never afraid of ghosts. He would lie beside Wolverine's grave and when I came back from the store he would make scratching noises and talk in low gruff tones. I would be stiff with fright and would walk by the grave looking straight ahead. As I climbed over the fence he would groan louder and scratch harder. I would pee my pants from fear while running up the hill, and he would pound the ground to make a sound like footsteps right behind me. When I burst into the house babbling and screaming, Daddy would go out and see nothing. This happened several times and one night I couldn't stand any more. I came through the graveyard and heard those noises again, the groaning and scratching, and as I climbed the fence there was an awful scream and noises like someone falling and running towards me. I crumpled down and fainted.

I came to, at home, with Mom rubbing my wrists. Uncle Robert sat in a corner with a most terrified look on his face, all scratched up and bloody. He said that he was coming from the store behind me and Wolverine grabbed him and knocked him down, bawled him out for using his graveyard and chased him away. He was too frightened to go home alone, so when Daddy came back he went with him. After Dad returned he laughed until he cried, then told us what had happened. He had followed Robert to the graveyard one night and watched him scare me, so this night he asked Mom to send me to the store again while he went ahead and hid in the bushes behind the grave. Then, when Robert came sneaking down, he waited until I had gone by. Robert was so absorbed in making his noises he heard nothing. Daddy had on an old fur coat and hat and he grabbed Robert's arm and groaned in his face. Poor Robert nearly died. He screamed and started to run, so Daddy grabbed his feet and when he fell, climbed on his back and berated him for sitting on his grave. He said he would haunt him forever if he came near again. Poor Uncle, he finally got away and raced to the hill, but forgot the barbed-wire fence and ran right into it. He picked himself up, and ran past me, racing to our house. Mom came and found me and carried me home. I had no more trouble with Wolverine after that, but I was still frightened of that graveyard. In a way I liked being afraid, and if Jamie had to go to the store instead of me I was disappointed.

Chief Peguis and His Descendants
(Winnipeg: Peguis Publishers, 1973)
by Chief Edward Albert Thompson

This biography of an historical figure, Chief Peguis (1774 - 1864), was written by Chief Edward Albert Thompson, a great-grandson of the famous Saulteaux chief. The story was given to him by his grandfather in writing, but the manuscript was lost so Chief Thompson relied on his memory for this biography.

In 1871 the Peguis band was given a reserve north of what is now Winnipeg. The reserve, known as St. Peter's, prospered with many good homes, farmlands, schools, and churches. Because this was prime agricultural and industrial land there was pressure for the band to relocate when settlers arrived. Government officials, whose job it was to protect Native rights, used graft, fraud, and other questionable methods to trick the Native people into surrendering the land in 1909. Depressed and angry, the band suffered great hardships as they were moved to where the Peguis Reserve is now located north of Hodgson, Manitoba. Their claim to land which they believe is rightfully theirs is still unsettled today.

The Saulteaux band had originally lived in Ontario, but they moved west in search of new territory under the leadership of Chief Peguis. Peguis was then a young man in his thirties who ably led the band throughout the years of resettlement in Manitoba, the turbulent years of Métis unrest and the coming of settlers in the Red River area. He died at the age of ninety in 1864. He is buried in St. Peter's churchyard north of Winnipeg, and a monument has been erected in his memory in Kildonan Park in Winnipeg.

In this excerpt, Chief Thompson tells about the arrival of the Peguis band in Manitoba in the 1790's.

This is the story of the famous Chief Peguis and a band of Saulteaux Indians who came from Sault Ste. Marie to the Red River country in the latter part of the 1790s. These people had no destination in mind when they left their old home in Ontario but decided to travel westward until they could find a location where fish, waterfowl and game could be had in abundance.

They travelled by canoe for weeks in their search, and finally entered Lake Winnipeg along the eastern shore and headed south, to the Red River. Not far from its mouth, the Saulteaux canoes came to a halt when they encountered a small stream flowing from the west.

On the banks of this stream a fairly large encampment was discovered which appeared to be deserted. After assuring themselves that this was not an ambush, a landing-party went forward to investigate. The teepees contained the remains of dead bodies. It was evident that the people had succumbed to disease. Their tools, cooking pots, clothing and totems revealed a tribe unknown to Chief Peguis and his followers.

The Saulteaux paddled further along this "river of the dead" and came upon a second silent camp where the teepees also held corpses. When an alert scout observed a movement in the willows he found a small boy hiding. The frightened child told Peguis how his people, the Plains Cree, had sickened and died of smallpox. He was the lone survivor.

The boy was adopted into the tribe and named Pockwa-now. They called the river Ne-poo-win, Death River. The white men named it Netley Creek.

The location seemed to be ideal for the band's needs. From the mouth of the Red to the creek fishing was good, and in the marshes on both sides of the river plenty of fur-bearing animals and wild fowl could be seen. There was also wild rice, and scrub maple trees that the people could tap for sugar in the spring, and fertile ground in which to plant the Indian corn that old Shag-koosink had carried in a deerskin bag from Sault Ste. Marie.

Now that the earlier occupants no longer required the area, the Saulteaux appropriated the land for their new home. Later when their explorations took them south along the Red to the mouth of the Assiniboine River, they found a large band of Indians encamped for the winter.

These were the Assiniboines, led by Chief Ouckidoat. They occupied the country stretching westward from the Red River far across the prairie. They subsisted wholly on the buffalo, and told the newcomers that they were welcome to the animals of the bushland and the fish of the waters.

Chief Peguis and Chief Ouckidoat smoked the pipe of peace and swore allegiance. Together, they would fight the Sioux, their common enemy since 1640, and jointly patrol the Red River, the route frequently used by their foe from the south. The Sioux, who claimed all the land about the Pembina River where it joins the Red (just south of the International Boundary) often made forays to plunder and kill as far north as the junction of the Red and the Assiniboine, known to voyageurs, fur traders and the Métis as the "Forks."

Returning to Netley Creek, the Saulteaux made preparations for their winter camp. From the inner bark of trees they braided a large net, some seventy feet long, weighted with stones. Several canoes carried it out into the water, where it was dropped, then slowly dragged back to shore filled with fish. The women prepared these for winter use by baking them in a long, low stone oven. They were then placed in birchbark or woven reed baskets, and buried in the ground to freeze. Bear-fat mixed with wild berries was also placed in the ground.

The women collected the largest shells from the lakeshore, filled them with fish and animal oil and a strip of rag to serve as lamps.

One hundred rabbits were killed for each family. The meat filled the cooking pots, and the skins were cut into strips and woven into mittens, blankets and hoods. The floors of the teepees were covered with animal skins and braided rushes, dyed with colour extracted from rocks and roots.

Medicinal plants such as wild ginger roots growing in abundance at the river's edge were dug and hung to dry. They would be used later in the treatment of colds and coughs. Seneca root was gathered by the midwives and a brew of the powdered herb administered to both human and canine mothers-to-be at the appropriate moment.

When roving bands arrived from the Great Lakes to visit and hunt on the Plains, they were made welcome by the Saulteaux encampment. With one of these groups there appeared a large bark canoe bearing a flag denoting the royal status of the occupant, Princess Net-no-kwa.

Recently widowed, she was travelling with her two sons. Her husband had lived in the Red River country when a young boy and often spoke of the fabulous prairie black with herds of buffalo, and the princess was hopeful of her sons becoming rich in the hunt.

Chief Peguis, observing the white skin of a fourteen-year-old boy, learned that he had been kidnapped from the settlers in Ohio six years before. He answered to the Indian name Shaw-Shaw-was-Be-na-se or The Falcon and appeared quite devoted to his foster-mother and older brother. His real name was John Tanner.

The Métis: Canada's Forgotten People
(Winnipeg: Pemmican Publications, 1975)
by D.B. Sealey and A. Lussier

The history of the Métis usually centres around the insurrection of 1870 and the rebellion of 1885. Other aspects of Métis history are often ignored, as are the Métis people who contributed richly to the development of Western Canada. James McKay (1828 - 1879), the son of a Scottish trader and a Métis mother, was born at Fort Edmonton but later he moved to the Red River settlement in the area that is now called Winnipeg. He did not participate in the insurrection of 1870, preferring to remain neutral. His sympathies, however, lay with the Métis. He was appointed a member of the first Manitoba government, where he served as Minister of Agriculture. He was especially sought after as a guide for the rich people of other countries who found that touring Western Canada was an exciting and unique experience. When the Sioux sought political refuge in Canada after the Battle of Little Big Horn, McKay was one of the first Métis people to offer sanctuary, even though the Sioux and Métis had been enemies for many years.

James McKay was a remarkable person in many ways, and, as is often the case with unusual persons, it is difficult to determine where factual information ends and fiction begins. The information included in this short biography is all factual; it can be verified by reading old letters, travel journals, government reports and records.

> James McKay, the Métis son of a servant of the Hudson's Bay Company, became one of Manitoba's wealthiest and most influential men. He had first worked for the Bay and later became an independent trader. Early in life, he built the famous Deer Lodge Mansion as his home along the banks of the Assiniboine. He owned thousands of acres of land, and, at one time, had a stable of horses valued at $100,000. This huge, 340-pound man was a most impressive person in every way. His strength was legendary and the stories about him legion. Once, when riding on the plains, he was attacked by a grizzly bear, a

species that preyed on the buffalo herds and is now extinct. McKay responded to the attack by lassoing the bear and subduing it. On another occasion, he came upon a man and woman in a horsedrawn cart that had become stuck in the mud. McKay unhitched the horse, put himself between the shafts, and pulled the vehicle out. As a member of the Palliser expedition, which was making a preliminary study of agricultural potential and other related matters on the prairies, McKay is said to have ridden a buffalo. In a spirit of adventure, he rode alongside a huge bull, leaped onto its back, stayed on through vicious bucking, and then regained the saddle of his horse, which had faithfully kept close to the buffalo. People naturally expected a huge man to be slow moving, so McKay took great delight in astonishing friends by leaping over the back of his horse. He was also considered a champion dancer of the Red River Jig, a dance that demanded grace and agility to perform well. It is recorded that he often wore out a pair of moccasins in one night of dancing. A number of Cree and Saulteaux Indians chose McKay, admired by all people, as a family name when they converted to Christianity.

McKay's reaction to the uprising led by Louis Riel in 1869-70 reveals the typical English-speaking half-breed view of the insurrection. Although some English half-breeds supported Riel, the majority tried to remain neutral because of their close ties with both the French-speaking half-breeds and the British crown. Many did not actively support the Canadians. McKay said, "I am loyal to my Queen, but I will not take up arms against Louis Riel's men, many of whom are related to me and my wife."

When Treaty One was being negotiated with the Indians, he was chosen the interpreter because of his complete mastery of English, French, Cree and Saulteaux. At one time in the negotiations, it appeared that the Indians would not only refuse to sign but that an outbreak of violence might occur. Late at night, a speedy messenger was sent from Lower Fort Garry to Deer Lodge. McKay responded by driving all night to reach the Fort and then, in a marathon, four-hour speech, managed to persuade the Indians to continue to negotiate. The Indians later blamed McKay for deceiving them, but such a charge is not supported by the facts. James McKay wrote Ottawa on several occasions in the years following the signing of the treaties and condemned the government for not living up to the promises he, as interpreter, had passed on to the Indians. He was also the major interpreter for Treaties Two and Three. James McKay rose in politics and became the Honourable James McKay when he was made a member of the Executive Council of the new province.

James McKay should be given a special place in the pages of history for his role in preserving the buffalo. Realizing that buffalo were becoming scarce, McKay had some calves captured and he raised a thriving herd of buffalo at Deer Lodge. The offspring of this private herd, later split and sold to Donald A. Smith, a private citizen, and Colonel Bedson of Stony Mountain Penitentiary, were used to stock Assiniboine Park in Winnipeg and Banff National Park. From McKay's original herd have come many of the buffalo in parks throughout North America.

Fifty Dollar Bride: Marie Rose Smith - A Chronicle of Métis Life in the 19th Century
(Sidney, B.C.: Gray's Publishing, 1977)
by Jock Carpenter

Jock Carpenter researched family letters and other records to compile the life story of her grandmother, Marie Rose Smith (1861 - 1960).

Marie Rose was born on the White Horse Plains area of Manitoba. She spent much of her childhood travelling with her parents as they hunted buffalo and traded with the various Native bands. At the age of sixteen she married Charley Smith, a Norwegian trader who was twenty years her senior. They settled in the Pincher Creek area of Alberta where they lived as ranchers and traders. Marie Rose bore seventeen children. Eleven of the children died before she did — some in infancy, some through illness or accidents, and two were killed on the same day in World War I. Marie Rose died at the age of ninety-nine.

Life was hard for pioneer women since families were large and few work-saving appliances existed. From her mother,

Marie Rose learned the skills of preparing whatever foods nature provided, sewing, nursing, and childcare. She also played an important role in running the ranch and made extra money to buy necessary supplies by sewing and selling gloves. She became a very strong woman who not only looked after the physical needs of her family but also served as the source of emotional and spiritual strength for all those around her. No friend or stranger was ever turned away from their door.

This excerpt shows her as a very shy sixteen-year-old girl and tells how her marriage was arranged.

At the end of two years, Mother Gervais decided her girls had had ample education and made arrangements to have them leave the convent.

Marie Rose and Eliza had grown accustomed to convent life and were quite happy, but the excitement of a trip was overwhelming and they eagerly said their farewells to the Sisters, promising to remain the modest young women they had become. After two years under the watchful eye of Mother Superior, the girls were quiet and submissive, having the usual fits of girlish giggles but becoming withdrawn and silent whenever strangers appeared.

Father Gervais was freighting for the Hudson's Bay Company, making long journeys to Fort Edmonton, with stops at Fort Carlton and Fort Pitt along the way. On his return trip he carried furs and robes back to Fort Garry for the Company.

The first part of the journey was uneventful, with no hint of what was to take place. They made the same camps, making and renewing acquaintances along the way, exclaiming over new babies in moss bags, remembering people and places from earlier journeys.

One day a rider rode in from his lookout far ahead.

"Camp ahead," he called to Father, pointing to the north, "many carts, many horses, not Indian."

Turning his heaving horse, he rode off in the direction he had come.

Father Gervais, with a wide sweep of his arm, signalled a turn to the north. They sighted the camp as the carts pulled up on a small rise in the land. Below was a sprawling encampment, the carts forming a very large ring with animals grazing inside. Two teepees stood to one side, the smoke from their fires wafting overhead. The outfit belonged to a big trader judging from the number of carts and horses.

On nearing the camp a tall, raw-boned man came out to greet them. He wore the usual buckskins, which were dirty; a belt with a knife in its sheath was buckled over his shirt. His hair was shoulder-length and fair. He was full-bearded and his blue eyes twinkled under scraggy brows. When he smiled, his eyes reflected that smile, and his greeting was sincere. When he spoke his accent stamped him with the unmistakable brand of the Norwegian.

"Velcome, my name is Charley Smith," he said. "Da day is youst about gone. Vy don't ya stay da night?" He gestured with his arm to his camp.

It was time to stop and Father Gervais was pleased with the invitation. Here was a chance to swap information and visit; the man seemed friendly enough. Father Gervais had killed a bear earlier that day and there had been no time to dry the meat. Maybe he could trade some of it; there were no signs of fresh meat here. Mother Gervais nudged him to reply and again Father Gervais gave the signal to the waiting riders. She grunted as she climbed down, thinking that a train with this many carts would surely have goods to barter. The riders were tired and eager for rest so they busied themselves, swinging the wagons into position for the night. A full belly and a pipeful of tobacco would soon be theirs. Maybe the tall stranger would pass around a jug. Tipped up on an elbow, a swig of its liquid burned all the way down before spreading out fingers of warmth. Mother Gervais recruited Pezzan and Charlie Ross to gather buffalo chips before they disappeared into the other camp. Liza and Marie Rose started the supper, frying bear steaks over the fire.

Charley Smith hung around the camp, volunteering the information to Father Gervais that several of his horses had been stolen or strayed away. He had four riders in all, but two of them were away looking for the missing stock. He accepted the supper offered to him and then invited the adults to taste his liquid refreshment. He had more than his permit allowed him to carry. The Gervais were happy to accept and they sat on robes around the fire, passing the jug and smoking. Far into the evening, yarns were exchanged and tales of earlier travels noted. Liza and Marie Rose fetched water, washed the tin plates, and then prepared the teepees for the night, spreading robes and blankets for their beds. Marie Rose cooked for the next day's journey while Liza searched for the boys. Marie Rose busied herself with her work, stooping to stir the roots cooking over the fire. Keen senses told her she was being watched and she shivered. Every time she looked across the fire, the trader nodded to her and smiled. The young girl did not understand his attention; this had never happened before. Maris Rose was happy to escape to bed, away from those watchful eyes.

Charles Smith left his Norwegian home at the very young age of twelve and went to sea. The son of Maerward Smith and Anna Peterson, he was born in 1844 aboard ship on the coast of the Mediterranean. Time then covered his travels until he became a fur trader, travelling and amassing wealth in furs, carts and horses. An adventurer and daredevil, he suited his buckskins as if he had been born to them. His light-colored hair fell to his shoulders underneath a broad-brimmed hat. His fair skin absorbed the brunt of the elements, weathering to a ruddy glow. He was good-natured and friendly. His eyes reflected his spirit, one of daring and mischief under a calm exterior. He loved children, and in loving them, would turn his attention from the adults to enter their world, teaching them games and playing with them. For all his kindness Charley was still a man's man, could drink with the best of them and hold his own in a fight. He had had many skirmishes with the Indians in his trading career; he did not give in to their demands like other traders and his robust body showed the scars of these encounters.

In the morning after breakfast, Father Gervais and Charley Smith stood with large cups of steaming tea. Smith argued that their horses needed rest and they should stay another day. When his riders returned he said, the whole camp could travel together for he too was heading to Fort Edmonton. Father Gervais argued that the riders would have trouble locating the horses in the brushy land; they could have strayed for miles and maybe the Indians had picked them up by now, if they had not taken them in the first place.

"No," he said, "we must be on our way." Finishing his tea, he tossed the dregs into the fire and turned to his stepdaughter. "Marie Rose, get the boys, help to hitch up. Come, we must be on our way."

The trader stepped up to the horse Marie Rose was hitching saying, "Are ya Marie Rose?"

Startled, she lifted her head, looking directly into his lively blue eyes. Flustered, she looked away, wondering what this tall man wanted of her. Why did he address her so?

Hearing no reply, Charley stayed around helping her hitch the teams, while a faint smile played around his lips.

The riders started the teams moving with calls which echoed across the prairies. The trader was thanked for his hospitality and gifts.

"Monsieur Gervais, vere vill ya be makin' yor vinter camp?" Charley asked.

"Well, my friend," was the reply, "it will be where the greatest of Indian camps are, where the trapping and meat are the best."

They left his camp and continued their journey. Marie Rose hoped this would be the last she would see of the strange man.

The Métis roamed the prairies for some weeks after the freight had been taken to its destination. Needing fresh meat they moved along, unhurried, hunting for buffalo herds. Moving gently along, life returned to its normal ways and once again Marie Rose and Liza were carefree girls, picking flowers for their hair and learning from Mother Gervais the way of the Métis. The days were gentle and soft and the young girl soon forgot the tall stranger. . .

As the Gervais caravan left, Charley Smith watched till they disappeared over the prairies and made a decision that was to affect Marie Rose and change her life completely. Narrowing his eyes with determination, the man planned a course of action and made a decision to have the girl for a wife.

In making the decision, Charley Smith wondered about the responsibility of taking a wife and raising children. The picture of the slender girl came back into his mind again and again. He liked her ways, her energy and resourcefulness; she had been well trained in the ways of the prairie. Her skin was dark and smooth, her young body like a willow, supple, but firm and sturdy. She would be the perfect mate to accompany him over the plains, to bear and nurse his children, to work beside him on long and lonely journeys to the west. She was obedient to her parents, and as Father Gervais said, she could read and write English and French. She spoke Cree which would be of help in trading. Charley appraised all her fine points while making his decision. He wanted her and in dreaming and thinking about her, the big fur trader succumbed to the pangs of love.

Impatiently he waited for the return of his riders and when they appeared several days later he wasted no time in following the now cold trail of the Métis caravan. He hailed all the riders he saw and asked the same query:

"Have ya seen an outfit, a trader named Gervais, got two girls fresh from da convent?"

"Yah," one rider replied, "they are on the Edmonton trail, and are to winter near the old Bear Hills."

With a satisfied glint in his eye, Charley Smith turned his riders in the direction of the Edmonton Trail. The Gervais camp was well on its way to making winter quarters when the lanky rider reined in his horse, and looked down toward the smoke of many fires rising through the pines.

There were a lot of Roman Catholics wintering along the creek. Their devotion was strong and the families often walked through the crunchy snow to a hut that served as a church. When the priest came from St. Albert, the whole encampment was alerted; a confessor was here, a Mass would be said. Mother Gervais gave the girls permission to walk to confession one evening, sending Charlie Ross to accompany them. They walked along, talking as they watched the northern lights pulsing with vitality in the night sky. Marie Rose did not know that Charley Smith was in camp. He had not put in an appearance, being busy with his own preparations for the winter and building a small hut of his own.

After confession, there was Mass and they stayed to attend, following the ancient service in the Latin tongue. Coming out of the church into bright moonlight they started the long walk home. The snow was ankle-deep, powdery stuff that crunched and squeaked under moccasined feet. Talking and laughing they followed the trail, walking animal file, passing snow-shrouded cabins, some with smoke plumes rising against the blue-black sky, others cold and empty.

Sleigh bells tinkled in the clear night air. A flat sleigh caught up with them, the horses decorated with melodious bells.

"Very nice evenin'," Charley said as he came abreast, "but ya should come in da sleigh."

The girls walked a little faster, not replying, keeping their eyes straight ahead.

"Have ya bin to church?" he questioned.

Getting no response, he now joined the group, walking and leading his horse. Frightened, the girls hurried as they were near home. Marie Rose was stiff with fright; she had had no conversations with any man because the girls never spoke to the riders of the outfits. She stumbled and nearly fell and Charley caught hold of her, saying something she did not understand. As if in a dream Marie Rose felt numb and her mind went blank. She did not understand what he was saying with his strange accent.

"Yes, yes, let me go," she cried.

He kissed her quick as a flash, and she wrenched out of his grasp, drawing the back of her hand over her mouth as she ran away. A strange man-smell of tobacco and whiskey made her swallow hard and she feared she would be sick. Trembling, Marie Rose caught up with Liza and Charlie Ross as they ran for the cabin.

"What is the matter?" Mother questioned. "Why do you look so strange? What Mooniyas (white man) say?"

"Oh Mama, I do not know, I just kept saying, yes, yes, let me go, but first he kissed me."

Marie Rose wanted the safety of the cabin, and huddling in her bed under the skins, she cried herself to sleep.

The next day Marie Rose tried not to remember the events of the previous night. Busying herself with decorating a fire-bag she tried to blot out of her mind the smell of the man and the hardness of his kiss. She heard bells, and looking up from her sewing, listened - every fibre of her body willing the sound to go away! He was coming - and coming to her house. Soon the room seemed to be filled with the presence of the big fur trader as he greeted the Gervais, giving gifts all around.

Mother was pleased with her gifts; he was generous and had spared nothing to impress her. He brought a bottle and roast of deer meat from his sleigh and was soon pressed to stay for dinner. Marie Rose mumbled a stiff thanks for the lush furs he offered, with Mother Gervais prodding her to accept. The alarmed girl longed to escape but in one room there was no place to hide. She was afraid to go out into the snow-shrouded camp in case he should follow.

Dinner was made, using the fresh meat Charley had brought, along with little luxuries he had purchased at the Hudson's Bay trading post near Edmonton. Charley and Cuthbert sat over their pipes and whiskey. The family could see that Mother Gervais was impressed by the attention paid to them by the wealthy trader. Soon the talk turned to something that made all heads come up in alarm.

"Father Gervais, I would like to have da hand of Marie Rose in marriage. I vant to take her as my vife," he said.

Mother Gervais was taken aback by this turn of events and she looked askance so Charley continued on.

"I asked her yesterday night, an she said yes," he said.

Interrupting, forgetting her manners in her agitation, Marie Rose flew from her bench to the fireplace saying, "Mother, I knew not what he said."

"Marie Rose, you promised to marry this man, he has said so."

Ignoring the girl's pleas she settled with Charley for her daughter's hand in marriage. Charley gave her a present of fifty dollars, a great fortune in those days. With a nod to his future bride, and a pleased smile on his face he left the cabin saying he would be back.

I Am Nokomis, Too
(Don Mills: General Publishing, 1977)
by R.M. Vanderburgh

Verna Patronella Johnston (1909 -) was born on the Cape Croker Reserve in Ontario and recalls with nostalgia the days when Native people lived in more traditional ways. Her childhood was a life of warmth, sharing, and cooperation among reserve residents. Girls spent most of their time in the company of older women. The most influential person in Verna's life was her grandmother. By the time Verna was twelve she was a capable housekeeper.

School was a mixed experience for her. She was an excellent student and especially good at making things with her hands. However, she experienced terrible feelings of inadequacy because she was a Native, a feeling that stayed with her until well into adulthood.

She married Henry Johnston when she was sixteen and had five children. Her husband proved to be very uncommunicative and domineering. Verna became fully involved in reserve life, joining organizations such as Homemakers and Women's Institute, and actively working for the church. She became the first Girl Guide leader. She also had to work very hard to look after her family and she helped her husband with farming and fishing. When her children were grown she left Henry, the first woman to leave her husband on that reserve, in search of a life where she could have more freedom. She went to Toronto and, although she was keenly aware of how reserve life was changing and old values were being lost, she was very lonely in the city and soon went back home.

A very happy period of her life started when she opened a foster home on the reserve — the first Native foster home ever to be established. She found out later that she was paid only half as much as non-Native foster parents. Because of poor health she had to give up her foster children, but when her granddaughters went to the city to further their education, she went with them.

This led to another first — Verna ran a boarding house for

Native students in the city. She became well known for her work in helping young Native people in the city and was greatly in demand as a speaker and teacher. She wrote a book called *Tales of Nokomis* and at the age of sixty she took in her great-granddaughter, Randa, to live with her. When she was sixty-five she had to retire because of poor health. In 1976 she was named Native Woman of the Year by the Native Women's Association of Canada.

This excerpt from her biography tells about her retirement on the reserve at the age of sixty-five. The chapter it is taken from is called "You can never go home again."

> After Verna moved back to Cape Croker she wrote to all the organizations she had been involved with and told them that she was retiring. Then she wrote to Indian Affairs and told them that too; that she had closed the boarding house and had moved back home to live. She would have plenty of time to write more stories and to put together her book of Indian medicines. She expected to be able to help out in her family too, with her granddaughters who were raising their own babies now. She hoped that there would be the kinds of community projects that there had been when her children were young, and she looked forward to visits with her cousins and friends on the reserve. Randa, at eight years of age, was full of excitement at the thought of living right on the lake and finally being able to have a pet of her own.
>
> For years now Verna and Randa had looked forward all during the week to those weekend trips home to the reserve. Indians who worked in Toronto and other cities made the long drive to Cape Croker almost every weekend. They saw their families, they went to church, and they went to parties. That trip home was the focal point of the week for many of them. Verna and Randa had been that way, waiting for that feeling of coming home that begins when one drives through Wiarton and turns off to the Cape. That feeling gets stronger as you turn off past Colpoys toward Purple Valley, and at Purple Valley, you are nearly home. Then you turn the final corner and head onto the reserve, and suddenly the road curves down and away and there

is your home spread out at your feet. The great bluffs brood over the road, and beyond is the water of Sidney Bay with a big hook of land in the distance framing McGregor Harbour and far out in the bay a little black cloud that is Rabbit Island.

Cape Croker is a very beautiful place. Everyone who lives there and leaves remembers its beauty always. Whatever the time of year, the beauty always makes you catch your breath as you come down that first hill. And where Verna's cottage stands is beautiful too. You look from her house down a rocky beach to the water and across the water to the high bulk of Hay Island, with all its mysteries. Once Hay Island, and White Cloud and Griffiths' Island belonged to the people at Cape Croker. Then, all of a sudden, it seemed that Indians couldn't use those places anymore, and yet those islands were part of the land reserved for the Indians in the Peter Jones Treaty.

Anyone who has enjoyed such beauty always wants to go back to it again. Cities have excitement, but a place like Cape Croker is remembered as a haven after years of living in Toronto. A haven of beauty, of friends, of family, of happy times.

Well, the beauty lasts. But after Verna moved back to her home, she began to remember the other things about the reserve, things she hadn't liked so much all those years ago. When you are just going home on weekends everything is good. When you live there all the time, it's very different. But the beauty lasts. Even with all the changes it is still a beautiful, beautiful place.

And there had been many changes in the ten years that Verna had been in Toronto. There were children, and teenagers all over the place. You could usually tell by their faces what family they belonged to, even if you didn't know their names. But it seemed strange to see so many young people she didn't know, and who didn't know her. There were new houses too, all over the reserve. There were even little clumps of new houses on roads laid out in subdivisions off the main road. The old stone schoolhouses had been converted to different uses. One was a teacher's residence, and another had been sold and turned into a private home. The third stone school had served first as a furniture factory, and later as a drop-in centre for young people during the years of her absence.

Parts of the reserve were serviced now by a community water

line, and there were plans to extend that service eventually to most of the homes. One of the old stores had burned down, and there was a new general store attached to Stella's house. The Cape Croker Indian Park had grown, with many new campsites and improved public facilities. There were three places now where tourists could stop and buy Indian craft work. Some of the craft things were made right at Cape Croker, and the three women who ran the stores all travelled to buy crafts from other parts of Ontario. The tourist trade was really a big thing; there were more cottages at Hope Bay and North Bay, on land that was rented from the Indians. And the park brought in people too.

The churches were the same, and the old Council Hall still stood there at the crossroads. The three cemeteries were filling up. People had been dying at Cape Croker for over a hundred and twenty years, so those old cemeteries were pretty crowded. They were better kept than they had been when she went away. The young people got government money for community projects and one of those projects was to clean up the graveyards. When she was a girl the people never needed any special incentives to keep the graves clear. Later it got so that you couldn't pay your respects to your dead without wading through poison ivy. It was a pleasure now to see those graves all underbrushed and the poison ivy cut back.

Verna fell back at once into the old habit of stopping everything to look out of the window when anyone went by on the road. All the houses at the Cape face onto the road, and whenever anyone goes by on foot or in a car, people look out of their windows. Every time you go for a walk or take a drive with a friend everyone knows about it. The city may be impersonal, but there is something to be said for neighbours who mind their own business. In a small community one of the big things to do is to mind your neighbour's business! It always had been like that, people always could see where you were going, and who you were with and how long you were gone. But Verna found there was something different and very ugly in this public aspect of living at Cape. The teenagers, sitting around with nothing to do, watch people's comings and goings and find out when a house is left alone for a day, or an evening. They break in and steal things, or even smash things up if they don't find anything worth stealing.

Verna was dependent on her old age pension and if people broke into her house she couldn't afford to replace the things they took. Maybe that's why old people are afraid to leave home. They are afraid they'll be robbed while they're gone. There's no safety out on the roads either. Sometimes those gangs of young people will beat up an old man who is out on the road visiting his friends. That is another reason to stay home. This pervading feeling of fear seemed strange to Verna. You hear about the crime and violence in the cities, but you don't expect to run into them in your own community.

It was a very, very bad feeling. And it even spread to the youngsters on the school buses where little ones were threatened and tormented by gangs of older students. Poor Randa, who was going to school on the reserve for the first time, had never run into this sort of thing in the city. It is a terrible thing to live always in a state of anxiety.

Making ends meet was another anxiety. For the first time in many years Verna had no job. The old age pension didn't go very far with a growing youngster in the house to feed and keep clothed. Her own expenses weren't that big, she wasn't paying rent. But she had to pay for heat and electricity, and her telephone. And people she had known in Toronto came to visit her on weekends. It was good that they cared enough about her to come all that way to visit, but the need to be a generous hostess put a real strain on her resources.

The men in her family used her nets in the fall and she got half the catch for her freezer, but it seemed that everyone who came to visit wanted to feast on that good whitefish and trout. Her pride made it impossible for her to set a less generous table, and she was amazed at how hard it was to make ends meet. After all, in the old days she had got by perfectly well on very little cash. She had produced most of her own food then. No one at Cape did that anymore. There was only one man now doing any real farming.

But what Verna had done once she could do again, so she got her son-in-law to build her a chicken house and she fenced in a yard and began to raise chickens. That meant that she didn't have to buy eggs and that she could always have fowl for the table. Then she thought about rabbits. They grow fast and are good eating. So she built a rabbit pen and started raising rabbits. Poor Randa! She loved those little animals and couldn't bear to think of them as food. But she had a pet now, a dog, and Verna let her keep two special rabbits as pets. Those two little things kept turning up in the house, in Randa's bed, or wrapped up in her sweater.

Verna wasn't content until she put in a garden. Over at the old homestead the garden hadn't been plowed for years and there was no one with the equipment or the time to plow it for her. So she really went out on a limb, and with the last of her money from the sale of the boarding house furniture she made a down payment on a small tractor and she got her garden in. All that summer she had fresh vegetables and it was just like the old days, seeing those things grow and knowing that there'd be plenty of potatoes and carrots and onions for winter. The garden was isolated, tucked away beside the old house, at the end of a long lane. Because the gangs of teenagers didn't know it was there it was more or less left alone. But they raided most of the other gardens, stealing things as they ripened and smashing squash and pumpkins just for the fun of it. No wonder the people at the Cape don't bother to plant gardens any more!

She baked fruit pies all that summer and sold them at Stella's store. She'd send over a dozen or so every other day and the customers couldn't get enough of them. They never stayed around long enough to get stale! The success of her pies is a great satisfaction to Verna. She says, "I'm really famous for my fruit pies," and never thinks that she might be known for other things, such as her book, and her work for Indians. She sees those pies as her real claim to fame; apple, blueberry, cherry, date, and raisin testimonials to her skills.

But there was no closeness at the Cape, as there had been in the old days. No friendliness, no neighbourliness. There was no visiting back and forth, even though many people had cars now and could get around easily. In the old days people used to walk long distances to visit their friends. You'd look up from your work and there would be a friend on your doorstep. "Ahnee neetchee, hello my friend." You heard that all the time. Today nobody wants to go visiting, only the old people, and some of them live in very isolated parts of the reserve so they are really stuck. And they are all afraid to go out.

There are no community projects anymore, the feasts at Pay Day or the fund-raising programs they used to put on to raise money for the hockey team. One of the first things she tried to do when she went home was to get involved in a community project. She wanted to work to raise money for hockey again, the way she had worked when she had had foster children. But they told her that they didn't need the money now. They got a recreation grant from the government, and it covered everything the teams needed. Everything she wanted to do, there was no need for. Nobody in the community needed to worry about recreation, about supporting the churches, about working for anything for the community. The government handed out grants for everything.

Grants can be very bad. They make people dependent on the government, not themselves. Anything you want, you write up a report and send it to the right place, and wait for your grant. "I'm not trying to make a joke, but grants mean that people take everything for granted!" Then there is the problem of spending grant money on a reserve. Who is going to say how it should be spent? Of course the Council and the people in the Band Office have to make decisions, and then people blame them and accuse them of lining their own pockets. At least in the old days you could blame the agent. Today the Indians blame each other and the grant system sets one family against another.

Every time Verna tried to get into something, somebody would tell her to be quiet, not to stir things up, to relax and enjoy being retired. "They sort of put me in a rocking chair. I can't sit around. I must work at something, or I'd be climbing the walls." She didn't like what she saw happening around her, and when she complained, they put her down and told her she was trying to stir things up. They didn't want their gravy boat rocked! It was this business of not being able to speak her mind, and not being able to be involved in things, that made her see that she couldn't stay at home.

They gossiped about her friends who came up, they criticized her for criticizing the school bus system, and for transferring Randa from the Catholic school to the Protestant school, which was within walking distance. They rejected her attempts to be a good citizen of the community. They really made it clear that she was on the shelf, ready for Gateway Haven, the old people's home in Wiarton. Nobody listened to her any more.

This was the real reason she finally went away, back to Toronto where she could be a respected, independent person again. Of course it was easier to tell people that she had to live in the city, near the hospital where they monitored her condition. And that was important too, to be able to get her regular doctors, in an emergency. But the real reason was that things weren't the same at home any more. All the people of her age at Cape Croker were looking back, at the old days, and when she was there she looked back all the time too. When she was in the city she was living for the work she was involved in, she was looking ahead. She intends to work as long as she is able. There will come a day when she will have to go home, and accept the changes, and put herself on the shelf. Maybe then she'll go into Gateway Haven. But in the meantime there is still plenty to do.

Defeathering the Indian
(Agincourt: The Book Society of Canada, 1975)
by Emma LaRocque

Defeathering The Indian is a social commentary on the Canadian educational system and its failure to respect both Aboriginal history and Aboriginal students. While this book was published in 1975, many of its themes are relevant today. Emma LaRocque is a Plains-Cree Metis originally from northeastern Alberta. Despite encountering many obstacles in schools and society, she went on to earn a B.A. in English/Communications, an M.A. in Religion and an M.A. in History. She has been a professor of Native Studies for 14 years at the University of Manitoba where she is also completing her Ph.D. in Aboriginal History. Emma LaRocque is author of numerous articles and is a frequent guest lecturer on Native education, human rights, racism, colonization, literature and women's issues. Her poetry and an essay on Native literature are featured in *Writing The Circle: Native Women of Western Canada, An Anthology,* edited by Jeanne Perreault and Sylvia Vance with a Preface by Emma

LaRocque, Edmonton: NeWest Press, 1990.

A personal essay on poverty

Liberalism has made much of poverty in our last decade. Statistics on poverty have been flying around from all directions. And as I mentioned before, Native people have been closely associated with it; so closely in fact that some very significant questions have been bypassed.

What is poverty anyway? Is it the failure to reach beyond that magical Poverty Line established by the Economic Council of Canada? Or is it "...relative to the living standard the rest of society enjoys." And more important, what is so sacred about what the majority enjoys?

To me it seems obvious that poverty is relative all right; but not necessarily relative to the wealth of the majority, but rather to one's own perceptions of material possessions.

My two brothers, one sister and I grew up in a one-roomed but well-managed log cabin. Many of our clothes were handsewn by my very resourceful mother. All our wooden furniture (two beds, one table, a cupboard, several night stands, three chairs and a bench) was put together by my practical father. Our diet consisted of a large variety of wild meats, berries, bannock, potatoes, some vegetables and herbal teas and so on, all of which were usually cooked with originality and imagination.

At the age of nine, against my father's perceptive advice, I howled my way into school. He knew only too well that sooner or later I would come home with new desires. As predicted, a few months later I wanted juicy red apples, oranges, bananas, trembling jello, bread and even red-and-white striped toothpaste! Once, my father teasingly wondered what I could possibly do with toothpaste and brush because my teeth were all falling out! Toothless or not, I found the pictures at school powerfully suggestive.

Other school pictures also played with my mind. I saw Dick, Jane and Sally's suburban home and their grandparent's expansive and, oh, so clean farm. Not for a long time was I to appreciate my home again.

The point is, I had been perfectly content to sleep on the floor, eat rabbit stew and read and play cards by kerosene lamp until my perceptions were swayed at school. Neither had I suffered spiritual want. I had been spellbound by my mother's ability to narrate Cree legends and enriched by my father's dreams, until the teacher outlawed Cree and made fun of dreams.

From then on I existed in poverty; not with reference to our log cabin, our food and our small wood-stove as compared to the brick schoolhouse, its food and its huge, coal-burning pot-belly stove, but because I was persuaded by my teacher's propaganda and the pictures.* The teacher's authoritarianism, coupled with his failure to reinforce whatever world we came from, effectively weakened our respect for our parents.

Still, there is more to poverty than its relativity. Even if I had believed in my home and its simple beauties, it is true that I had no money. And without that commodity, eventually I could not be mobile. And to be immobile in any society is to be quite choiceless. It is at this point that equal opportunity becomes meaningless.

It is psychologically cathartic to know that one has a choice. Ultimately, poverty in the North American context is not having enough money to choose among alternatives. Poverty exacts its toll on people not always because of a mere lack of material possessions, but often because of choicelessness.

Today, there are hundreds of urban dwellers who are suffering from "cabinitis." Come Friday afternoon there is a mass and speedy exodus to the "simple" life of their cabins. These people are often happy there because they are there by choice. They feel a sense of self-direction.

People may be "culturally deprived" perhaps only in that they are deprived of choice. In this sense then, most of us are "culturally deprived" in some area because most of us cannot choose everything we want out of life.

Now I live in a city, and I often see children playing on concrete, at artificial playgrounds and in overcrowded parks or swimming pools. I always feel a profound sense of sadness that these children cannot have what I had as a child. No spruce branch from which to master a Tarzanian swing. No soft moss to

* It must be said that this teacher meant well. He was by nature a disciplinarian but not malicious. Apparently, he sincerely believed that his ways were for the good of the Native children.

land on if you fall. No moonlight rendezvous beside a creek, watching a beaver tirelessly build his dam. No place to build an honest-to-goodness, creaking, but functioning, ferris wheel! No pond or lake or river to try out a self-made raft, row boat or canoe. Or to skinny-dip in. No green space to just run and run and run. No wooded meadow in which to lie and sleepily feel akin to the lethargic clouds. No crocuses, wild roses, tiger lilies or bluebells to sniff.

Cultural deprivation?

Yes, we must work towards equal opportunity for all. We must help people reach a sense of self-direction and mobility. We must lift people to the place of choice. But we cannot, we must not, dictate what people should choose.

Native people have been stereotyped in many different ways and literature has reflected these stereotypes. Writing from within the cultures shows that these stereotypes have little substance. Biographies and autobiographies, like traditional poetry and memoirs, show that Native people were neither primitives nor pagans and savages. The most common stereotype of the 1970s and 1980s are those of cultureless nomads or disoriented, displaced persons caught between two cultures, unable to cope with either. These stereotypes are strongly refuted by these biographies and autobiographies. Native people led rich, full lives, some largely in traditional fashion; others were strongly influenced by new life styles and new religions.

Many of these biographies and autobiographies show how the education system undermined the self-concept of Native students. But they also show how regaining pride in their heritage has led Native and Métis students toward a future of personal satisfaction and contribution to their society.

CHAPTER 5
Short Stories

Introduction

Short stories are fiction. Though often the story is based on some factual occurrence they do not have their origin in reality but rather in the writer's imagination. Traditionally oral narrative and poetry were used to transmit spiritual beliefs, the values of the society, or to record history. Every effort was made to be as accurate as possible. For a society to compose and enjoy purely imaginative works a certain amount of leisure time is required. Most traditional societies had relatively little leisure time; some had virtually none at all. What time was not taken up with the pursuits of daily survival was spent in celebration and ritual with spiritual significance. Fiction, with purely imaginary characters doing imaginary things, was viewed as untruth, hence to be avoided. In fact, in most cultures fiction was considered immoral during some phase of their evolution.

In technological societies like ours, however, there are whole industries devoted to the prodution of fiction, whether in the form of short stories, novels, poems or drama it is one of the greatest pleasures of life. Radio and television are also sources of fictional enjoyment, but for literate persons they cannot equal the enjoyment provided by a written masterpiece where every word can be savoured and re-read.

Fiction serves many purposes. Readers can become emotionally involved with the story and relate it to experiences of their own. It is entertaining because it may have unusual, funny, exciting, or scary plots. It may satirize or burlesque, that is, use ridicule to make a point; exaggeration is also often found. On the other hand, it may also present serious ideas about life where the author is trying to teach, present a specific point of view, or transmit certain values and beliefs. The author may be hoping to influence the readers. Characters are used to portray and dramatize emotions; often insights are given into the feelings of the characters and readers empathize with their dilemmas.

Short stories have been described by some writers as being to literature what a microscope is to a scientist. Through the medium of the short story a small portion of life, or one isolated incident in a person's life can be examined minutely. Through this examination readers can come to better understand human nature.

Native writers are using the medium of the short story more and more to express their ideas. Three of the stories in this anthology are historical anecdotes. No doubt the events, or similar events, actually happened and the stories were passed down from generation to generation. Each storyteller embellished the story with details, many of which came from the creative mind of the teller.

Several stories in this chapter comment on social and political issues — issues as diverse as family ties, the Indian Act and environmental pollution. Basil Johnston and George Kenny write about what it is like to be contemporary Natives living in two cultures. D. Bruce Sealey's story about Joe Bignell and the Weetigo is an excellent example of the combination of traditional and contemporary storytelling.

Short stories, like myths and legends, also entertain and instruct. Through fiction, Métis and Native writers are expressing what is going on in their hearts and minds. Some of the stories are similar to the myths, legends and anecdotes passed on through oral narrative; others use sophisticated literary devices borrowed from Western literatures. The message in the story may be poignant, sad, disturbing, thought-provoking, or simply highly entertaining. The variety of stories included in this anthology shows how the writers have adopted the genre as their own. Though the authors have used a genre that was not a part of traditional story telling, the stories are uniquely Native in content and theme.

Short Stories

An Act of God

In the summer of 1972 seven Métis university and high school students researched Métis history in order to shed some light on the daily lives of their ancestors. The result was a book called *Stories of the Métis* (Winnipeg: Manitoba Métis Federation Press, 1973) edited by D. Bruce Sealey. This story comes from the "golden age" of the Métis when they were lords of the plains and their lives had not been disrupted by encroaching settlement.

The fall hunt, although plentiful, left the Métis with very little meat as winter progressed. Whenever their provisions ran low, the Métis were forced to return to the prairies and hunt the buffalo. So it was that on a cold winter morning, a number of Métis hunters organized themselves to go and hunt their staple food. They left Grantown and proceeded in a southwesterly direction.

The buffalo hunt in winter was very much different from the fall hunts. In winter, for the most part, snow fell so heavily on the open prairie that horses were much less useful than one would imagine. At times, the snow would fall for days on end, and banks of snow drifting ten feet high would exhaust the horses. For this reason, dogs became most treasured friends during the winter hunts.

The half-breed would dress himself in a wolf-costume, and with two or three sturdy dogs bundled inside his sled, he would anxiously await the arrival of the herd. Here, the bow and arrow would be very useful. As the buffalo would advance towards the awaiting hunter, the sled would be completely hidden by the beasts. The hunter would kill with silent ease as many animals as was necessary to feed his hungry family. Once the kill was over, the dogs would swiftly pull the heavy meat through the deep snow.

At the same time that the hunting expedition was leaving Grantown, Pierre Desrochers and his dog sled were leaving Fort

Carlton on their way to Grantown. Till now, Pierre and his Cree Indian wife had had a hard and tiring journey. They were anxiously looking forward to being in the warm, comfortable cabin of their relatives in Grantown. However, their troubles were just starting. Not long after sunrise, a snow storm had made travelling almost impossible. They decided to make camp and rest in a bluff shielded from the biting wind.

Hurriedly, Pierre set up a shelter made of buffalo skins. His wife could do little to help for she was heavy with child, and Pierre knew that very soon he would be a father. It took very little time to set up camp, and Mary, bitten by the cold, crawled into the hovel. Pierre was outside, cleaning his rifle, getting ready to go and hunt for small game. Just as he was leaving, he heard the cries of a new born child. In the midst of this open prairie, during a blizzard, this hearty Cree woman gave birth to Ti-Pierre, their first son.

Time could not be wasted. Pierre's wife, his new-born child, his dogs and he himself were nearing starvation. Off he went to find food over the next hill, and it was here that he first caught sight of the hunting party. He was wild with excitement, for now he knew that his small family would be saved. He ran back to camp and told his wife to make ready for travel. They tucked the child between layers of buffalo skin, and hurriedly travelled to join the party.

The hunting party was setting up camp, for the blizzard had reached its height by mid-day. The buffalo herd had been spotted not more than one mile away. But the hunters realized that it would be impossible to hunt in the blinding snow. Plans were made for an early morning hunt.

Morning came fast and the sun shone brightly on the snowclad prairies. Within an hour, the party, composed of men, women and children, was making its way towards the buffalo. These were not visible until the last moment because of their position in the narrow valleys. Suddenly there arose a most beautiful sight! Thousands upon thousands of these cumbersome beasts stood pawing the snow trying to uncover bits of grass.

Little Ti-Pierre was nestled cozily in the warmth of the buffalo skins. Although the landscape was rough, the sled provided ample comfort as the dogs trotted in unison over the snow. It was Desrocher's dogs who were the first to spot the herd. Without delay, they started in mad pursuit of the buffalo, leaving the father and mother in astonished despair for the safety of their only child, as they saw him pulled behind the runaway dogs. The dogs soon reached the buffalo, and all were mixed pell-mell; the dogs running, the sled swinging to and fro, and the buffalo kicking. At length, a bull gored one of the dogs, and the horns getting entangled in the harness, the frightened buffalo went off at the gallop, carrying the dog on his horns; the other was suspended by the traces and the sled and child were dragging behind. The frightened animal ran a good half mile before he shook himself clear of the encumberance. He was pursued by a large party, who fired many shots without effect. The state of the parent's feelings may be imagined. Yet to their amazement, although all dogs were killed, the child escaped unhurt!

Many curious and astonishing incidents happened on the open prairie. This miraculous happening is but one of many that took place in the arduous and exciting life of the Métis.

Catharine of the "Crow's Nest"

Pauline Johnson (1861 - 1913) is best known for her poetry, but she also wrote some short stories. She was the daughter of a Mohawk chief and an English mother, and much of her writing tells of the interaction between the two culture groups. This story is set in an historical time period — the building of the railway through the Crow's Nest Pass. There is no evidence that any of the characters in the story existed, but Pauline Johnson used the recorded incident of a child's bonnet found on the shores of Kootenay Lake to give her story authenticity. The story first appeared in *The Mother's Magazine* in 1910 and is now available in the book, *The Moccasin Maker*. (Tucson: The University of Arizona Press, 1987)

The great transcontinental railway had been in running order for years before the managers thereof decided to build a second line across the Rocky Mountains. But "passes" are few and far between in those gigantic fastnesses, and the fearless explorers, followed by the equally fearless surveyors, were many a toilsome month conquering the heights, depths and dangers of the "Crow's Nest Pass".

Eastward stretched the gloriously fertile plains of southern "Sunny Alberta," westward lay the limpid blue of the vast and indescribably beautiful Kootenay Lakes, but between these two arose a barrier of miles and miles of granite and stone and rock, over and through which a railway must be constructed. Tunnels, bridges, grades must be bored, built and blasted out. It was the work of science, endurance and indomitable courage. The summers in the canyons were seething hot, the winters in the mountains perishingly cold, with apparently inexhaustible snow clouds circling forever about rugged peaks - snows in which many a good, honest laborer was lost until the eagles and vultures came with the April thaws, and wheeled slowly above the pulseless sleeper, if indeed the wolves and mountain lions had permitted him to lie thus long unmolested. Those were rough and rugged days, through which equally rough and rugged men served and suffered to find foundations whereon to lay those two threads of steel that now cling like a cobweb to the walls of the wonderful "gap" known as Crow's Nest Pass.

Work progressed steadily, and before winter set in construction camps were built far into "the gap," the furthermost one being close to the base of a majestic mountain, which was also named "The Crow's Nest." It arose beyond the camp with almost overwhelming immensity. Dense forests of Douglas fir and bull pines shouldered their way up one-third of its height, but above the timber line the shaggy, bald rock reared itself thousands of feet skyward, desolate, austere and deserted by all living things; not even the sure-footed mountain goat travelled up those frowning, precipitous heights; no bird rested its wings in that frozen altitute. The mountain arose, distinct, alone, isolated, the most imperial monarch of all that regal Pass.

The construction gang called it "Old Baldy," for after working some months around its base, it began to grow into their lives.

Not so, however, with the head engineer from Montreal, who regarded it always with baleful eye, and half laughingly, half seriously, called it his "Jonah."

"Not a thing has gone right since we worked in sight of that monster," he was heard to say frequently; and it did seem as if there were some truth in it. There had been deaths, accidents and illness among the men. Once, owing to transportation difficulties, the rations were short for days, and the men were in rebellious spirit in consequence. Twice whiskey had been smuggled in, to the utter demoralization of the camp; and one morning, as a last straw, "Cookee" had nearly severed his left hand from his arm with a meat axe. Young Wingate, the head engineer, and Mr. Brown, the foreman, took counsel together. For the three meals of that day they tried three different men out of the gang as "cookees." No one could eat the atrocious food they manufactured. Then Brown bethought himself. "There's an Indian woman living up the canyon that can cook like a French chef," he announced, after a day of unspeakable gnawing beneath his belt. "How about getting her? I've tasted pork and beans at her shack, and flapjacks, and - "

"Get her! get her!" clamoured Wingate. "Even if she poisons us, it's better than starving. I'll ride over to-night and offer her big wages."

"How about her staying here?" asked Brown. "The boys are pretty rough and lawless at times, you know."

"Get the axe men to build her a good, roomy shack - the best logs in the place. We'll give her a lock and key for it, and you, Brown, report the very first incivility to her that you hear of," said Wingate, crisply.

That evening Mr. Wingate himself rode over to the canyon; it was a good mile, and the trail was rough in the extreme. He did not dismount when he reached the lonely log lodge, but rapping on the door with the butt of his quirt, he awaited its opening. There was some slight stirring about inside before this occurred; then the door slowly opened, and she stood before him - a rather tall woman, clad in buckskin garments, with a rug made of coyote skins about her shoulders; she wore the beaded leggings and moccasins of her race, and her hair, jet black, hung in ragged plaits about her dark face, from which mournful eyes looked out at the young Montrealer.

Yes, she would go for the wages he offered, she said in halting English; she would come to-morrow at daybreak; she would cook their breakfast.

"Better come to-night," he urged. "The men get down the grade to work very early; breakfast must be on time."

"I be on time," she replied. "I sleep here this night, every night. I not sleep in camp."

Then he told her of the shack he had ordered, and that was even now being built.

She shook her head. "I sleep here every night," she reiterated.

Wingate had met many Indians in his time, so dropped the subject, knowing well that persuasion or argument would be utterly useless.

"All right," he said, "you must do as you like; only remember, an early breakfast to-morrow."

"I 'member," she replied.

He had ridden some twenty yards, when he turned to call back: "Oh, what's your name, please?"

"Catharine," she answered simply.

"Thank you," he said, and, touching his hat lightly, rode down towards the canyon. Just as he was dipping over its rim he looked back. She was still standing in the doorway, and above and beyond about her were the purple shadows, the awful solitude, of Crow's Nest Mountain. . .

Catharine had been cooking at the camp for weeks. The meals were good, the men respected her, and she went her way to and from her shack at the canyon as regularly as the world went around. The autumn slipped by, and the nipping frosts of early winter and the depths of early snows were already daily occurrences. The big group of solid log shacks that formed the construction camp were all made weather-tight against the long mountain winter. Trails were beginning to be blocked, streams to freeze, and "Old Baldy" already wore a canopy of snow that reached down to the timber line.

"Catharine," spoke young Wingate, one morning, when the clouds hung low and a soft snow fell, packing heavily on the selfsame snows of the previous night, "you had better make up your mind to occupy the shack here. You won't be able to go to your home much longer now at night; it gets dark so early, and the snows are too heavy."

"I go home at night," she repeated.

"But you can't all winter," he exclaimed. "If there was one single horse we could spare from the grade work, I'd see you got it for your journeys, but there isn't. We're terribly short now; every animal in the Pass is overworked as it is. You'd better not try going home any more."

"I go home at night," she repeated.

Wingate frowned impatiently; then in afterthought he smiled. "All right, Catharine," he said, "but I warn you. You'll have a search party out after you some dark morning, and you know it won't be pleasant to be lost in the snows up that canyon."

"But I go home, night-time," she persisted, and that ended the controversy.

But the catastrophe he predicted was inevitable. Morning after morning he would open the door of the shack he occupied with the other officials, and, looking up the white wastes through the grey-blue dawn, he would watch the distances with an anxiety that meant more than a consideration for his breakfast. The woman interested him. She was so silent, so capable, so stubborn. What was behind all this strength of character? What had given that depth of mournfulness to her eyes? Often he had surprised her watching him, with an odd longing in her face; it was something of the expression he could remember his mother wore when she looked at him long, long ago. It was a vague, haunting look that always brought back the one great tragedy of his life - a tragedy he was even now working night and day at his chosen profession to obliterate from his memory, lest he should be forever unmanned - forever a prey to melancholy.

He was still a young man, but when little more than a boy he had married, and for two years was transcendently happy. Then came the cry of "Kootenay Gold" ringing throughout Canada - of the untold wealth of Kootenay mines. Like thousands of others he followed the beckoning of that yellow finger, taking his young wife and baby daughter West with him. The little town of Nelson, crouching on its beautiful hills, its feet by the waters of Kootenay Lake, was then in its first robust, active infancy. Here he settled, going out alone on long prospecting expeditions; sometimes he was away a week, sometimes a month, with the lure of the gold forever in his veins, but the laughter of his child, the love of his wife, forever in his heart. Then - the day of that awful home-coming! For three weeks the fascination of searching for the golden pay-streak had held him in the mountains. No one could find him when it happened, and now all they could tell him was the story of an upturned canoe found drifting on the lake, of a woman's light summer shawl caught in the thwarts, of a child's little silken bonnet washed ashore. The great-hearted men of the West had done their utmost in the search that followed. Miners, missionaries, prospectors, Indians, settlers, gamblers, outlaws, had one and all turned out, for they liked young Wingate, and they adored his loving wife and dainty child. But the search was useless. The wild shores of Kootenay Lake alone held the secret of their resting-place.

Young Wingate faced the East once more. There was but one thing to do with his life - work, work, work; and the harder, the more difficult, the work, the better. It was this very difficulty that made the engineering on the Crow's Nest Pass so attractive to him. So here he was building grades, blasting tunnels, with Catharine's mournful eyes following him daily, as if she divined something of that long-ago sorrow that had shadowed his almost boyish life.

He liked the woman, and his liking quickened his eye to her hardships, his ear to the hint of lagging weariness in her footsteps; so he was the first to notice it the morning she stumped into the cook-house, her feet bound up in furs, her face drawn in agony.

"Catharine," he exclaimed, "your feet have been frozen!"

She looked like a culprit, but answered: "Not much; I get lose in storm las' night."

"I thought this would happen," he said, indignantly. "After this you sleep here."

"I sleep home," she said, doggedly.

"I won't have it," he declared. "I'll cook for the men myself first."

"All right," she replied. "You cookee; I go home - me."

That night there was a terrible storm. The wind howled down

the throat of the Pass, and the snow fell like bales of sheep's wool, blanketing the trails and drifting into railroad cuts until they attained their original level. But after she had cooked supper Catharine started for home as usual. The only unusual thing about it was that the next morning she did not return. It was Sunday, the men's day "off." Wingate ate no breakfast, but after swallowing some strong tea he turned to the foreman. "Mr. Brown, will you come with me to try and hunt up Catharine?" he asked.

"Yes, if we can get beyond the door," assented Brown. "But I doubt if we can make the canyon, sir."

"We'll have a try at it, anyway," said the young engineer. "I almost doubt myself if she made it last night."

"She's a stubborn woman," commented Brown.

"And has her own reasons for it, I suppose," replied Wingate. "But that has nothing to do with her being lost or frozen. If something had not happened I'm sure she would have come to-day, notwithstanding I scolded her yesterday, and told her I'd rather cook myself than let her run such risks. How will we go, Mr. Brown; horses or snowshoes?"

"Shoes," said the foreman decidedly. "That snow'll be above the middle of the biggest horse in the outfit."

So they set forth on their tramp up the slopes, peering right and left as they went for any indication of the absent woman. Wingate's old grief was knocking at his heart once more. A woman lost in the appalling vastness of this great Western land was entering into his life again. It took them a full hour to go that mile, although both were experts on the shoes, but as they reached the rim of the canyon they were rewarded by seeing a thin blue streak of smoke curling up from her lodge "chimney." Wingate sat down in the snows weakly. The relief had unmanned him.

"I didn't know how much I cared," he said, "until I knew she was safe. She looks at me as my mother used to; her eyes are like mother's, and I love my mother."

It was a simple, direct speech, but Brown caught its pathos.

"She's a good woman," he blurted out, as they trudged along towards the shack. They knocked on the door. There was no reply. Then just as Wingate suggested forcing it in case she were ill and lying helpless within, a long, low call from the edge of the canyon startled them. They turned and had not followed the direction from which the sound came more than a few yards when they met her coming towards them on snowshoes; in her arms she bore a few faggots, and her face, though smileless, was very welcoming.

She opened the door, bidding them enter. It was quite warm inside, and the air of simple comfort derived from crude benches, tables and shelves, assured them that she had not suffered. Near the fire was drawn a rough home-built couch, and on it lay in heaped disorder a pile of grey blankets. As the two men warmed their hands at the grateful blaze, the blankets stirred. Then a small hand crept out and a small arm tossed the covers a little aside.

"Catharine," exclaimed Wingate, "have you a child here?"

"Yes," she said simply.

"How long is it that you have had it here?" he demanded.

"Since before I work at your camp," she replied.

"Whew!" said the foreman, "I now understand why she came home nights."

"To think I never guessed it!" murmured Wingate. Then to Catharine: "Why didn't you bring it into camp and keep it there day and night with you, instead of taking these dangerous tramps at night and morning?"

"It's a girl child," she answered.

"Well, what of it?" he asked impatiently.

"Your camp no place for girl child," she replied, looking directly at him. "Your men they rough, they get whiskey sometimes. They fight. They speak bad words what you call swear. I not want her hear that. I not want her see whiskey man."

"Oh, Brown!" said Wingate, turning to his companion. "What a reproach! What a reproach! Here our gang is - the vanguard of the highest civilization, but unfit for association with a little Indian child!"

Brown stood speechless, although in his rough, honest mind he was going over a list of those very "swears" she objected to, but they were mentally directed at the whole outfit of his ruffianly construction gang. He was silently swearing at them for their own shortcomings in that very thing.

The child on the couch stirred again. This time the firelight fell full across the little arm. Wingate stared at it, then his eyes widened. He looked at the woman, then looked back at the bare arm. It was the arm of a white child.

"Catharine, was your husband white?" he asked, in a voice that betrayed anxiety.

"I got no husban'," she replied, somewhat defiantly.

"Then - " he began, but his voice faltered.

She came and stood between him and the couch. Something of the look of a she-panther came into her face, her figure, her attitude. Her eyes lost their mournfulness and blazed a black-red at him. Her whole body seemed ready to spring.

"You not touch the girl child!" she half snarled. "I not let you touch her; she mine, though I have no husban'!"

"I don't want to touch her, Catharine," he said gently, trying to pacify her. "Believe me, I don't want to touch her."

The woman's whole being changed. A thousand mother-lights gleamed from her eyes, a thousand measures of mother-love stormed at her heart. She stepped close, very close to him and laid her small brown hand on his, then drawing him nearer to her said: "Yes, you do want to touch her; you not speak truth when you say 'no.' You do want to touch her!" With a rapid movement she flung back the blankets, then slipping her bare arm about him she bent his form until he was looking straight into the child's face - a face the living miniature of his own! His eyes, his hair, his small kindly mouth, his fair, perfect skin. He staggered erect.

"Catharine! What does this mean? What does it mean?" he said hoarsely.

"Your child -" she half questioned, half affirmed.

"Mine? Mine?" he called, without human understanding in his voice. "Oh, Catharine! Where did you get her?"

"The shores of Kootenay Lake," she answered.

"Was - was - she alone?" he cried.

The woman looked away, slowly shaking her head, and her voice was very gentle as she replied: "No, she alive a little, but the other, whose arms 'round her, she not alive; my people, the Kootenay Indians, and I - we - we bury that other."

For a moment there was a speaking silence, then young

Wingate, with the blessed realization that half his world had been saved for him, flung himself on his knees, and, with his arms locked about the little girl, was calling:

"Margie! Margie! Papa's little Margie girl! Do you remember papa? Oh, Margie! Do you? Do you?"

Something dawned in the child's eyes - something akin to a far-off memory. For a moment she looked wonderingly at him, then put her hand up to his forehead and gently pulled a lock of his fair hair that always curled there - an old trick of hers. Then she looked down at his vest pocket, slowly pulled out his watch and held it to her ear. The next minute her arms slipped round his neck.

"Papa," she said, "papa been away from Margie a long time."

Young Wingate was sobbing. He had not noticed that the big rough foreman had gone out of the shack with tear-dimmed eyes, and had quietly closed the door behind him. . .

It was evening before Wingate got all the story from Catharine, for she was slow of speech, and found it hard to explain her feelings. But Brown, who had returned alone to the camp in the morning, now came back, packing an immense bundle of all the tinned delicacies he could find, which, truth to tell, were few. He knew some words of Kootenay, and led Catharine on to reveal the strange history that sounded like some tale from fairyland. It appeared that the reason Catharine did not attempt to go to camp that morning was that Margie was not well, so she would not leave her, but in her heart of hearts she knew young Wingate would come searching to her lodge. She loved the child as only an Indian woman can love an adopted child. She longed for him to come when she found Margie was ill, yet dreaded that coming from the depths of her soul. She dreaded the hour he would see the child and take it away. For the moment she looked upon his face, the night he rode over to engage her to cook, months ago, she had known he was Margie's father. The little thing was the perfect mirror of him, and Catharine's strange wild heart rejoiced to find him, yet hid the child from him for very fear of losing it out of her life.

After finding it almost dead in its dead mother's arms on the shore, the Indians had given it to Catharine for the reason that she could speak some English. They were only a passing band of Kootenays, and they journeyed on and on, week in and week out, they finally came to Crow's Nest Mountain. Here the child fell ill, so they built Catharine a log shack, and left her with plenty of food, sufficient to last until the railway gang had worked that far up the Pass, when more food would be available. When she had finished the strange history, Wingate looked at her long and lovingly.

"Catharine," he said, "you were almost going to fight me once to-day. You stood between the couch and me like a panther. What changed you so that you led me to my baby girl yourself?"

"I make one last fight to keep her," she said, haltingly. "She mine so long, I want her; I want her till I die. Then I think many times I see your face at camp. It look like sky when sun does not shine - all cloud, no smile, no laugh. I know you think of your baby then. Then I watch you many times. Then after while my heart is sick for you, like you are my own boy, like I am your own mother. I hate see no sun in your face. I think I not good mother to you; if I was good mother I would give you your child; make the sun come in your face. To-day I make last fight to keep the child. She's mine, so long I want her till I die. Then somet'ing in my heart say, 'He's like son to you, as if he your own boy; make him glad - happy. Oh, ver' glad! Be like his own mother. Find him his baby.' "

"Bless the mother heart of her!" growled the big foreman, frowning to keep his face from twitching.

It was twilight when they mounted the horses one of the men had brought up for them to ride home on, Wingate with his treasure-child hugged tightly in his arms. Words were powerless to thank the woman who had saved half his world for him. His voice choked when he tried, but she understood, and her woman's heart was very, very full.

Just as they reached the rim of the canyon Wingate turned and looked back. His arms tightened about little Margie as his eyes rested on Catharine - as once before she was standing in the doorway, alone; alone, and above and about her were purple shadows, the awful solitude of Crow's Nest Mountain.

"Brown!" he called. "Hold on, Brown! I can't do it! I can't leave her like that!"

He wheeled his horse about and, plunging back through the snow, rode again to her door. Her eyes radiated as she looked at him. Years had been wiped from his face since the morning. He was a laughing boy once more.

"You are right," he said, "I cannot keep my little girl in that rough camp. You said it was no place for a girl child. You are right. I will send her into Calgary until my survey is over. Catharine, will you go with her, take care of her, nurse her, guard her for me? You said I was your own son; will you be that good mother to me that you want to be? Will you do this for your white boy?"

He had never seen her smile before. A moment ago her heart had been breaking, but now she knew with a great gladness that she was not only going to keep and care for Margie, but that this laughing boy would be as a son to her for all time. No wonder that Catharine of the Crow's Nest smiled!

The Torch Woman

Alex Grisdale (1895 - 1973) came from the Brokenhead Reserve in Manitoba. At the age of twenty-four he set about recording the stories he had been told by his father and grandfather. In all, he wrote over eight hundred pages of stories, and gave them to a teacher at the reserve mission for safe keeping. The mission burned down shortly afterward, but he soon returned to the task and recorded them again. Finally at the age of seventy-seven his stories were published in a book called *Wild Drums: Tales and Legends of the Plains Indians* (Winnipeg: Peguis Publishers, 1974) edited by Nan Shipley. In this story he tells of inter-tribal warfare between the Sioux and Assiniboine before the coming of the Europeans.

Many years before the white man came to this country a band of Indians set up their tepees by the Assiniboine River near where Brandon city now stands. These were Stone Roasters, people who dropped hot roasted stones into water to make it boil. This tribe is now called the Assiniboine. The band made their camp near a cut bank where the land dropped fifteen or sixteen feet over the rocks into the water. The chief chose this safe place because enemies could not approach by river.

There was a widow in this camp, and because she was young and childless she was expected to look after herself. Her husband had been killed by the Sioux and she was still in mourning for him when the scouts rode in to report a large herd of buffalo about a day's ride out on the plains. At once the people prepared to break camp and move closer to the hunt.

"I will remain here until you return," the widow said.

Her friends were alarmed. "What will you do if the enemy comes while you are alone? We will be gone for the days of one hand."

She shrugged and continued to scrape fat from a buffalo hide with her sharp flint stone scraper. "If this happens then I shall surely die."

When the chief saw that the woman was determined to remain in her tepee by the river, he ordered that three other lodges remain standing. This might deceive any spies into believing several families were here instead of a lone woman.

The people rode away to the buffalo hunt and the widow slept one night without fear. Only the sound of the river and far away coyotes disturbed the dark stillness. But she knew that if enemy scouts were about and had seen the departure of the band they would lie patiently watching the four tepees to count the men who went in and out. It would not be long before they would discover that she was alone. But she was prepared to die, for her husband had been dead two moons and she still grieved for him. To live or to die was of no consequence to her.

She performed her work as usual about the quiet camp. Even when the sun set and there was nothing for her to do, the widow carried her tanning frame into her tepee to work by the light of her fire and the birchbark cone she had thrust into her beaded headband, like a torch.

As she scraped the hide, the widow became aware of strangers just outside her lodge. A moment later the door flap was raised and six Sioux warriors entered. They carried bow and arrows and tomahawks in their belts. She knew she must die.

"Sit down and eat before you slay me," she said quietly.

Without a word the men sat down, three on each side of the entrance. The widow's invitation was not strange. Many warriors facing death committed an act of supreme courage or service, and it was the custom to permit those doomed to die, a last request.

The woman with the torch on her head set fresh meat and berries on birchbark platters. She passed these to the men seated on the ground. When their hands were full she darted from the tent and ran towards the river.

The torch on her head made it easy for the Sioux to follow her and the warriors were right behind, shouting and yelling their rage. When the widow came to the edge of the cut bank she tore the torch from her headband and threw it ahead, and then dropped to the ground crouching low.

The Sioux chasing the light plunged over the cut bank to their death on the rocks below.

The woman listened to their cries for a time to see if all had really fallen and she was safe. Now she was too frightened to spend the night in her own tepee so she began to run westward where she knew her band would be camped in readiness for the big buffalo hunt.

She ran all through the night and it was sunrise when she saw the familiar lodges in the distance. The guards had seen the lone figure and rode out to discover who it was. Onc was waving his blanket in a friendly signal. They were certainly surprised to see the widow.

The people of the camp listened in disbelief as she told her story. Could a lone woman outwit six cunning Sioux? Was she telling this wild story to win honour for herself?

The chief ordered a fast pony for the widow and he with twenty of his men rode back to the four tepees by the Assiniboine River. As the men peered over the edge of the cut bank and saw the six bodies they knew that the woman's story was true. They made their way down to the rocks below and six scalps were taken as proof of what had happened.

The widow rode back with the chief, his men following, all singing the Hero Song to let the women in camp know that they must prepare a feast in the widow's honour. That night all sat around the campfire and watched as she who was now called the Torch Woman danced and enacted the story of her experience.

The chief proclaimed the widow a heroine. "Had our enemies killed her they would have hidden in our lodges there and waited our return and killed us all. Truly this woman is one of the great hero-queens to be honoured for all time."

Torch Woman was greatly admired for all her life after that. She received many gifts and many offers of marriage.

Abandoned

Eleanor Brass, who has already been introduced through excerpts of her autobiography, told Cree legends on an educational radio broadcast in Regina. Response from her listeners was so enthusiastic that she compiled a book called *Medicine Boy and Other Cree Tales* (Calgary: Glenbow Museum, 1978). Included in this book of legends is a short story about more contemporary times.

Hortense happily anticipated the forthcoming exhibition in a nearby city. Sitting beside the campfire she was baking bannocks that she and her family could take along with them to the fair. Her mother had shown her a certain kind of wood to use on the fire that would produce large glowing embers to bake the bannock to a golden brown. Joe, her husband, liked it that way.

Hortense knew that according to the customs of the Cree tribe, her father gave her to Joe to marry. She had lived with him since she was a little girl and after they were married she did her best to please him.

In preparation for going to the exhibition, Hortense saw that her children's clothes were clean and mended. She was always bothered by the way people always stared at her when they went into a town or city. She also wondered why she didn't have black hair and dark skin like the other Indians. Joe had often told her in his quiet way, that she was all right for him, even though she had fair skin, blue eyes and blond hair.

Hortense sometimes felt that she looked forward a little too eagerly to being with the throngs of people on the midway and watching the shows. Why should it take hold of her like this? Why should she feel a desire to be part of it? Could it be true what the children in camp used to say, that she was an abandoned white child? Could this be the reason for the strange stirrings in her heart?

Hortense always fought these feelings down, for they made her feel disloyal to Joe and their children. She never mentioned these thoughts to her mother who had carefully brought her up in the customs and traditions of the Cree tribe.

The day of the fair dawned clear and bright. Joe hitched the ponies to the wagon and they loaded their tent, bedding, clothes and food, before joining in the caravan of wagons and rigs from the reserve. It was a six-hour drive till they reached the outskirts of the city, where they pitched the tent and tethered the horses out to graze.

They saw the exhibition open with the usual procedure, a parade led by Indians in costumes, beads and feathers, followed by bands, floats and clowns. As before, Hortense watched breathless and wide-eyed.

She wandered down the midway to watch the rides, and to see the performers, chorus girls, and animals come out on the platforms in front of the marquees. Then she came to a group of dancing girls, clad in light fluffy costumes. Hortense watched them fascinated; then suddenly a woman in a fluffy costume rushed up, embraced her tightly and wept. Before Hortense could catch her breath to enquire what it was all about, the weeping woman had released her and disappeared into the tent. Hortense's mother, who had witnessed the scene, walked over to her with a disturbed expression on her face, saying; "I expected something like this would happen sometime."

"Why?" asked Hortense, still bewildered.

"Twenty years ago," said her mother sadly, "a frightened young white girl walked up to me, placed a small bundle in my arms and ran off into the crowd. I stood astounded on the same spot where you are now standing until the bundle started to move and cry. I looked down into the tiny face and saw a newborn baby. I waited and waited for the mother to come but she didn't so I took the baby home and looked after her like one of my own. That bundle was you, and the frightened young girl is the same woman who just embraced you. She is your real mother." She added sadly, "I suppose now, you'll be leaving us."

Hortense felt sick inside. Her mother had abandoned her own flesh and blood, which was unpardonable according to the tribal laws. All the previous thrills and awe of the midway suddenly died away.

"No, Mother," she said, "you are my real mother and my family will never be abandoned by me."

Stories by Hubert Gunn

Hubert Gunn is a Saulteaux who attended Marieval Residential School in Saskatchewan, receiving a grade six education. This, he says, qualified him for "manure-forkin', hay-pitchin' and wood-choppin'."

He is a veteran of the Korean War and today is a band councillor on the Cowessess Reserve as well as a Land Claims Specialist, researching illegal land surrenders and other treaty-related issues.

His stories tell of everyday life on the reserve when farms were not yet mechanized and a few dollars could be earned by selling wood or performing casual labour for farmers.

A Question of Rights

Back in the not-so-long-ago-days, when Treaty Indians were forbidden by law to buy or consume liquor, "Shingles", a bachelor from the reserve, was hovering around the door of the Government Liquor Board Store. He was waiting for any Whiteman he knew, or even a Métis, to happen along. If he saw one or the other he would ask him to buy a gallon of wine for him; he had the price in the pocket of his faded overalls. The money was folded away and had been since that morning when he got ten dollars from old Steve Miller, for whom he had been fixing fences for three days.

"That was good money just for fixing fences," thought

Shingles.

He stepped away from the building he had been leaning against when he saw Jim Cross, another farmer he worked for occasionally. Jim was apparently heading for the liquor store.

Shingles had been stone deaf since childhood. He always blamed this handicap on the brothers who were the boys' supervisors at the Indian residential school he attended, graduating with a grade-three equivalent. Shingles said that one day he was caught eating stolen cream from the milkhouse at the mission. He was around twelve years old then, old enough to perform chores for half a day and attend class the other half. He and another boy were eating this cream with bread, also stolen, when one of the brothers came in behind them silently. Suddenly he hit Shingles over the head from behind with a piece of electrician's wire. The wire made a deep cut in his scalp which became infected. The final outcome, Shingles said, was deafness. His brooding thoughts were broken when Jim asked,

"Hello, Shing, what brings you to town?" Jim made every effort to make Shingles hear him by yelling. Of course, Shingles, stone deaf as he was, couldn't hear a thing Jim was saying. But by reading the man's lips and watching the signs he made with his hands he finally made out what was asked of him.

He answered in his high pitched voice, and not even bothering to pass the time of day or anything else that would endanger this opportunity of getting a jug, said, "Hidy, Jim! Say do you think you can see your way clear to buy me a jug while you're in there buying your own stuff?"

At the same time he pointed to the store with his chin. "I can give you the price of it." He reached into his pocket for the money that was practically burning a hole the size of a duck's egg. He turned his head to spit at a cricket that was chirping away for all it was worth, without taking his eyes off Jim.

Jim was in a difficult spot. If he refused, Shingles might not work for him again. Worse yet, the old boy might tell some of the other Indians not to work for him either.

"These people are scarce sometimes," Jim thought to himself. "Just when you need them in the worst way to do some work on the farm you can't find a single one." It always puzzled Jim how they could disappear all at the same time like that. Jim scratched the stubble on his chin.

"My chin sounds like when you smoothen a brand new tip of a pool cue," he said aloud to himself. Feeling foolish, he stopped scratching and talking to himself abruptly. "Hell!" he said, "This guy is deaf anyway."

Gazing down the street and as far out of town as he could, he took a blue and white polka dot rag that served as a handkerchief out of the back pocket of his overalls. He removed his floppy, faded old engineer's cap from his head and wiped his sweating brow. "Sure is hot!" he said to no one in particular except maybe the cricket who didn't hear him either because it was busy rubbing sticky stuff off its body. Stalling for time, he inspected his cap closely and wiped the band dry. All the while Shingles' nose was practically inside the cap, watching closely.

A fellow could get in trouble buying liquor for the Indians if they got caught and squealed on him. Still stalling for time and wondering how he could get out of this predicament, he took a package out of the bib of his overalls. Old Chum tobacco — this would keep Shingles busy, at least until he could think up some excuse without making Shingles mad. He offered Shingles the package and papers after rolling one for himself. Shingles declined.

Just then an RCMP car passed slowly by with two constables looking at them closely. The car went around the corner, its wheels sending up little clouds of dust that hung in the hot, still air before grudgingly settling to the ground again. As Shingles followed the car with his eyes to see what the cops would do, Jim saw his chance. He hurried across the street and ducked into the hardware store, glad to have got out of the tight spot he was in.

Shingles watched the police car go out of sight, headed in the direction of the highway. When he turned around to talk to Jim he found himself standing alone. He decided to take a chance since the cops were gone. Looking up and down the street, he quickly entered the store.

The man behind the counter watched Shingles shuffle in and go directly to the list of liquors available. Should he ask this man for his "blue card" he wondered? A person who was non-treaty, but of Indian ancestry, was given a card addressed "To Whom It

May Concern", stating that he could buy liquor or enter a beer parlour. Sometimes he did not bother to ask a man for this card because some of the Métis were as Indian as the Indians and it seemed a waste of time.

Shingles laboriously finished writing out the form that was provided for buying liquor. It was not written out too well. He took it to the counter to have his order filled, at the same time unfolding the worn bills; he was obviously familiar with the procedure for buying liquor.

The storekeeper noticed the poor handwriting and reasoned, with sympathy, that most of the Métis had little or no schooling. He also noticed at the bottom of the form the "Tax" was not included. By yelling until his face was red, and scribbling figures on the back of the form, he finally made Shingles understand that he had forgotten to include tax.

Immediately, Shingles sprang to defend his rights. He yelled at the man while jabbing his finger at the form.

"What do you mean, tax?" His face was close to that of the storekeeper. "Don't you know the law? I'm treaty Indian and I don't pay tax!"

Two minutes later Shingles was busy brushing the dust off the seat of his overalls where the man's foot had kicked him out of the liquor store, without his jug of wine. Leaning against the building, scratching his head, he wondered why the man got so mad and threw him out like that. . .

A Lamp To Read By

It was a nice, warm, sunny fall day. A good day to haul a load of wood to town and sell it in that district the Indians call "German Town." The residents in that end of town were predominantly of German extraction and most of them liked to get a deal on a load of wood. The sharp blade of the axe bit deep into the dry poplar tree. Old Gus grunted as he pushed the tree down and started trimming the limbs off. The ring of the axe echoed through the bush. He guessed that there were at least twenty or thirty loads of good dry wood left in this part of the reserve. He would be back again soon, but this log would complete today's load.

Old Gus stopped to take a grey, nearly empty package of tobacco out of the little bib of his faded overalls. The cigarette papers that accompanied his tobacco were Chantecler's. There was a rooster on the red cover, drawn in black ink. Gus referred to them as the "Rooster" brand.

Gus now fashioned a cigarette, rolling expertly. Then, lighting a match by whipping it across the seat of his overalls, he puffed contentedly on the cigarette. He was eyeing the team of blacks who were trying to reach a tuft of grass, causing the wagon to creep ahead a few feet.

"Whoa!" yelled Gus, at the same time grabbing the lines and jerking the animals' heads up.

"Allus tryin to eat when there's work to be done," he grumbled.

Gus was still peeved about events earlier that day. At times, the horses were hard to catch, like this morning when they somehow sensed there was work to do. At other times he could fool them by putting a handful of gravel in the pail he usually fed them from. They would come trotting up to him, expecting to get a treat of grain when he shook the pail. But this morning they must have remembered and were not fooled by the old trick. They came close, necks stretched way out, trying to sniff at the pail to see if there was really oats in it.

Just as he going to drop the pail and grab their halters, Old Dick, the wiser one, turned around as fast as a cutting horse and after kicking his heels up in the air a couple of times and bucking, he raced out of sight into the bush, switching his tail with Old Billie close behind.

It was at times like this that Gus felt like shooting his horses. He ran crashing and tripping through the bush, swearing. At last, his chest heaving, Gus stopped to lean against a tree to catch his breath and plan other strategy. Rolling a smoke, but looking out the corner of his eye under the brim of his tattered straw hat, he spied Dick's head, only partially concealed by the brush, calmly peering back at him. Gus began to whistle as he walked over in that direction, at the same time trying to make it look as though he had given up trying to catch them. Suddenly he made a dive and grabbed Dick's halter.

"Just for that -- no oats for you," he said triumphantly. Billie followed meekly behind.

Gus cut four three-foot stakes and squared the ends. He put them in the stake holders of the wagon and loaded the poplar poles. He stepped back and surveyed the load. "Damn nice load," he said to himself. He threw his axe on top of the load and climbed up after it. He drove out of the bush, carefully skirting old stumps sticking up out of the ground.

Getting near town, he stopped and rearranged the logs to make it look like a really good load, which it was. He generally had to haggle the deal for the five dollars he got for his wood.

He pulled into town under the railroad overpass. The yard engines passing back and forth overhead made the horses nervous. They lifted their heads and pranced. "They'll think I have a fine team of lively horses," said Gus, proud of the way the team was acting. When he got to Herman Buckt's place, he pulled into the yard and noticed the curtains fluttering inside the kitchen window.

He got off the wagon and knocked on the door. Herman came out the door, pretending he had not seen Gus before. He shook Gus' hand and said,

"So, I see you vant to sell me a load of vood, yah."

Herman walked around inspecting the load of wood. He peered under it and over it and slipped in behind the team to see if the bottom of the logs were rotten. He went back to see how small the ends were, and was trying to climb up on the load when Gus stopped him.

"Four dollars," said Herman.

"Four fifty," Gus answered.

Herman was adamant, "Four dollars."

"But I worked hard and had to come a long way to bring such a nice load of wood to town for you."

"No matter, all the money me and the vife get is the old age pension."

"I need the money, and besides I didn't have my dinner yet. If you won't buy the wood, I'll go someplace else."

"Vell, four fifty. No more."

Gus knew he had won. "Four fifty and dinner to boot."

"All right, all right," said Herman, throwing up his hands as if he were being robbed. But he, too, had won.

While Gus unloaded, Herman went inside to tell his wife to prepare a meal. Gus tied a horse on each side of the wagon and split the bundle of hay he had on the wagon between them.

He thanked Mrs. Buckt for the baloney and potatoes and with the money in his pocket, hitched up the team and drove down town. He tied up near the pool hall, where the Indians from the reserve gathered whenever they came to town. As soon as he walked in he was greeted warmly by his friends who were standing by the first table playing poker pool.

"Grab a cue, Gus," said one. "We just started."

At that moment Gus thought about his old lady and her last words when he left the house that morning.

"And don't forget the lamp chimney this time. Come home early and no pool and no drinking!" At the awful impact of the thought, he backed out of the pool room and went to the general store.

"Well, Gus, long time no see," Mr. Lesser, the store keeper greeted. "What would you like?"

"Well, Mr. Lesser, my old wife's been nagging at me all week."

"What for?" asked Mr. Lesser.

"Well, the last time I came in, I forgot to buy a replacement for that damn lamp chimney our grandchild broke on us. Before I go and play pool and stay till midnight, like last time, and catch hell again, I thought I'd better get what I need first."

"Wise move," beamed Mr. Lesser, starting to get the items on the list Gus presented him with. "Come here, Gus, I'll show you a lamp chimney the kids won't be able to break so easy."

The store keeper took a package from the shelf and unwrapped a lamp chimney and threw it on the floor. It smashed into a hundred pieces as Gus jumped back in alarm. He then took another chimney from the shelf and throwing it on the floor, laughed as Gus jumped back again, expecting to see glass all over the place. Gus was amazed as he looked down at the fragile looking chimney, still in one piece.

"Well, I'll be dawgonned," said Gus. "Let's see that trick again."

"That was no trick, it's a new kind of lamp chimney," said Mr. Lesser. "You just have to be careful it don't hit any iron, like a nail or anything like that."

Walking out with his box of groceries and looking at the lamp chimney in its brown paper wrapping, Gus kept saying to himself over and over, "Well, I'll be damned, just wait till I show Sarah this one."

Twenty miles away, Sarah, Gus' sharp-tongued old wife, was cooking supper for herself, knowing that she would eat alone. She put another stick of wood in the stove. Gus did not get drunk every time he went to town, only once in a while, just when she least expected it. If he got drunk today, her mood would not let him hear the end of it for days on end.

Seeing that it was getting dark, Sarah cut a piece of cloth from one of Gus' old flannel shirts and placing it in a saucer, poured some melted grease over it. She lit the wick and watched as the room lit up dimly with the makeshift "bitch lamp."

It was nearly midnight when she heard the dogs barking and going outside, she heard the wagon creaking in the distance. She went inside and made another fire in the stove. Gus would be hungry. The dogs were setting up a racket, yelping and barking as they recognized their master.

The wagon stopped and Gus came in carrying the box of groceries and, looking at the sputtering bitch lamp, he started to unwrap a parcel. Sarah was trying to sniff at Gus' breath to see if she could detect the smell of liquor. She was looking at him closely in the fitful light.

His wife waiting, Gus finally got the wrapping paper off the lamp chimney and said,

"Look, Sarah. I bought a lamp chimney, a new kind, if you drop it, it won't break." Sarah, her suspicions now aroused, stepped closer, wondering what Gus meant. Gus said, "Watch this."

He threw the chimney on the floor. It hit a nail and smashed into a hundred pieces. Only then did Gus remember the store keeper's words "...as long as it doesn't hit anything iron, like a nail or anything like that..."

Sarah, frustrated after waiting all these days for a lamp chimney so she could read, grabbed the broom and chased Gus outside, yelling at the top of her voice,

"Get out, you drunken old fool! You can sleep outside with the dogs again."

Old Gus unharnessed the horses and giving them each a syrup pail of oats before letting them go, grumbled to himself, "Now what do you suppose got into the old lady to say that I was drunk like that?"

The dogs were staying away from Gus, just in case he was really drunk. They did not want to be within kicking distance. They watched him uneasily ... but with some sympathy.

The Kiss and the Moonshine

Basil Johnston, whose myth "Nanabush, Kitchi Manitou's Emissary" is found elsewhere in this anthology, also wrote short stories. In his stories he tells about life on a modern reserve, using humour and gentle satire to comment on both Native and non-Native societies. This story was originally published in the *Tawow* magazine. Later the short stories were published in *Moose Meat and Wild Rice* (Toronto: McLelland and Stewart, 1978).

"Avoid women and get an education. Women can wait."

Such was the admonition and advice that I received from the wise and the experienced. So scrupulously did I follow it, that I graduated from Loyola College in Montreal.

Even after graduation I wasn't particularly interested in females; nor they in me. Whether they grew weary in the wait or were simply disinterested, I am unable to say; it was probably for the latter reason.

I did eventually form a liaison with Early-in-the-Morning, who possessed among other attributes an automobile. As my affection for her grew, so did my resolve to kiss her. However, my fibre remained weak and static; and Early-in-the-Morning unkissed.

I had to do it right. I was convinced that the act of kissing was not merely the application and pressure of mouth to mouth. There was something more to this wondrous business. Moreover, I was college educated. Consequently, I should bring something extra to the basic elements of kissing.

But alas, having fastiduously avoided women and girls during my college and high school days, my proficiency in the craft of kissing was deficient. To go out to practise at that point was out of the question.

So I planned the kiss. I had to decide upon the technique; the opportunity would come later. I tried recalling all the techniques used by Roy Rogers, Tom Mix, and John Wayne, but they were not very illuminating. In my deliberations I remembered Humphrey Bogart. His was the method; his was the technique. It was manly, honest, direct and forceful. Early-in-the-Morning would like that. I shivered in excitement.

My opportunity came months later. On my next visit back to the reserve I sought out Early-in-the-Morning. That evening we went out, and though it was warm, I shivered. We went bowling; I shivered. We drank coffee in a restaurant; I shivered. I had one purpose, one resolve, the kiss. For it I shivered.

Later that evening Early-in-the-Morning transported me home, to my uncle's place. At the gate she stopped; kept the motor running. We talked. I edged closer. We talked some more. I occupied a little more of her territory until I couldn't move over any more. I placed a friendly shivering hand on her shoulder. She didn't object. I moved my friendly shivering hand to her other shoulder. She was ready; I was ready.

Early-in-the-Morning looked at her watch and announced,

"It's getting late. I'd better go home."

I made my move, but I never completed the assault, for the car horn blasted the stillness of the night and interrupted my ambitions. Only when I removed my elbow from the car horn did the trumpeting cease.

Early-in-the-Morning rocked with laughter. I retreated from the car and walked toward my uncle's house.

Disconsolately I looked up. All the lights in the house were ablaze. The front door opened. My uncle, dressed only in underwear and rubber boots, burst out. With a pail in either hand, he scudded across the open field.

Early-in-the-Morning drove away.

I waited at the door for uncle. He came back puffing, his two pails empty.

"Holy Jeez, you scared me. I thought it was the police. I just threw out two pails of moonshine," he said scornfully.

We commiserated with one another.

On the Shooting of a Beaver

George Kenny was born on the Lac Seul Reserve and grew up in small towns in Northwestern Ontario. He lived in Toronto and other cities. Much of his writing deals with the ambivalence all young people feel as they leave the ways of their ancestors to live in a different cultural milieu. This story is taken from his book *Indians Don't Cry* (Oakville, Ont.: Chimo, 1977).

Joe Rivers stood in front of an irregular line of spruce. He rubbed his leather mitted hands together. The air was still quite cold. The sun of spring in early April had not yet begun to melt the snows of the winter past, here in this region of Northwestern Ontario.

Joe's brown deep-set eyes scanned to his left and right as he faced a hole in the frozen creek surface. Careful not to move too much, he removed the leather covering of his new Olympus OM-1. He wanted to get a photograph of any creature, likely a beaver or a muskrat, that might crawl out of that watery opening.

His father, a trapper, had positioned him in this spot so that Joe might be able to shoot any furry animal using this hole to get a look at the above-water surroundings of its habitat. The elder Rivers had left Joe a Winchester 30:30 for this purpose.

Joe, who had spent most of his twenty-one years in town going to various schools, had not been too eager to act on his father's wish. Maybe it was because he never had to depend upon trapping and hunting in order to live, Joe reasoned, consenting nonetheless to follow his father's instructions.

What a contrast, being a bushman compared to life in the town of Dryden. Where did he belong, really, he wondered.

If the education counsellor from the Department of Indian Affairs had had his way, Joe, a grade twelve graduate should have gone to college and worked at getting some "real education." Though he had not been an outstanding student, he had the marks to go on.

He had decided, however, to work, and he had worked at the Dryden Paper mill ever since.

Joe shook a lock of hair out of his eyes. He began to feel his leather-booted feet getting cramped as well as cold. Maybe living in town had its advantages, he thought ruefully, as he shifted his hundred and seventy pounds; then again, it was really something out here.

He took his eyes away from the watery hole and gazed around. To his left, the snowy shoreline could not totally conceal golden strands of bulrushes, nor hide the broken pieces of aged trees lying down in natural death. Across the frozen stream a wall of balsam, cedar and birch trees stood in uniform - nature's vanguard, he thought. To his right, the curve of shoreline ended at a shrub-tipped point. Beyond it lay the wide expanse of Moose Lake, across which he and his father had come on snowshoes. Squinting his eyes, he looked up at the sun, a round saucer coloured bright yellow in the empty blue sky.

The breeze rippled the water of the opening, making Joe's heart seem to bob up to his throat; but as no furry animal appeared, he slowly exhaled and found that he was relaxing muscles of his body. Come on, you dumb beaver, he thought, and then smiled at the idea of a beaver hurrying out to be shot.

His legs sore from standing, Joe sat back on his haunches as he thought of where he was.

He was by a small stream, deep in a forest somewhere to the north-west of Dryden, Ontario. Town life had gotten to be too much for him. Joe had gone to the foreman in the finishing room of the plant and had asked for a leave of absence for a couple of months. His boss, he first thought, would be disgusted, but instead had broken into a grin and said, go ahead, but come back if you still want to work. He seemed to understand this need that Joe, and others before him, had had. Joe began to feel a sense of freedom he had never experienced before.

For three years, he had visited his father along the shores of Moose Lake. On his visits, during winter weekends, he had used a friend's ski-doo, roaring up the forty miles or so, on old logging trails. His father, a small and tough Indian, had never ceased to fish, trap, and hunt as so many of the men from the reserve had done. Joe recalled those days and nights of his weekends off when he and his father would drink tea brewed in a cast iron pot, munch on fried bannock, and talk in the comfort of the well-insulated log cabin. Measuring no more than eight by twelve, the cabin was warmed by the heat of an old oil drum stove. Ah, those were the days, he thought, his chest aching with the memory of his father. On those occasions his father had hinted how nice it would be if his only son would come to share his few remaining years. Joe had wanted that. Yet, he had been too dependent upon living in electrically heated homes with their flush toilets, the town's offerings of a library, picture shows, a coffee and talk in the small Chinese-owned restaurants. Sighing, Joe gazed blindly at the hole, remembering his father's gladness and smile when Joe told him that he had come to stay with the elder Rivers for at least a couple of months. And so wrapped in his thoughts was he, that Joe didn't see. . .

A brown, furry head with a black nose peeking from the water, its button eyes sliding around in a circling watch, its rounded ears pointing to the other shore. The head of the beaver was barely above the water level, when with a catch of breath, Joe became aware of it. Apparently satisfied no danger was near, the large rodent put its front paws on the far edge of the ice, and slowly started to climb onto the ice.

With a sudden throbbing of his temples, Joe instinctively recovered from his initial surprise; bending swiftly, he exchanged items. For one long drawn out moment he held his breath, focusing, as the large beaver swung around to face him, droplets of moisture rolling down its glistening fur. Joe seemed to see sudden shock in the beaver's eyes as he fired, and then a red spurt of liquid came from just above the animal's right temple, as it fell backward onto the icy surface. Feeling sick instantly, Joe watched, frozen, as the large adult beaver spat out scarlet, its heated breath substance coming into the cold air as steam. Its wide flat tail pounded hard, then gradually stilled as the animal thrashed out its death throes.

Bending down, Joe picked up the expensive camera he had so quickly forsaken. I really only wanted a picture, he thought. What does this say about me? The first cloud of the coming spring day seemed to chill the sun as he swung both the camera and the Winchester over one shoulder. With his hands he picked up the now-still creature. One man, he knew, would be pleased with his choice.

Joe Bignell's Fight with the Weetigo

D. Bruce Sealey is a Métis from southern Manitoba. He has held many different positions in both northern and southern Manitoba. He is best known for his historical and cultural writings about Métis people; his biography of James McKay was included earlier in this anthology. He also has a reputation as a master storyteller. This story was originally published in the magazine *Prairie Fire*.

Following Joe's failure to become a member of the Aurora Borealis Club he returned to York Factory in disgrace. Of course, everyone was too polite to talk about the ice worm incident but Joe remained very down-hearted. He was itching to do something that would redeem himself to his friends so when the troubles with the Weetigo started Joe was eager to help.

For those of you who live down south, I better give you some information about the Weetigo. It is a huge creature about eight feet tall, with unshorn hair, unshaved face and had black, peeling cheeks and nose for it seems always to be recovering from severe frost bite. A Weetigo is feared because it lives mainly on human flesh and if it gets around a trapper's bush camp, is likely to pick off members of the family one by one. Without doubt it is the most feared creature in the north and wise trappers flee their trap line if one is sighted. Libraries have all sorts of books about this cannibalistic monster and the most up to date science textbooks mention it. However, if you want to read about it in a scientific textbook like *Vertebrate Paleontology*, you will have to look it up under its fancy Latin name, *homo-nonexistus*.

There is one characteristic of a Weetigo that is very fearful. Its spirit can move from its body and, when it wishes, enter a human body. If a person is attacked by a Weetigo and manages to kill it, you never know where its spirit may go. It might even enter the body of your wife who will then murder you to satisfy her new cannibalistic cravings.

During January the village was surprised to notice that Obadiah Bluecoat, one of the best trappers, had returned from his trapline. Puzzlement gave way to fear when it was discovered that Obadiah and his partner, Isaiah Beardy, had been attacked at their bush camp by a Weetigo. They had fought back with axes and killed it. Later Isaiah's body was entered by the spirit and Obadiah killed him and then fled to the village. For weeks everyone stayed close to the houses and even when carrying wood and water the men kept a loaded rifle handy. Parents would not let their children attend school and I had to close it. When I got my school supervisor, Bernie Grafton, on the radio and told him about the temporary closing, he asked rather cautiously, "Do you think there is anything to it?"

"Yes," I replied. "It is out there."

"We better fly you out," said Bernie. "I'll get Tom Lamb in with his plane as soon as possible."

It took some arguing but finally I persuaded him of my good health and to leave me for another month to see if things settled down. Sure enough, when a month had passed without incident the village forgot its fears and normal activities were resumed.

Things went well until spring break-up when Obadiah and his son, Ezra, canoed a couple of miles upstream from York Factory to where a creek flowed into the Hayes River. It was a good trout stream and they hoped to catch a few dozen.

Upon arrival they were amazed to discover some dark clouds had rapidly built up and seemed to hover over them. There was a fair bit of thunder and then suddenly a stroke of lightening flashed and split their canoe into small pieces. They clambered up the bank while other strokes of lightening hit the ground around them. They set out running for the village and the lightening bolts never let up the attack until they were a half mile away from the creek. Of course, everyone understood that the spirit of the Weetigo was in the clouds and out for revenge. And likely it wouldn't leave the area until it had killed a number of people.

We were sure scared and took the only action possible. We got together a collection of tobacco; cigarette makings, snuff and six plugs of Big Ben chewing tobacco and went to see old Jonah, the Medicine Man. He took the tobacco, said prayers, burned some sweet grass and other herbs but those black thunder clouds never moved from over the creek. Finally he admitted his powers were of no avail against such a powerful Weetigo. It was then that Joe offered to fight the spirit monster. But, he reasoned, if Indian medicine wouldn't work, White medicine must be used. So Joe went to the Bay store and asked the manager for the most powerful White medicine he had. The manager just laughed and said the only thing he had that made White men feel powerful came in bottles. The result was that Joe headed out for the creek to do battle with the Weetigo armed only with two bottles of Hudson Bay Rum.

When Joe got to the creek he opened one bottle and took a big drink and then several more. As rumbles of thunder came from the cloud, Joe stood up and yelled at the Weetigo to come down and fight. As the thunder got louder, Joe drank more and screamed his challenge again and again. Soon lightening bolts were shot at him but Joe was drinking the second bottle by then and was feeling more powerful all the time. The larger the lightening bolts the louder were Joe's challenges. Finally after three hours of this battle the Weetigo in the thunder cloud realized it was beaten and disappeared, never to be seen again in that region.

To this day the Métis call the stream Weetigo. The White people, not fully understanding these things, named it Drunken Creek.

The Serpent's Egg

Gilbert Oskaboose is an Ojibway from Serpent River Reserve in Ontario. He has worked as a logger, a miner, a guide, a deckhand, a catskinner, a manager of a trading post, a reporter, and an editor of an international Native newspaper. In 1985 he was forced to retire because of a stroke. Now, confined to a wheelchair, he spends his days moose hunting from a specially designed truck, working for the Band, and writing.

This story is an allegory which deals with a pressing contemporary issue — nuclear power. Residents of the Serpent River Reserve have suffered severely from radiological and chemical pollution of their water source as a result of uranium mining. Moreover, the reserve has been left with 9,000 truckloads of dangerous wastes — acidic soil, sulfur, iron pyrite and a host of other toxic chemicals. These are the result of a sulphuric acid plant which was established on their reserve without their consent. Though the plant has been closed the waste has not been cleaned up.

Long ago, when the world was young, a great Serpent came down from the north, and by its passing carved a mighty river through the Cambrian Shield in a land now called Northern Ontario.

Anishnawbek elders say it is so.

As she moved ponderously south the Serpent searched with a growing sense of urgency for she was ripe with new life and her time was near. In the wild barren lands between Elliot and Quirke Lakes she laid millions of tiny eggs, ominous little nodules that sank away from the light, deep into the bedrock, to lie dormant for millennia, waiting for their time to come.

And all around life went on. Her passing had created a river and the rains came and the river took on a life of its own. Schools of pickerel and bass swarmed through its cool depths; silver trout knifed through its brisk eddies, its warm shallows were patrolled by Giant Northern pike and shimmering dragonflies foraged up and down its length. On the glossy surface of the still backwaters black whirlyjig beetles spun in delirious circles. Otter and mink prowled its banks and in the air above the tumbling flights of teal and mallard were the wind.

In time a wandering Ojibway scout found the sacred river and brought his people to live there in harmony with the land and its wild creatures. The men hunted bear and moose, the women gathered acorns, blueberries and the wild, sweet strawberries that grew in the meadows at the river's edge. Life was such that the children ran with wolves and the elders spoke with eagles.

In the time of the Moon of Popping Trees they sat around their fires and the elders told about the great Serpent. It was a good life, the way the Creator meant it to be. "But only the mountains live forever," it is said. For the First People change came in the form of The Others - a new race of humans that moved into the territory, strange people with pale faces, cold icy eyes and hair the colour of dry grass. The newcomers said they were trappers. In no time at all they had trapped all the beaver, otter and muskrats. They went away leaving the People with only trees and rocks.

A few years later they returned. This time they said they were loggers, and that was true because soon they had cut down all the big timber, the white pine and red pine and jackpine. Then they went away again, leaving the People with only the rocks. Everyone thought they had gone for good and the elders burned tobacco and thanked the Creator for small mercies.

But it wasn't meant to be. Somebody discovered a thing called uranium and The Others came back - this time for the rocks. They called themselves miners and they came armed with little black boxes that chattered like angry squirrels whenever they walked near the Serpent's nest. That made them happy and they started digging there, and didn't stop until they had found the Serpent's eggs.

The elders tried to warn them not to bother the eggs but the miners sent them away, and said they were old and foolish. They kept digging and wouldn't listen to anyone, not even their own medicine men who told them something was very wrong. The men were becoming ill. Their lungs blackened and they coughed up blood. But they kept digging and what they couldn't sell they threw into the river and the lakes. Then the river and the lakes died and still nobody paid any attention.

The miners ground the Serpent's eggs into a fine yellow powder they called "yellowcake" and sold it south of the medicine line to their brothers who were called 'military tacticians' and 'nuclear technicians'. They cooked it up in big pots and made strong medicines from it. Many of them became sick and died after handling the yellowcake and the other medicines but nobody seemed to notice.

One of the medicines was called "radium" and they had their women paint it on dials that went into the cockpits of their tanks and airplanes so that their warriors could see to fight at night. The women put the tiny paint brushes into their mouths to wet and sharpen them into fine points, so that they could paint thin, neat lines. After a while the radium ate away their faces and those women died too.

Two sub-tribes known as the "peace-niks" and the "anti-nukes" became worried and tried to stop the military tribe but they were too small and weak. The military tribe was strong and had powerful allies who said that something called "acceptable loss factor" made it okay that a few people died from the medicines.

Another thing they made from the yellowcake was "nuclear bombs." They were long and slim and cold - just like the Serpent - and whenever they dropped one on another tribe that tribe disappeared in an instant, just as if the sun had fallen on it.

Two of them had been dropped on Japan. One of the bombs was called "Fat Boy" and Fat Boy must have been very heavy because when he landed on Japan 100,000 people died instantly. When the other tribes saw this they became frightened and asked The Others not to make any more but they wouldn't listen and kept on building "bigger and better bombs."

When they wouldn't stop other tribes figured they had better make some too, and pretty soon there was a big race to see which tribe could make the biggest and most. Very soon many of the tribes had bombs, enough to destroy the Earth 30 or 40 times over, even if a powerful medicine man could bring it back each time it was destroyed. In all of their recorded history the Others had never invented a weapon that - sooner or later - they didn't use on each other.

And so, that's the way the final war began. It started off with a lot of bad words that led to threats that ended up with them shooting their flying bombs at each other.

It wouldn't have been too bad if they just shot a few and then quit. Maybe their "acceptable loss factor" would have worked and only a few hundred thousand would have died, with a hundred thousand more dying later when the Serpent's breath settled to the ground. But it didn't work out that way, they just kept shooting more and more. One or two fires might have gone out by themselves or they could have been put out but ten thousand fires raged in an inferno that took on a life of its own. Giant firestorms never dreamed of created winds up to 1000 miles an hour. The event screamed and writhed and sucked whole cities and tribes into the serpent's opening jaws. The Serpent had returned, lingered, and then gone - taking the entire Earth with it.

And in a galaxy far away a tiny green planet hung in deep space, in the gossamer web of another solar system, waiting for the white light from an incinerated planet as it sped across the dark chasm of a billion light years.

It was in the dead of winter when the light arrived and on the southern hemisphere of that tiny green planet peaceful people tending their flocks on rocky hillsides looked up, and a great shining light appeared in the eastern sky, and they were afraid, and stood in fear and awe, and wondered what this great sign could mean.

THE BEGINNING

CHAPTER 6
Novels

Introduction

Many of the comments in the chapter about short stories also apply to novels. Short stories, however, lack the power of novels by the fact of their brevity; there is not the opportunity for an identification with the characters, and the insights into human nature are not as profound.

Readers must enter novels imaginatively and they must learn to examine their own experiences constantly for relevance to the world presented in the novel, recognizing symbolism where it exists. Realistic, or true-to-life stories, are always popular but in fiction as in everyday life not everyone perceives events in the same way and while readers may have firmly held beliefs that they may not wish to change, a work of fiction may present opposing ideas or a different point of view.

Fiction brings alive the significance and beauty of the world. Sounds, sights and people are presented with heightened clarity. Through these descriptions everyday experiences can be evaluated and the significance of the world can be judged. But readers must also be willing to go beyond immediate meanings and think of allegorical or symbolic meanings. Themes emerge as characters and events are described. A novel may not be fully understood until the reader reflects on it later; often many readings are required.

Excerpts from four novels and one novella have been selected for this anthology. They represent widely scattered cultural groups and diverse life styles. Markoosie's book, *Harpoon of the Hunter*, is about Inuit life before European contact, but the other four are written by young Native writers describing the life of contemporary Native people. In *In Search of April Raintree*, Beatrice Culleton tells about the life of two Métis sisters in Winnipeg, Manitoba. Ruby Slipperjack, in *Honour the Sun*, tells about life in an isolated Ojibwa community in northern Ontario. Jeanette Armstrong's story, *Slash*, is about an Okanagan Indian from British Columbia who is searching for a meaningful life. Jordan Wheeler has written three novellas on the same theme - the relationship between Native brothers and their efforts to re-establish contact after years of estrangement.

The stories presented by these five writers are so diverse that no definition of a "typical" Native novel can be developed. The stories reflect the diversity of life styles, geography, social conditions and social change. They all explore how human beings relate to one another and to their environment, and they have in common a deep committment to a Native identity and the values of Native cultures.

Harpoon of the Hunter
(Montreal: McGill-Queen's University Press, 1970)
by Markoosie

Markoosie, an Inuit pilot who flies in the Arctic, makes his home in Resolute on Cornwallis Island. He has an excellent repertoire of traditional stories and legends. He also creates his own. Though he speaks English well, he chose to tell this story in the language of the Inuit since it was written for Inuit readers. It was originally published in syllabics in the magazine *Inuittituut* and later translated into English by Markoosie.

The story opens with Kamik and his parents, Suluk and Ooramik, waiting out a storm which had already raged for three days. Sixteen-year-old Kamik felt he was almost as good as a man; he felt he was ready to become one of the community's hunters. As they waited, Kamik and Suluk sharpened their harpoons while Ooramik made them new sealskin boots.

It was a season of scarcity and they were anxious to get on with their hunting. Though Suluk had killed several seals the meat, shared by humans and dogs, had not lasted long. Suluk was hoping to kill a polar bear, though hunting bears was the hardest way of procuring meat in the north.

That night tragedy struck. Kamik was the first to hear the dogs howling and roused his father. Without dressing, Suluk rushed out to see a great polar bear attacking the dogs. He managed to wound the animal in the hind leg with his harpoon before it escaped. Paralysed with fear, Kamik watched from the door of the igloo. Other hunters had arrived, but it was too late; the bear was gone, the dogs mutilated. Kamik was ashamed and humiliated, realizing that he alone could have helped his father — if he had been man enough to act promptly.

The bear's actions had been strange. Not even a polar bear comes into a settlement just to fight the dogs. The hunters concluded the bear was rabid and that it must be tracked and killed. No one else was safe until this horrible menace was removed, for it might infect other animals.

Suluk hoped that all the men would go on the bear hunt even though it would be the most dangerous hunt they had undertaken. He asked anyone who did not want to go to speak up. Kamik felt he had been a coward and should not go, but he could not make himself speak up, so his silence was taken as assent.

Suluk selected two men to stay behind to look after the people of the settlement. The next day nine men and sixty dogs set off in pursuit of the bear. Their first day of travel brought them to an island where they had killed many bears. Because darkness was falling they made camp, hoping to track the wounded bear by its bloody footprints in the snow in the morning.

The barking of the dogs woke the hunters up all of a sudden. Before anyone realized what was happening, the igloo came down on top of them. A great roar followed. Kamik knew what was happening. He had heard stories. This had happened too often. They were under attack by the bear.

Kamik had difficulty getting up from under the blocks of snow. He took his harpoon and started to run towards the bear. He saw his father raise his arm, harpoon in hand, but the bear made its move faster. It leaped toward the lone figure. Kamik screamed a warning, too late. The bear had its powerful jaws around Suluk's waist. Kamik screamed and ran towards them. He could see the bear shake its head, the body between its jaws. Kamik threw his harpoon without thinking of aiming carefully, just throwing it toward the bear. The harpoon struck. The bear roared, dropped the still figure of Suluk, and leaped for Kamlik. While the bear was in midair, another harpoon struck its side. The harpoon came from Kisik's hand. Kamik fell with the bear on top of him. Before it could move, other hunters came and struck it from all sides, draining the life out. Kamik was helped from under the bear. As soon as he was free he ran to his father, who was lying in the snow, very still. With tears in his eyes, Kamik took his father on his knee.

Slowly Suluk opened his eyes, breathing very weakly. "I am done for, Kamik. But for the sake of the others, get that bear. For the first time in my life, I feel there is a peace for me somewhere. At last I find peace. I shall rest forever in the peace which only dead people find. Someday you will find such peace, Kamik. I'll be waiting for you and for our people there."

Kamik did not understand what his father meant about getting the bear. But then he realized that this was not the bear they were seeking. The bear they were after had a wound on its hind leg. This one hadn't. The hunt was not yet over. Now Kamik understood Suluk's words.

Next morning they buried Suluk on the island, and they covered the grave with the hide of the polar bear that had killed him. "We will stay here the rest of the day and leave tomorrow," Kisik said. "I made a silent promise to Suluk that I shall not stop until that bear is dead."

But that night the sound of rising wind and snow told them that tomorrow would not be the day to travel; they would have to stay here until the blizzard was over. They couldn't go anywhere. Once in awhile someone would go out to relieve himself, and when he came back he was covered with snow and shaking with cold. For two straight sunrises they couldn't go any place. On the third night the wind went calmer, and they knew this would be the day to start hunting again. At the first sign of dawn they began to make plans.

"We will travel for half of the day only, and use the other half to hunt for food for ourselves and our dogs," Kisik said. "This way we will not tire our dogs so much and have a good chance to get food. And you all know how it feels to be hungry in this weather."

"That reminds me," Kamik said. "We only have enough meat for one more sunrise. When the meat is gone, what will we and the dogs eat?"

"Don't worry," Kisik said, "we have enough time to get seal. Or if we don't get seal in two sunrises from now, we have enough dead dog to eat and enough for our dogs too. I hope you have realized by now that after the blizzard some of our dogs are sure to be dead."

Everyone went out to check on the dogs. Sure enough, two dogs had not survived the days of the blizzard.

"But I have never eaten dog in my whole life," Kamik said.

"This time you may have to, Kamik. It takes a lot of will power to survive," Kisik said sternly.

"You ever eat dog?" Kamik asked.

"Yes."

"How does it taste?"

"Terrible, just terrible!"

"That doesn't help much!"

"I know, Kamik. But maybe this time you will just have to taste one. I hope it won't be necessary. Now let's get ready to travel."

They didn't travel far that day. The snow was soft, which made things harder for the dogs; but though they were tired they kept going. That afternoon they made camp near a large ice ridge. This ice would act as a shield against the wind. After they had built an igloo, they went out hunting on a crack in the ice. They found three seal holes, and three of the hunters began to watch. For a long time they waited. Nothing came. The cold wind won and they had to walk to keep warm. After the sun had set, they decided to destroy the two holes and take turns on the one they did not destroy. Kisik was the first one to wait. But his feet couldn't take the cold and he had to quit. Immediately Naoolak took his place. Naoolak fought against the cold wind. His feet wanted to move, but he fought to keep still. Finally his mind began to go.

"Come on, you dumb animal," he whispered. "You better come up. If you don't come up I'll kill you!" At that moment he lost his temper. He broke his harpoon in half as he yelled and went down in the snow, beating his head against the ice and crying. Kamik, who was not far behind him, realized what was happening. He began to run toward Naoolak. Then his heart jumped. He saw Naoolak getting up slowly. Naoolak took his harpoon, which was broken in half, and put the sharp point to his throat, ready to take his own life. Kamik jumped and got his hands on the harpoon. He tried to get it away from Naoolak's hands, but Naoolak being older and stronger, threw Kamik down. Kamik was down, and he could see Naoolak above him ready to throw the harpoon of death at him. Just as Naoolak threw, Kamik rolled to one side and the harpoon missed him by only inches. Kamik got up and swung with all his might. His fist found its mark and Naoolak went down. At that moment the others arrived, got between them and brought Naoolak back to his senses.

"Another dead man is not the answer to our problem," Kisik said toughly. "If we are to survive and get the bear, we must think hard and straight. There will be no more violence, Naoolak. We have more of that than we care for, and I am sure there is more to come. But we must fight violence, not create it. Losing our tempers will help no one. Now control yourself." Without saying anything, Naoolak walked away in shame. Now it was Kamik's turn to wait for the seal.

It was getting dark now and Kamik was getting cold, and as he waited he felt small in this dark world. He felt like crying. So many things had happened in a few sunrises — the mad bear, his father's death, dogs lost, and now this fight between him and Naoolak. He didn't blame Naoolak for what had happened. He didn't blame him for the way he acted. Maybe all of them would act that way in time. But no! Nothing like that must ever happen again. To survive in this land they must be brave. The tears ran down his cheeks as he began to think about his mother. Suddenly he was brought back to the present by a bubbling sound from the seal hole.

Seal!

The seal was near. Kamik's heart pounded hard. He stopped breathing. Would the seal come up for air? He held his breath. An eternity later he heard a soft sound of breath from the seal hole. Wait! Wait for the right time. Don't strike too soon. Must strike at the right time. Kamik aimed his harpoon directly at the seal hole and waited. Then he heard the heavy breathing of the seal. It suspected nothing. With all his might, Kamik struck.

A hit! Quickly he put his hands through the hole: the water was cold. He searched for seal. Was he strong enough to kill it?

Was his aim true? Then he felt it. It was dead. He began to yell for help. The hunters came and wasted no time chopping the ice from the seal hole. Then they pulled the seal up. They began to jump and cheer and dance. For a few minutes there was no thought of all the things that had happened before.

"No dog meat for breakfast, dinner, supper!" Kamik cried as he danced.

That night they had a good meal, but they were careful not to eat more than necessary. They had to save some meat to make it last as long as possible. Later, in bed, Kamik began to think of the bear again. Where will the bear strike next? Who will be the next victim? When will the people of the north, the Inuit, find rest?

Early next morning they set out again. Before the sun was up, they were travelling again, and all day they travelled without seeing any sign of the bear. Evening came and they made camp. They had hunted again without luck.

"We will not tie up the dogs this time," Kisik said. "They will have more of a chance in case the bear attacks." It was to be one of the deadliest mistakes.

Early next morning they began to get up slowly, one by one. They had a little meat for breakfast. Kamik was thankful this was not dog meat.

"It sounds like a nice day to travel," Naoolak said as he was getting out. To his surprise there were no dogs in sight. "Hey! There are no dogs," he said as he quickly went back in.

"What do you mean?" Kamik asked.

"I don't see a single dog." The same fear hit them all. They all went out quickly.

No dogs.

They saw dog tracks and followed them. Then they all stopped. In front of them were bear tracks. Fresh. Then they all knew why. The bear had come to their camp during the night. The dogs, being loose, had sighted the bear and had gone after it.

"This is all we need!" Kisik said angrily.

"Do you think they will come back?"

"There is a chance they will come back, but that might take a day or two, or even a week."

"What will we do next?"

"We will wait a day or two, and if they are not back by that time, we will start walking home."

"Walk? But that is impossible. We are many sunrises away from home."

"I know that, but it's all we can do. We can't wait here for long, the sooner we start the better. But we will wait here for one sunrise, and if they don't come by then, we start walking."

"If we met a bear without dogs, we wouldn't have much power," Kamik said.

"There are eight of us, and we have harpoons," Kisik said. "We have a chance."

"Let's say there are seven and a half hunters," Kamik said. "Remember, I am only half a hunter."

" I wouldn't say that," Kisik said. "Anyone who can kill a bear is a full hunter."

Then Kamik remembered. His harpoon had struck the bear first the night his father was killed. According to the hunter's law, he had the right to claim the bear as his.

With all the provisions they could carry, they started walking toward home. They had waited for one sunrise, but no dogs had come. On the move, Kamik went to Kisik, who was leading the hunters.

"How long do you think it will take us to get home," he asked.

"Maybe ten sunrises, or maybe more — or less if we are lucky."

"And what if we aren't lucky?"

"We won't get home."

"Do you think we will get home?"

"I can't say. It is a long way and there are dangers."

"What will happen to our families if we don't get back?"

"I guess they will have to move to another settlement."

"Think we have a chance to get home?"

"Yes, if we can go on without meeting any danger, and if we can kill some food on the way."

With their harpoons in their hands, the hunters went on, armed only with their harpoons and their courage.

In Search of April Raintree
(Winnipeg: Pemmican Publications, 1983)
by Beatrice Culleton

This is a story of two Métis sisters who were placed in non-Native foster homes. The author, Beatrice Culleton, was herself a foster child and spent many years of her adult life trying to come to terms with her identity. Though the story is fiction, Culleton drew on many actual experiences, either her own or those of people around her, and wove them into a coherent story.

Upon completion of this book Culleton wrote *Spirit of the White Bison* and worked for Pemmican Publications. She now lives in Toronto where she is continuing her writing career.

The story is about two Métis girls, April and Cheryl Raintree, whose parents were originally from northern Manitoba, but were forced by illness to move to Winnipeg. Though they were poor, they had a basically happy home until alcoholism took its toll. The parents explained to the children that it was "medicine" they were drinking. Being an observant child, April was greatly puzzled by the medicine that did not make her parents well, the rowdy drinking parties, and the violence.

When April was six and Cheryl was four-and-a-half, social workers arrived to take them away. Most devastating for April was the fact that her mother did not fight to keep them; in fact when April clung to her mother, she pushed her away.

The girls were first placed in an orphanage and then in separate foster homes. April's foster family was kind and loving, and her foster mother, Mrs. Dion, did her best to help April adjust. April came to love her and called her "Maman". Family visits were arranged for the girls, and though it was a chance to see each other, April was always very depressed afterwards. Her foster family was sympathetic and understanding. April's relative happiness did not last long; when she was eight her foster mother died and she was moved to a new home.

The DeRosier's home was a shock to April. She was made to work in true Cinderella fashion while the two children, Maggie and Ricky, ridiculed and tormented her. Two older foster children, Gilbert and Raymond, silently came and went doing the work they were assigned to do outside, and kept to their room the rest of the time. For April to complain was futile; her social worker did not believe her, Mrs. DeRosier invariably championed her children and Mr. DeRosier lived in his own silent world. April lived with malice, tension, and humiliation. The fact that she did better in school than Maggie did created additional problems.

April was soon made aware of the fact that she was Native. She came to believe that all that was Native was worthless and evil. As she grew older she also understood that the "medicine" that caused her parents' illness was alcohol.

April became a very self-contained little girl, hiding her emotions, trusting no one, and loving only Cheryl. When she was beaten for things she did not do she did not cry. She lost the faith in God that Mrs. Dion had so carefully taught her. She harboured a deep feeling of anger toward her parents. Though Cheryl was in a good foster home she yearned for her sister's company so was moved to the DeRosier's. This created complications for April as she again felt responsibility for her sister. Cheryl was a strong-willed, defiant child who would not accept unfairness.

Events reached a climax when Ricky tricked Cheryl into entering the bull's pasture and it was April's quick thinking that saved Cheryl's life. In a fury, April thoroughly beat up Maggie and Ricky. Much to April's amazement, Mr. DeRosier, who had witnessed the incident from a distance, championed the girls, so no retribution took place — at least not right away.

> At the beginning of the summer holidays, about a month after the incident, I was in the house one morning, when I noticed a car enter the driveway and saw that it was Miss Turner. Then it hit me. Miss Turner was here to take Cheryl away. Of course, that's what their secret had been. That's why we had never been punished. I panicked. I couldn't be separated from Cheryl again! I just couldn't! But what could I do to stop it? Nothing! Nothing, except run away with Cheryl! But where could we go? Cheryl was outside somewhere. I didn't stop to think what we

would take. I just ran out the kitchen door and looked around the farmyard. I saw Cheryl coming towards the house. Ricky and Maggie were still upstairs, sleeping. I heard the DeRosiers calling for Cheryl from the other side of the house. I ran towards Cheryl and urged her to duck behind a building.

"Cheryl, Miss Turner is here. I'm sure she's come to take you away." I was shaking. I was glad to see that Cheryl had her jacket on.

"April, I don't want to go away from you. They told me I'd never see you again."

"I know, Cheryl. We are going to run away. Right now."

I looked around the corner of the building. There was nobody in sight. We ran across the open grain field as fast as we could, trying to keep low. When we were into the safety of the woods, I said, "We're going to Winnipeg. I'm sure I know the way there. We'll just follow along the roads through the fields. When we get there, I'll try to find the Dions. I'm sure they'll help us. I know Mrs. Semple. She'll just believe whatever DeRosier tells her. Okay?"

Cheryl nodded, and we started on our journey. I had no idea how far it was or how long it would take. We followed alongside Highway 200, the same way we went to Winnipeg by car. We walked all that day, ducking low in the tall grasses whenever we saw or heard a car. Sometimes, we walked through the nearby woods. Once, we saw a car moving slowly and when it came closer we saw that it was an RCMP car. I knew they were looking for us, and that we'd have to be more careful. It grew dark and the darker it got, the harder it was for us to walk through the weeds. We waited until it was pitch black and returned to the road. Cheryl began complaining that she was hungry and tired and wanted to stop and rest.

I urged her on, saying that we had a better chance to make it if we continued through the night. In the middle of the night, Cheryl insisted she just couldn't go on anymore. I knew how she felt because I was dead tired myself. We left the road and found ourselves in a field. Cheryl fell asleep, her head resting on my lap. I sat for awhile to guard her, but I soon lay back and fell asleep too.

I was awakened by someone who prodded at me. The sun was

shining down on us and when I remembered where we were, I felt exposed. I blinked and was dismayed to find a police officer standing over me. Cheryl was already sitting up and she was still rubbing her eyes.

We were told to get in the car and I sat there, glumly. The Mountie talked to us but we ignored him and didn't say anything. I was so disappointed that I couldn't think of anything except that we had been caught. I wondered if running away was a crime. We couldn't possibly go to jail just because we wanted to stay together. I was surprised when we got to Winnipeg after all. But we were taken straight to the police station. We were told to sit in the waiting area. After a while, the officer came back and gave us milk and cinnamon buns. I was wondering why we were waiting there.

"We almost made it, didn't we?" Cheryl said, "If I hadn't gone to sleep, we would have made it."

"I went to sleep, too, Cheryl. Don't worry, we'll explain everything to them." I had read about the RCMP. I knew they were good guys and that they would listen to us. I began to wish that I had talked to the Mountie in the car, after all.

We never did get another chance to talk to the Mounties. Mrs. Semple came in first and she gave us a disapproving look.

"I never expected this of you, April. Mrs. DeRosier is worried sick. Don't you know how much she cares for you? You girls put a scare into all of us. You should be ashamed of yourselves. Do you know what could happen when you hitchhike? Why you...you could have been hurt."

"We didn't hitchhike. We walked," Cheryl said, sullenly.

"Don't try to tell me that you walked all that way. You girls have had a very bad influence on each other." She turned to stare at Cheryl. "And you, young lady, I won't be surprised if you land in reform school."

"Why should she land in reform school?" I said, bitterly. "I'm the one who talked her into running away. I didn't want us to be separated again."

"And I suppose you're the one who attacked Maggie?" Mrs. Semple asked.

"I beat her up. And Ricky too. They tried to kill Cheryl."

After I said it, I realized it must have sounded ridiculous.

Nothing was coming out right. I had wanted to explain everything in a very sensible manner. Instead, here I was sounding almost hysterical.

"You have too much imagination and not enough common sense," Mrs. Semple said. "Mrs. DeRosier brought her poor daughter in and showed us what happened. Now they have no reason to lie about who did what. It was a very vicious act, Cheryl. Especially when Maggie refused to defend herself. Furthermore, Mrs. DeRosier brought a report from school to back her claim that you are a troublemaker. April, it's touching that you want to cover up for your sister. But if we don't do something now, she'll end up in reform school."

"I'm not covering up! I'm telling the truth! " I shook my head in disbelief. How come they couldn't see through Mrs. DeRosier and Maggie? How could I convince them of our honesty? Then I remembered Mr. DeRosier and the boys. He had spoken up for us once. If he knew about this, surely he would speak up again.

"Did you talk to Mr. DeRosier and Raymond and Gilbert?" I asked excitedly.

Mrs. Semple eyed me suspiciously and said, "April, you're a beautiful girl. I advise you to keep your charms to yourself. Mrs. DeRosier told us that you've been flirting with them."

Of course. The old hag had that covered too. After that, I just didn't know what to say. Then Mrs. Semple gave us a little speech about what she called the "native girl" syndrome.

"...and you girls are headed in that direction. It starts out with the fighting, the running away, the lies. Next come the accusations that everyone in the world is against you. There are the sullen and uncooperative silences, the feeling sorry for yourselves. And when you go on your own, you get pregnant right away or you can't find or keep jobs. So you'll start with the alcohol and drugs. From there, you get into shoplifting or prostitution and in and out of jails. You'll live with men who will abuse you. And on it goes. You'll end up like your parents, living off society. In both your cases, it would be a pity because Miss Turner and I knew you both when you were little. And you both were remarkable youngsters. Now, you're going the same route as many other native girls. If you don't smarten up, you'll end up in the same place they do. Skid row!"

I thought if those other native girls had the same kind of people surrounding them as we did, I wouldn't blame them one bit. Much of the speech didn't make sense to me anyway. I'd never heard the terms shoplifting and prostitution and I didn't even know what drugs were. I'd been into drug stores and they sold all sorts of useful things. So far, I hadn't had a crush on a boy, well, not a major crush. And what the heck was skid row? All I knew for sure was that somewhere in that speech, she had insulted our parents and I could see that it rankled Cheryl. I held her hand.

I thought of once more trying to reason with Mrs. Semple but then Miss Turner walked in. Mrs. Semple went over to her and they talked for a few minutes. Then they came to us and told us that we were going to the Children's Aid office.

There we sat alone in one room while they discussed our futures in another. I was still angry and felt like a criminal. We hadn't done anything wrong. Well, maybe I shouldn't have laid such a beating on those two brats. But it was Cheryl who was getting all the blame. Between the two of us, she was the more innocent. It was unjust.

"Cheryl?" I said quietly.

"What?"

"I'm sorry."

"You're not the one who should be sorry. All of them are the ones who are doing wrong. They're the ones who ought to be sorry," Cheryl said, vehemently. After a few minutes, she said, "I guess I'm going that syndrome route, huh?"

"Of course not. Why do you say that?"

Cheryl smiled. "I just kind of accused everyone of being against us, didn't I?" We both laughed.

It was a while before Mrs. Semple and Miss Turner came back into the room. Mrs. Semple said to me, "April, we've decided it's in your best interest for you to return to the DeRosiers. You never got into any trouble until Cheryl came to live with you."

"No. Don't send her back there. They're mean people. Mrs. DeRosier said we'd never see each other again," Cheryl shouted.

"Cheryl, we've arranged for you to go to the Steindalls. If you give them a chance, you'll be happy there. And don't you worry. There'll be visits between you and April," Miss Turner said.

"Please don't send April back to the DeRosiers. They'll do something bad to her. I just know it. Why can't she come with me?"

"Because you're not good for each other. Now, I don't want anymore nonsense, Cheryl. April, if you can talk any sense into your sister, you'd better try," Miss Turner said to me.

"I want to talk to Cheryl alone," I said. The two women looked at each other, shrugged and left the room.

I knelt before Cheryl and said, "Cheryl, we can't fight them. I know I'll be okay with the DeRosiers. I don't want you to worry about me, okay? And I don't want to have to worry about you. I want you to be good at the Steindalls. I want you to keep your grades up. This won't last forever. When we're old enough, we'll be free. We'll live together. We're going to make it. Do you understand me? We are going to make it. We are not going to become what they expect of us." I sat back on my heels and looked her in the eyes. She nodded and smiled through her tears.

"Okay, April, I'll try to be good."

Honour the Sun
(Winnipeg; Pemmican Publications, 1987)
by Ruby Slipperjack

Ruby Slipperjack lives in Thunder Bay, Ontario, where she is enrolled in university and is an artist as well as a writer. Slipperjack has created a small, isolated community of Ojibwa characters for this book. It is told from the point of view of "The Owl" and spans six years of her life, from the age of ten to sixteen.

The Owl kept a seasonal diary of her life in this small community. The only contact with the outside world was when the train brought new school teachers, relatives from other communities and such delicacies as chocolate bars, bananas, and Kool-Aid. The Owl's diary tells of events big and small, happy and unhappy, in her daily life as she shared a one-room cabin with six other family members.

Her mother was a solid woman weighing a couple of hundred pounds. She had curly brown hair and dark brown eyes. Though she appeared brusque and matter-of-fact, she was a tower of strength and a source of security for her family. Life in the home revolved around the mother who, since her husband's death, was responsible not only for the children but also for relatives and community members.

The small cabin was a place of shelter from the elements; much more of their time was spent outdoors. Nature was as much a part of The Owl's experience as the house and its furnishings. Catching fish could be an adventure, as were picking blueberries, gathering firewood, camping with her mother, and minutely observing nature around her.

Life at home was full of excitement as The Owl's older brother came home to visit and her sisters' budding romances ended in marriage and babies. She enjoyed listening to adult conversations between other community members.

School was not of great importance to The Owl, though she enjoyed it. New teachers were always a novelty and unusual events happened in school. One December they were introduced to a Christmas tree, on another occasion they received skates and crayons. They also received biscuits which were appreciated by children whose families were short of food. Her mother did not speak a word of English so the children had to translate when she had to talk with the teachers.

Not all the events in The Owl's diary were happy. She told of practical jokes that got out of hand, of forest fires, trips out of the community by train when illness struck, and of the deaths of village members. She told of hiding quietly in the bush while the men of the village were drinking and described the dreadful night when her mother did not get out of the cabin in time.

When she was twelve she had reached grade six, the highest grade taught in that community. Further education meant going to a boarding school in the city. Many changes were in store for her. An ominous climate pervaded the community as she and her friends were growing up. Despair set in for her mother as her children left home and as poverty became more severe. When she no longer had the strength to do the backbreaking physical work required of her, her mother, too, began to drink.

Mom hums under her breath. It's very calm on the lake. In the evening sun, the lake shines like a mirror. I can see the clear reflection of trees of the island. Smoke from the camp fire gets in my eyes. Mom always lights the fire in the evening. She's drying trout over the open fire by smoking the fish, which she'll pack away for later. We have only one dog left, Rosiak. The man across the lake needs a lead dog on his team and has been asking Mom for her. Mom says that this fall she'll let him have her. She says we can't afford to feed her anymore. Rosiak lies on her side occasionally flicking her ear against the flies which continually buzz around her head. Laughter erupts from the cabin again. We have a record player now and there's music in the cabin most of the time.

Vera is in there with Greg. They're getting married in the fall. Wess has already married Laura and she's at his side most of the time when he comes home. Annie's gone with Barbara and her husband, Allan, to a place down the tracks where he works. Maggie's gone to live with her mother. The only ones left here now are Brian, Tony and me. I find myself spending a lot of time with Mom which is strange but nice. I help her with the fishnet that she's making, sew the beads on the moccasins she's sewing, scrape the moose hide when she gets too tired and clean the fish for her while she starts the fire. I never realized that fish could be cleaned in so many ways.

Mom pokes me and says, "Here he comes again!"

I look up to see Greg's friend, Jere. Whenever he finds out that Greg is here, he comes down to see him from where he works. He hung around Annie quite a bit, but she didn't like him. Annie likes Ross now or maybe has as long as I can remember. Anyway, Annie was always running away from Jere. Now she's gone and he still comes. Mom smiles at him and says, "They're all inside."

Jere walks by. His hair shines light brown in the setting sun. He looks nice. I'd never noticed that before.

The fish are all done and Mom goes next door to see Aunty. I sit down on the swing. The knots up on that branch don't look too secure so I scramble up the tree, edge along the branch and tie several more knots. I slide back down and jump the last four feet to the ground. I hear a chuckle from the open doorway. It's Jere, looking at me, smiling. I sit down on the swing again feeling suddenly quite shy. Imagine him watching me when I thought there was no one around. The music in there is still quite loud. I don't bother going in when they're in there. Suddenly, I feel a pair of hands grip the seat of the swing and pull back. Released, I sail away, free and far only to swing back to the same pair of hands. I giggle and glance back.

"Higher!" I yell.

He laughs again and pushes harder. Away I go, higher than the branch that holds me. He comes around the front and watches me sail by. Then I become conscious of my long feet sticking out in front of me. Oh no! I jump down and run away, toward Aunty's cabin. I don't look back. How embarrassing! He must have seen my long feet. Oh, he must think I'm crazy, dashing off like that. Mom and Aunty are talking about going camping with the Widow. I think of her son, Freddy. I don't talk to him very often. They went away for awhile this summer and it's almost fall right now. Our Out House Gang is quite broken up, too. Well, maybe it's for the best; the guys were getting out of hand. The conversation catches my attention, just as Mom is saying, "I'll ask her tomorrow if she'd like to come with us for the weekend."

I can't wait. I dash back toward the cabin again. No one is around. The record player sits quietly in the corner. They probably went to Greg's place. Vera practically lives there now, anyway. Greg moved into the empty cabin on the other side of the tracks when he came into town last year. He's really nice. Our gang used to go there often just to listen to his records. None of us had a record player then, just radios. I wish everybody was still here. I get bored quite often. Rita and Hanna hang around together all the time now. Sarah is still my friend but her brother Bobby is getting strange. I've been hearing stories of his weird behaviour; like torturing animals and always being mean.

I never liked him for as long as I can remember. I have a very bad feeling each time I see him. That strange look on his face — he stares at me in a way that makes my skin crawl. So I only play with Sarah when she comes here but I never go to her house anymore.

I hear a loon calling out on the lake. The smell of pine needles fill my nostrils. I love waking up in the tent. We always put a layer of pine branches on the ground and load down the sides and corners of the tent with rocks. Someone is breaking branches. I poke my head out from under the blanket. Mom is gone already. That must be her out there. No matter how early I think I wake up, she's already out there. I kick off my blanket and crawl out of the tent. Where are my shoes? Mom clicks her tongue at me from over by the fire. "You should have taken your shoes inside the tent. What if it had rained?"

"But it didn't rain," I smile, before running into the bushes on our side of the camp. Deep into the bushes I walk. The ground is very spongy with moss. There are some holes at the base of the pine trees. Squirrels? I wonder if I'd catch anything if I put a snare over that hole in the ground. Well, I don't need to catch squirrels anyway. Not much I could do with a squirrel; besides, they're full of bugs in the summer. I find a good place to squat. Oh, look at the bright pink Lady's Slippers over there. They're so beautiful. Mom gets mad when I pick flowers for her. She says I should just tell her where I saw them so she can see them again and again. I always figured that it's funny how wild flowers die when you touch them.

On the other hand, the teacher got off the train once with flowers he wanted to show us. And they lived for a long time. Are white men's flowers able to live longer than our wild flowers? The ones Teacher brought were big, bushy, white flowers. When I asked Mom why his flowers lived so long, she just got mad at me for asking so many questions. I wish I could move some of the beautiful wild flowers and put them all around our house.

I'm almost back at camp and I smell bacon frying. Mom must like frying bacon when we camp because she doesn't buy it very often when we're at home. I see Freddy coming up from the lake with a dripping face towel. Oh, he looks so fresh and clean this morning. Mom is giving me a strange look and Freddy openly smiles at me, teasing. I get uncomfortable; I don't undertand something here. I duck into the tent. My heart is pounding as if I'd been running. Why? I don't know and I don't care. I'm hungry. I rummage around the packsack for a clean pair of socks.

I kick at Brian's feet sticking out of the blankets. "Wake up, sleepy heads! Always sleeping in," I tease, as Brian rubs the sleep out of his eyes. Tony stretches and his feet stick out. I slap at his feet, muttering, "Keep your stinking feet under the blanket." Giggling, I crawl back out.

Oh, it's such a beautiful, bright, fresh morning. I dash over to Mom by the camp fire. "Need some water?" I ask. She shakes her head and hands me the towel. I take it and run down to the lake. The surface of the water is smooth, showing a crystal clear reflection of the trees along the shoreline. It's going to be hot though, if a wind doesn't come.

Whenever we put face soap in the water, the bloodsuckers come by the dozens. I wonder if they come because of the soap or because of the water disturbance? I see a hook go sailing up and over in a graceful arch and plop into the water. That was a beautiful cast. I toss the towel on the rock and skip over the boulders till I come to the point where Freddy stands. He looks so beautiful to me this morning. He reminds me of Tarzan in Annie's comic books. He pulls out a cigarette and lights it. I watch the smoke drift into the still morning air around his head. He offers the package to me. The package is white and blue. I don't see those at the store very often and I've never smoked them either. I shake my head. Suddenly, his fishing rod jerks and he quickly holds out his cigarette to me. I take it while he starts reeling in the fish. Oh, it's a beautiful fish, a pike and it's a big one! I find myself giggling in delight while he reels the fish in. The fish is flapping back and forth on the ground behind us. On impulse, I throw my arms around him. Then I remember the cigarette in my hand and also, that this is Freddy. I should not be doing things like this anymore. He's laughing at me, his arms tight around my back. I pull away to cover my embarrassment. I put the cigarette to my mouth and puff. I make a face and hand it back to him. He throws his head back and laughs. I like the way he throws his head back to laugh. His eyebrows go up and he softly says, "Remember the partridge?"

Then I remember the partridge he caught last summer. I nod and run back, skipping over the rocks, back to the campsite. I stay with Mom all day, drying fish while Freddy and his mother paddle over to the point to check the fishnet. They return with another tub filled with fish. We clean and dry the fish over the open fire; some to be smoked, the rest to be made into pemmican. Mom doesn't like fish pemmican too much, so we're making it all for the Widow. Freddy's little sister just sits by her mother. She won't play with Brian and Tony. But then, those boys are always gathering rockfish that live under the rocks and pebbles on the shore. I carve out little canoes and paddles for them to play with. I make a miniature birchbark canoe for the little girl, but she doesn't want to play with anything. I think she's sick.

In the evening after supper I'm sitting on the big rock by the shore, when a whiff of cigarette smoke reaches me and I see Freddy. He comes to sit down beside me. I point to the bearskin draped over the back of the overturned canoe. "That would look like a bear to someone across the lake, wouldn't it?" I ask. The canoe is green. Set against the green bush background, the black fur is draped over the front bow of the canoe.

Freddy whips the skin off the canoe and walks to a shield of roots from an old windfall. It is about six feet high intertwined with numerous roots holding the soil and Freddy drapes the bearskin over it. I giggle and energetically fashion a dark head and legs for our moose. We stand back and admire it. Yep, that looks like a moose all right. I grin up at him and share a newly lit cigarette. We settle down to talk about the coming fall and the possibility that Freddy will be going away to school. Suddenly, his mother sets up a cry for my mother to come quickly and look at this thing the kids have made. "Who did this?" the Widow demands.

Sheepishly, Freddy and I walk to the camp fire. Our "moose" has his skin unceremoniously yanked off his back and shoved under our noses by the Widow. She yells, "What's got into your heads? Don't you realize that this is where the Americans are hunting now? They'd think nothing of riddling our camp with a million bullets trying to kill that thing you put out there. We'd all be dead in a few minutes. What's the matter with your brains?"

Freddy and I looked at each other. Gee, I never thought...

The next day, we prepare to go home. We've had a nice weekend. Freddy says that in a couple of days, they will be taking the train back to his aunt's place in the next town. He will be going to school from there. I'm beginning to feel quite lonely already.

Sure enough, in the following weeks, Annie, Jere and Freddy go off to school far away. Tony and Maggie have been sent away to boarding school too, because their real mother wouldn't look after them. Barbara, Cora and the baby have gone away again to live with Allan. Even Aunty and her family have gone to live with her oldest daughter in the next town. Of the whole busy household, only Brian, Mom and me are left.

We have another new teacher with a family. The kids like him so far. Mom likes the teacher's wife. She always comes over to visit, talking and laughing with us since Mom doesn't understand her. Hanna is off to the bush with her parents again this year. Rita isn't in school either. I don't know what she's doing at home. Only Sarah and I walk to school together now, except when her brother, Bobby, is with her. Then I usually wait till they go by before I start off to school. He has me really scared.

I'm the only one in the grade six row this year. That's the row that's always empty for fear of being sent far away to school. Hardly anyone has the guts to sit there all year. I'll be leaving next year. I have gone from the grade one row, one row each year, and now I'm in the last row of the school room. I feel at times like I'm sitting on death row. I get to thinking — where do all those people go who go away on the train? Where does the train go? What's it like where Annie is? I would like to see what's out there. All I've seen so far is from the occasional hospital trips. Then, I'm usually too sick to care. What will it be like when I go off to Boarding School?

Vera lives in another town too. She and Garry got married last month. Wess and Laura live somewhere else. I hear they are going to have a baby by Christmas time.

Jed is turning out to be the town drunk. I don't even talk to him anymore and Ben is back again. He was gone all summer to the bush with his parents. He's still in grade four. He keeps failing his grades. Maybe he does it on purpose so he never gets sent away.

Maybe I can go and visit Vera and Greg sometime. Yeah, that's a good idea. Tomorrow is school day and I feel like everyone's gone and left me all alone.

It's hot so I kick off my blankets. The top bunk squeaks under me. Yeah, I'm back on the bunk again. Brian sleeps beneath me and Mom has the whole double bed to herself in the corner. We've curtained off the little room at the back because it gets too cold in winter. Mom has put the extra double bed back there. I yawn. Mom doesn't even feel like telling nighttime stories, anymore. Nothing's the same.

Slash
(Penticton: Theytus Books, 1985)
by Jeanette Armstrong

Jeanette Armstrong is an Okanagan from the Penticton Reserve in British Columbia. She studied under some of the most knowledgable elders of the Okanagan as well as receiving a degree in fine arts from the University of Victoria. She is an artist whose works have received numerous awards and she has written two children's books, *Enwisteetkwa - Walk in Water* and *Neekna and Chemai* as well as a book of poems and visual arts called *Breath Tracks*. She is presently the director of a multifaceted Native education centre called En'owkin and is a Band councillor on the Penticton Reserve.

Slash is the story of a fictitious Native youth, Tommy Kelasket, as he grows to manhood. He attempts to come to terms with his identity during the turbulent years of social unrest in the 1960s and 1970s. Though he finds no solutions, he does come to appreciate his people, their traditions, and the social and community practices which led to the people's unity.

Tommy had a happy home life with loving parents and an extended family. His parents farmed "up the hill" from the village and Tommy had his share of chores to do before and after school. There was always plenty of game and food which they raised themselves. There was work which the children shared, all year round. Spring and summer were special times with planting, weeding and haying. The whole family worked during the day and enjoyed huge meals at night.

The village school only went to grade six so Tommy expected his education to end there. His father would not send him to residential school because his cousin Joe had gone there and, seeing Joe's example, he said the school made people mean from being hungry, cold, and lonely.

Visitors added excitement to their lives. Old Pra-cwa, a headman who still spoke their native language, was a master storyteller. Besides being knowledgeable in traditional ways he was also astute in the ways of white people's politics and advised the chiefs on political matters. Uncle Joe, a medicine man, taught Tommy to hunt, to recognize medicinal plants, and to appreciate the ways of the Native people.

Tommy's cousins and his best friend, Jimmy, lived in the village. Tommy visited there often but found life noisy and strange. He heard a lot about the ways of the world from Jimmy — about things like beer and drugs — but they were not a part of Tommy's world.

This idyllic life changed when the small village school was closed and children were bussed to an integrated school in town. Though the village schools were boring, it was a secure world for the children. They were not prepared for the treatment they received in town. Their heads were checked for lice and on the first morning the principal warned them against stealing. The white children jeered at them openly and soon fights broke out.

Tommy enjoyed the challenge of improved instruction even though teacher expectations of the Native students were very low. He would have enjoyed making new friends but the two racial groups largely kept apart. Tommy soon learned to loathe his looks and all the Native children felt keenly their lack of material things such as TV sets and bicycles. Tommy did well in school, however, because of his common sense and love of reading.

Changes were also taking place on the reserve. Tommy's father got a tractor, radios became common, and a new priest started a youth club. The young people in the club discussed current affairs — the threat of nuclear war and the black civil rights movement in the United States.

Tommy mulled all these things over in his mind. Sometimes he lay awake at night, wishing he would wake up in the morning and find all the white people gone.

"Come on, Tommy!" Jimmy hollered at me. "We're going for a ride up the creek in Johnny's car." We were all down at the old school talking at the youth group meeting when Johnny got there. Johnny John was from another reserve. He was a little older than us and he had quit school to pick apples in Oroville, Washington.

We went with Johnny in his new car roaring up the res with the radio turned on real loud. Johnny was seeing a girl named Denna. She was okay. We stopped at a place up the res called Elderbery Road. Everybody sat there in the dark smoking and kissing around. It was real cold and still outside, but there was no snow, even though it was January. Candy, my girl, squeezed between me and Jimmy.

Pretty soon Johnny said, "Hey, you guys know what? There's Sasquatch around here. I heard last week that Walleye and some of the older men were up here having a few beers and they seen one." Jimmy laughed, ". . . they were probably having the snakes." "No," Johnny said, "It walked out right over there in broad daylight."

I felt kind of funny because my Dad and them told me that there really were such things. He told me that they had seen them. But I knew these guys would only laugh like some of the white kids did about anything they thought was "superstition." While at the same time, things like angels and the devil weren't superstitious to them.

While I was thinking all this, one of the guys said, "I know a better place further up where my Dad says they come all the time. Let's go find out." "Okay," said Johnny, "I don't really think there are such things, but I hear some of the old people say there are."

We drove to the other place where there was a big pointed rock. We shut the car lights off, lit cigarettes and sat real quiet for awhile. It was pretty dark because of the big trees all around us and the steep high side of the mountain next to us.

After awhile everybody started talking again and we had almost forgotten why we were there, when all of a sudden, Jimmy said, "Shut up! Listen!" Everybody stopped real quick. We all heard a shrill, deep-throated whistle, almost human-like, way up the mountain. Everybody said at the same time, "Did you hear that? Was that a bird or what? Maybe it's somebody." Just a minute after that, it whistled again; this time definitely closer down the mountain. I got this real funny feeling like everything slowed down, even people's voices. I couldn't seem to move but I heard everybody yelling at Johnny, "Let's get the hell out of here! Dammit, Johnny!"

Johnny must have been scared because he started the car with such a helluva roar that we just jumped ahead and stalled. While he started it up the thing whistled again, this time only a couple of hundred feet away. It seemed like I heard it echo up and down my back and inside my head for a long time. Finally Johnny got started and he put the lights on and peeled out of there real fast. We drove down to the village in a great big hurry, everybody breathing real loud.

We never talked about that to anybody. I never even told my Dad and them because they would have lectured me about parking around in places we shouldn't. Most of us just wanted to forget it. It didn't make sense to most of us, I guess, because we knew it didn't fit in with what you learn in science books about animals and things that exist. So we didn't talk about it, even amongst ourselves.

Later on that year, about the time we heard about the black leader named Malcom X getting shot in New York, the priest had a big meeting with the Youth Club. Him and this older lady, who was on the council, asked us how things were at school. They asked us about discrimination and stuff. They said they were going to make a speech in town. They told us that some group in Ottawa did a study on Indian criminals to find out why they ended up in the slammer. They also talked about the civil rights marches in the States. They said that it wasn't right for whites to discriminate and that they mostly did it because they didn't know anything about other people.

We told them about how a lot of teachers and kids thought we lived in teepees and wore feathers on the reserve. We told them about Monty getting kicked out for fighting with Humphrey even though Humphrey started it by calling us "Injuns" and "full of lice" and stuff. We told them about all that but there were some things that we were too ashamed to even tell. Like all of the white girls laughing at Tony when he asked one of them to dance at the sock-hop. He quit school after that. Also how none of the Indian girls ever got asked to dance at sock-hops because us guys wouldn't dance with them because the white guys didn't. Another thing we never told them is how we always felt, like we just weren't good enough to mix with the white kids. I mean with things like using wrong words and laughing at the wrong times and we always felt shabby and poor, because we couldn't talk about new styles and things with them.

We left out the fact that sometimes out of "good manners" they would talk to us. We knew that it wasn't because they liked us or wanted to be friends with us. We left out why that was worse than not talking to us.

It felt good that somebody was trying to understand, so I spent some time talking to the priest after that. He said, "How come you don't come to church, Tommy?" I sat there for a long time wishing I could say, "Sure I will," just because I liked him. Finally I said, "I don't because I ain't a Catholic. Dad, Mom and my grandparents all don't either. Not because they are bad or anything. They pray a lot, all the time, in Indian way. They say we got to pray all the time no matter what we're doing. They say the whole world is our church and we go to church all the time." I looked at the priest for a long time; he never answered. Finally he asked, "Do you believe that?" I said, "Yeah, I do. I feel good when I pray Indian." I didn't tell him about praying in the sweat house or at the winter dance because I knew he might think it was wrong.

He said, "Tommy, don't ever change your way. You know, you are my good friend and you can visit me anytime at my home, if you need to talk or ask questions about school or about anything. Now, about church, some people really do need it because they don't see things the way you do. They need to feel good and clean sometimes and they feel they can only do that in a place like the church."

I knew what he meant but I wondered why all our people didn't think the same way as my Dad and them. Of course, I thought that a lot of them went to church, too, because of the priest. Mostly because they liked him.

Ever since the new priest came, more and more people seemed to go to church and other stuff they wouldn't do before. Like all the new clubs and organizations for adults, women, teens and kids. Seemed like everybody had a club they could belong to. The new priest had a certain way about him that everybody liked. He never talked hell-fire and stuff like the other priests. He didn't wear his black clothes, only when he was having church. He also played ball, sang and played guitar, drank beer, told jokes and talked serious politics with the men. Sometimes some of the Elders commented on these things saying, "He sure don't look like a priest." I knew what they meant. The only thing was, nobody liked to criticize him because they liked him too much. Besides, if he said things were alright then they must be alright, because he was a priest, wasn't he?

I did a lot of thinking about things that whole year, but I couldn't seem to straighten things out in my head too good.

At home, things were pretty much the same. I went out in the mountains quite a bit with Uncle Joe. He sure was fun to be with. He told me some pretty good stories about old timers. I thought he was probably the smartest man in the whole world. He taught me what he called "Indian medicine ways."

One time, while we were going to an art class at the old school house, we were visited by a lot of men and women from other reserves. A white lady artist was working with us at the old school; actually she was there as a sort of materials provider and encourager and she got along with us real good. The people who visited us were all in town for a leadership meeting organized by the new priest. These men and women came in and looked at everything and talked with all of us. They spoke to us about school, about "progress" and lots of other things. Also they talked about stuff like "Red Power". We didn't know anything about that stuff. We had heard a lot about "Black Power" because it was on the radio a lot. "Black Power" was about people who had kind of organized to fight against discrimination.

We had heard from Johnny John that some young Indians from Vancouver had talked about forming an organization like that for Indians. I guess that's what they meant by "Red Power". The men and women must have talked about it during the meeting which the new priest had helped set up. We told them that our Youth Club was really not for that. We told them that it was really organized because there was nothing much for us to do together on the res. The art nights were for that too. We would do art stuff and be together and tease and joke with the girls and each other.

It seemed funny that these men and women from all the reserves were together talking about such things, including us. An "Indian Affairs Committee" had been put together for that, with the help of the priest. Only younger men and women were on that committee, not any of the old people. I wondered why. It seemed to me that the older people always had the best advice about a lot of things but people said that wasn't so anymore.

One time me and Tony and Jimmy talked about it. Tony said, "Did you notice how all young Chiefs are getting elected in all the reserves? Well, maybe now things will change. What we need are young Chiefs and Councils to try out new stuff. Like in Inkameep, now, they're going to grow grapes to sell. Lots of people will be able to work and the band will get richer." "Yeah," said Jimmy, "I heard that in another reserve they are thinking about turning the reserve into a city-like, you know, part of it anyway." "What do you mean? Are you talking about the houses they want to build and lease out to white people?" I asked. "Yeah," Jimmy said, "my Dad told me that they are gonna do something like that here, too. We are going to build something for all kinds of animals and all of the Indians can work there and those that don't can grow hay and grain and corn and stuff to sell there for the animals to eat."

It didn't sound like a bad idea to me. I thought to myself that jobs were what people needed. Jobs would help because I knew a lot of people lived on welfare and a lot of people drank a lot more, too, since they opened up the beer parlours and liquor stores to Indians. There didn't seem to be anything to work on and stay home for because most people weren't farming or ranching anymore. People mostly picked apples. A few worked in the small sawmill on the reserve run by a white company.

Old Pra-cwa and some old men talked about it with Dad and my uncle in angry voices whenever they got together. The schooling the Indians got away from home was blamed for most of it. It was said that none of the young people wanted to work their land anymore to raise cattle and crops because they didn't know how, being away at school all the time. Also many people leased their land to white ranchers so they could get money once a year. Drinking was blamed for a lot of people not wanting to work their own land.

My Dad talked to Pra-cwa, his voice quiet but angry sounding. He said, "First it was the schooling, then it was the welfare and Band housing then it was the beer parlours and land leasing and now it's development. Pretty soon, Indians don't have to do nothing but get money and spend it drinking. They got nothing to get up for in the morning, nothing to occupy the hours in the day. Already lots are dead from drinking. Good young people, that might have had big families. Seems like the more Indians try new things, the worse off things get for them."

Old Pra-cwa nodded his head slowly, his heavy eyebrows jiggling. He said, "Yes, that is how I think and a few others of us, but you know our people are two now. There is us and there is them that want to try all kinds of new stuff and be more like white people. They don't even think like us anymore. What can be done? I just don't know. I don't like to feel sad and worried and ashamed of my people. I like to feel proud of them. I like to see them like long time ago; working and happy, strong and healthy, not selfish, lazy and weak." He sighed heavily, "I know they get mad at me and close their ears, because what I say hurts. They answer back in anger that if it wasn't for us stupid old people giving up in the first place and allowing many things to be done to us, things wouldn't be bad. They don't understand, we kept arguing against new stuff and we kept losing because more people wanted to go to schools, more people wanted to forget our ways, more people wanted to take welfare and Band houses and open beer parlours and all them other things. It was like that from way back and it's how it is now. It's how it will be for a long time. Our people are two now, that's why we have bad feelings at them Band meetings."

At the old school, during Youth Club, I had heard a lot of talk about it and other things. Mostly about the "old fashioned people" or "hill-billies" and how they were just against everything no matter what.

I listened one night to a young man who had been away living in Vancouver for most of his schooling. This guy looked so neat, almost like a white man, with his grey slacks that had sharp iron creases and a pink button-down shirt and blue polkadot tie. His hair was cut in what we called white wall style. We all had our hair in long duck-tails and mostly wore blue jeans and sweatshirts. His shoes were pretty crazy. They were shiny, like glass almost, and pointed so much they kind of curled up on the ends.

He spoke to us about how "we were living in the twentieth century," and how "we have a lot of catching up to do." He mentioned that young Indian people who were educated were now ready "to shape the future." He spoke about many things happening across Canada and United States. He said, "We must take our equal place in society. We no longer need to sit back and be forgotten second class people stuck on reservations living in the dark ages." He said, "We must learn to use new ideas and open our lands to development, because lack of money is at the bottom of all our social problems." He talked about making changes to the Indian Act which "would reflect changing conditions on reservations." He spoke about how reserves would change to be part of municipalities and how that would help "open up opportunities for Indian lands." He also spoke about how the liquor law was being changed to allow liquor to be served on the reserve.

All while he talked, I had this terrible urge to laugh. He kinda looked ridiculous, like a parrot does when it mimics a person. At the same time as I listened to him talk, I felt really scared at some of the things he said, although he made it sound right. I knew that a lot of young people there agreed with him. I knew a lot of them thought he looked pretty sharp too. Some of the things he said, though, made me feel really bad. I could see what old Pra-cwa talked to us about, wasn't being thought about. I really felt confused. I agreed with the young man but I also agreed with with Pra-cwa.

I told that to Jimmy, outside after the talk. I said, "You know, Jimmy, I don't know who is right anymore. I get real mad when white people make fun of us, but at the same time, I feel ashamed when I go into town with Dad and Ma and they get stared at. I know they ain't dumb and dirty. They're smart and kind and treat everybody good, even the ones that treat them ugly. In school it's like that, too. The only time you are talked to, is if you dress and talk like whites and act real smart and rich like that guy at the meeting. I found that out. Do you think that guy is right? Would things be better if we looked and acted rich and tried to change our reserve to be like town? How come we have to do that? My Pops and them live good. They're happy. None of them cares about clothes and fancy stuff. Why is everybody else all of a sudden saying things are no good, that we are not happy? Seems to me the ones that ain't happy is the people who try too hard to get stuff like new clothes and cars and want to be in town all the time. They drink lots, too. What do you think, Jimmy?" I guess I really wanted him to say that my Pops and people like them were right to be the way they were and everybody else was wrong.

He looked at me funny then he put his head down. "I don't know." He said, "All I know is, I like to feel good. I feel good when white friends of mine talk and joke with me as if I were like them. They only do that if I wear smart pants and shoes and have money to play pool with. I don't like them to think I'm like the rest of the Indians. I wish our people were like them. They have big clean houses and lots of stuff to eat. Not macaroni like us. Their dads make lots of money and they buy anything they want. They go to lots of places, like Vancouver, and see lots of neat things. Dad works but he gets drunk and spends all his money. Even his new car, he smashed the door and the front up so now it looks ugly. And my Mom, she gets drunk now, too, and the house is never clean, it stinks. Her and my Dad fight and argue and there's beer bottles all over and all we eat is bologna and macaroni. You know I never did have a new bike, so I went and stole one. I hate being an Indian. I hate Indian ways." Then he looked at me kinda defensively and said, "I know how you guys live up there, that's okay, because your folks don't drink and they work and all the kids in your family do stuff but down here, it ain't like that. Something's got to be done down here. Seems to me, the thing that can be done is what that young guy talked about. That's what I think."

I sat there smoking a cigarette and thought about what Jimmy told me. I really felt let down, like he slapped me or something even though I had to kinda agree with him. It left me with a bitter feeling inside.

"Yeah, I guess so," I said. "But why don't they want to live like us up the hill?"

"Because it's too damn Indian, that's why," he said. Then looking ashamed, Jimmy said, "Hell, let's go get old Donald to get us some beer. I don't even want to think about it anymore."

We got Donald to get us some beer. Donald was a strange guy. Some people said he was the smartest guy on the res. He always had some scheme or another going. I know of one time that he outsmarted a businessman from the States with a scheme. That time he sold my Dad's horses. Dad had these two really good-looking matched pintos he had raised. Well, Donald brought some guy in a Cadillac to "look at them." At least that's what he told Dad in Indian. A few days later the guy showed up in a truck ready to haul them away. He had given Donald a big down payment and had brought the rest of the cash that day. It took Dad a while to explain the horses were his, not Donald's and he knew nothing about a deal with Donald for them. Boy, that was one mad man. He cussed at Dad something awful. Dad said, "It wasn't my doing. You should have checked on what you buy. Somebody could sell you a bridge next."

Nobody saw Donald for a good three months after that. Donald didn't have much morals. He didn't mind buying beer and stuff for us young guys, if we gave him a couple.

It was the first time I drank beer. It tasted awful but I wanted to see what getting drunk was like. Every beer I drank I thought, "Hell with everything! I don't care!" Pretty soon, I started feeling really light and bouncy and everything seemed funny and all right. We laughed and told each other stuff about girls and sang, "It's Been A Hard Day's Night" real loud. That was a Beatles song and we thought it meant a whole lot.

Finally I must have gone to sleep or something because I woke up at Jimmy's the next day. I felt awful. My stomach and head were weak and my tongue was furry and ugly tasting.

I went home that afternoon, but I was kinda scared of what Pops would say. Sure enough Pops must have smelled me because he said, "You been drinking. That's why you didn't come home. How do you feel?" I felt real bad because he had a real hurt look in his eyes, and even though he was talking quiet

I knew he was mad. I said, "Yeah, I tried it. I feel real sick now, but when I was drinking, I didn't. I was mad and it made me feel happy. I didn't do anything."

Dad sat there and said, "You're too big to whip. But I'm going to talk straight to you. You listen real hard. I don't know why you were mad, but I can guess. There are lots of us feeling mad. I feel like saying, 'Hell with it!' sometimes, and joining all the rest of them down there. Sometimes, I used to, when you guys were small. But everytime I drank, I would have to face the next day, when I ran out of money, or I woke up in jail. Then I felt real awful because of you kids. You kids needed what little money I could get my hands on, and I would spend it in one night. The bad thing about it is, pretty soon you get to want it all the time to make you feel good. You can't feel good about anything, unless you got that drink in you. Then you're good for nothing. All you'll work for is that booze, and you'll feel empty inside all the time. Now you tried it. I guess everybody has to, but that don't mean you have to carry it on."

I felt pretty bad after that, but I saw what my Dad meant. I saw it in Jimmy's parents and lots of people like that. But I saw how they felt too. I went to bed that night and thought about Jimmy stealing a bike and probably other things too. I thought about him bragging about his new radio and phonograph player to some white kids. I thought about the older ladies getting all dressed up in lady suits and white high heels and gloves, and getting a taxi to town to have tea with white ladies, and how at home their kids got clothes from the Salvation Army and macaroni to eat. I thought about how some didn't do that either, just drank and let things go. I felt like I wanted to cry or holler or beat up somebody. I couldn't figure out what was wrong, and if there was anything anybody could do.

The only exciting thing that happened that summer was that a big feast and celebration was put on at the reserve park.

I did a lot of art work and things, just to get my mind off hard feelings that bothered me about all that kind of stuff. Me and Jimmy both liked to paint. We used to go to the white woman artist's place all the time to paint.

Later this guy named Dave, from some university, came to study our ways. He used to come to the reserve a lot. We found him to be really different; weird, kind of. He didn't seem to mind how we lived and he drank beer and talked to us a lot. He told us a lot of things going on all over the country. He also showed us some magazines that had a lot of girlie pictures. We used to read them and look at the pictures. One story I remember was about a professor, named Timothy Leary. He talked about a new drug that made people have visions and things.

I knew that some kids from school in town were smoking a drug called marijauna. They said it was pretty neat stuff. I asked this guy Dave about it. He said, "Yeah, I use marijauna. Lots of university people do. I won't give you guys any though. I need to keep my act clean here. It's against the law. Besides it don't do much that's different than alcohol, so forget it."

Me and Jimmy talked about it. Jimmy said, "Why don't we try some? Hell, if Dave smokes it, it can't be bad, Dave is real smart. Besides, it ain't like them other drugs our Dads tell us about, you know, the ones where they use a needle and then you can't go without it."

We tried marijauna on the reserve. I was sixteen then, in Grade Eleven.

Somehow after that, I let everything slip away that I used to like. None of it seemed important or good anymore. School was definitely the last place I wanted to be, after a long night getting high and talking about protesting against the establishment. After a few hassles with some teachers who used to give me looks that made me proud, I quit. At home too, Dad walked around looking grim and I wouldn't meet his eyes much.

He only talked to me once, but I knew without his repeating, exactly what he was saying with his looks. He said to me, "Look at you, Tommy. You're a smart boy. What's the matter with you? You could do all that school stuff easy, but you quit now. You know how to work on the ranch, too, but you don't anymore. You don't have anything to make you sad or mad. What's happening with you? Look at the morning and the birds singing. Look at the green grass and the mountains. Just clean and waiting to make you feel so light and happy inside that you could fly. Everything is good. We are free, Tommy.

"Maybe that schooling wasn't good for you. Maybe you're

spending too much time down in the village. Maybe you want more and more to be like some of them boys down there. Maybe you think they are happier than you or that they are luckier than you. Well, that ain't true. They are pitiful because they have nobody to teach them good things. Their moms and dads are all pitiful. They got broken spirits from going to residential school. Lots of them died when they came home, from drinking and T.B. sickness. The ones that made it okay, made it by learning how to please the priests and nuns and rejecting everything Indian. They were praised for that. That's how they are. They put the white man way up high above Indians and listen to them, and try to please them. We pity them. You quit school, now you have to do your share of work here at home. You understand?"

To me that sounded a lot like he had meant, either I could work if I was not in school, or could go out and support myself.

I resented that but I was ashamed, too, so I tried for a while to help out, but I didn't get a lot of work done at home. It seemed like they couldn't understand that I had to go to them places where there was talk about doing something. Just working and living didn't seem to accomplish anything. I wasn't sure what I wanted to accomplish or what was being done at these talks but I went again and again, night after night. Anyway, I couldn't feel really good, unless I had a toke or two a day.

Me and Jimmy started drinking a lot when we didn't have weed. It just seemed natural to take a beer that was offered instead. So, between long nights, beer parties and hangovers, I didn't exactly do any work for Dad anymore. We went to other places where Indians were, like Omak, Spokane, Vancouver and Seattle. We mostly went with Johnny John because he seemed to have friends all over; Indians that were sort of doing the same thing hippies were. Toking and partying a lot and having youth meetings where they talked about everything.

Johnny John was into dealing. I guess he had been for a while, that's how come he had a car and friends all over. He said I could stay with him, but I had to do my share. I did my share. I made pick-up and drop-off runs and scared up scores for him.

I didn't go to meetings very much, once I got there and got into the dealing with Johnny John. It was the crowd that I ran with that wasn't too keen on what the Red Power people were doing. I drifted away from that scene. Sometimes though when I walked down the streets and looked at the faces of people scurrying by, I would get a feeling inside of fear. When I looked at some of the Indians hanging around the skids, I got a sick feeling because all the faces looked so empty. Like they were dead people, walking fast to catch up with something I couldn't see. I would feel like stopping one of them and asking, "Why do you hang around here?" Somehow I was sure I was only there temporarily, not like them. I would flash on that play and think, "I'll never end up like that."

Things seemed to go fast and I just cruised with the pace for the next while. One night everything came crashing around me.

[Tommy was making a drug delivery when he was attacked by two men. Tommy was stabbed in the shoulder but managed to fight his way out before he was apprehended by the police.-*Ed.*]

I woke up in the hospital with this strange chick beside me. She said, "Hi, how's it going, Slash? My name is Mardi. I'm from the Friendship Centre. We need to know your name and reservation enrollment number before these doctors kick you out. Christ, I never seen anybody put ten cops on their backs. You know you're cut up pretty bad so you got to stay here for a while. In the meantime, we'll get somebody to try and sort out which charges we can get them to drop and stuff. Where are you from?"

I laid there feeling like somebody had taken the time to pinch every single part of me with a big pair of pliers. My shoulder throbbed and sent slow hot strings like worms inching along my arm. I looked at her and said, "Where am I? What the hell happened? Where is Johnny?"

"Johnny who?" she wanted to know. "What do you think happened? All I know is that you were at the Turkey Joint and someone thought to carve a few lines on your shoulder. I was there. All I saw was the john door busting open and these two guys stumbling out with big gashes in their shirts, and you slashing around and yelling, 'I'll slash the nuts off anybody that tries that again!' Man, the way you looked was enough to scare anybody that hangs around that joint. The cops came and they tried to stop you. It took a couple of billies to put you down after a few of them hit the floor. So here you are, Slash. Now, tell me what I need and I'll come back to see you later this evening."

I told her my name and the other things she needed to know and she left. Later on some cops talked with me. Seemed like I was being charged for assault and resisting arrest. I asked them about the other guys who started it, and they said they were also in trouble but that their charges wouldn't be heavy.

I never asked them what happened to my pack or its contents. I suppose somebody got lucky and picked it up. Probably the drop-off who motioned me to the john for the set-up.

Mardi did come back. She was extra deluxe. Tough with hard eyes and long black hair that hung below her hips. I could tell she knew her way around. Nobody could take her for a ride. She came back lots of times, until I was well enough to face charges. She sat and talked about stuff going on. She made things sound exciting, like something was about to happen. She told me about the meetings going on among young Indians. A lot of it she called hard talk about how to change things. She asked where I was from, and she told me about some things that were happening up home. She brought me Indian news bulletins and things like that to read.

I sure liked Mardi. She cared a whole lot about the right things. She didn't care too much for people who were just interested in building up a good image for themselves. She came almost every free chance she got. She wanted mostly to listen about my home life, about Uncle Joe, and how it used to be on the farm. She said it must have been good to live like that.

I guess we got to feeling pretty strong about one another. I couldn't wait to hear her footsteps coming. I thought about her at night, too. Sweet secret thoughts. I wanted to take her home and show her my hills and teach her our language. I wanted to put my arms around and hold her and never let anything hurt her again.

I was sure there wasn't anybody like her anywhere. God, I hoped then that things would work out. I didn't want to go to prison, I wanted to take her home. I wanted to help her to do the kind of work she was doing. Man, I just wanted her!

She got me a lawyer through the Friendship Centre. He talked to me and said that he could maybe get me off with a light or suspended sentence. Seeing as how I was not the instigator of the incident.

When I came out of the hospital I was put in Mardi's care. She had to see that I stayed put until a hearing was set. Those few weeks were the best I have ever spent, I guess, even though I was still weak and sick from my cuts, and even though I was facing a possible prison sentence.

I had a lot of chicks from the time I was fifteen upwards, but none made me feel so warm inside just by smiling. She took care of me those weeks. Sweet care. I fell terribly in love with her. I wanted to be near her every possible minute and breathe her soft scent. She smelled fresh like sage and cedar and her skin was even brown and smooth like those hills in the Okanagan.

I made all kinds of plans about going home. I wrote home and told my sister Josie that I was going home for good.

I said I was thinking of getting married, and where did she think would be a good spot to build a little log cabin. I knew she would tell Dad and them about it. I never mentioned about my hearing or my injuries.

One morning really early, we were sitting by the window in the basement she lived in... there were all kinds of birds chirping outside. Green branches almost covered the whole window. The window was open and the sunlight and a warm breeze poured through the leaves. The leaves whispered and seemed to tremble, just bursting with green life. A robin came and sat on a branch and just looked at us. Everything seemed to slow down. It seemed for a moment I was suspended in a shimmering timelessness filled with bursting green life and bird song. I felt an almost roaring in my ears as the robin looked and looked at me with his round shiny eye. I wanted to reach out and enclose the whole thing with my hands. I wanted to keep it so I could open my hand and look at it once in a while. The robin opened its mouth and whistled, then it was gone.

The day I went to court, I guess Mardi did what she could, but the facts remained. I was an Indian, and I had resisted arrest and had defended myself with a deadly weapon, after which I had apparently embarrassed a few cops. Nobody seemed to care that I hadn't instigated the fight, that the knife belonged to the other guys, and that I was the only one who was seriously injured while defending myself.

My lawyer kept saying those things were irrelevent and that I should act as polite as possible to the judge and say, "Yes, Your Honour" as much as I could. He told me to plead guilty to the assault charges, and I tried to tell him that I wanted to plead not guilty to that, because it was self-defense, and only plead guilty to the resisting arrest charge. He said we couldn't do that. I was either guilty or not guilty, but not both, and besides, I would get a better deal if I just pleaded guilty. He had told me to get my hair cut short and wear a white shirt and a tie.

I really felt like a fool with my short hair and those honky clothes. I didn't like Mardi to see me like that, and I couldn't see what that had to do with getting a fair deal in court. It was all for nothing anyway. The judge listened to the charges and asked me if I was guilty. I said, "Guilty, Your Honour," the way the lawyer told me to. The lawyer then talked for a while about how I was a first time offender. I guess the judge was in a hurry, or maybe they all were because that was it, sentence was passed, I got eighteen months.

I felt like somebody had knocked the wind out of me. Everything seemed so blank. All I could think of was, "Mardi, what about her? I can't live without her." I was eighteen that year.

You could say a lot of things about prison, not many of them good. One real thing is that you ain't free. You don't make many decisions for yourself, even ones you usually take for granted.

The time it really hits you is when you go through them gates, when they shut behind you and you see all them armed pigs up on the towers. It was the same with the guys who were riding the bus in from the lock-up. Most of them you could tell had been there before, by the way they talked. But when it came to the gates, it was like they suddenly deflated. You could see it in their eyes.

In there you have to learn fast. It's like everybody had to kind of fit in somewhere. It's not a matter of wanting to. It's that you had to. You were playing their game. You had to form a new attitude. You had to, or you got swept away.

One thing I noticed was that there sure were a lot of Indians. I couldn't believe it. Almost like more than half the people were Indian. Another thing that really struck me was that discrimination was kinda like in reverse, as far as the pigs were concerned. Us Indians were treated somewhat better than the white prisoners. It was like they didn't expect any more out of us than being in there, but their own kind, they really despised them when they saw them in there, so they were treated pretty awful. In general though, everybody was treated like dogs.

You just had to set your mind to live with it. I did that in a way and in a way I didn't. You had to take whatever was handed out and protect whatever small freedoms you had. Somehow little things became really important. I guess I functioned alright, but from the first month or so, I wasn't in a very good state of mind. Inside of me the hurt, anger and shame was like a pile of maggots gnawing away. Mostly, coming from shame, over having to swallow all the things dished out to humiliate you. I think they must have hired special people who train to do that kind of stuff because it broke you down, piece by piece until you're not really sure what's left is human. It made my days hard and the nights were long.

Sometimes I felt like I had cellophane stretched tight over me, and all it would take is just one wrong little move, and the cellophane would split and the maggots would come spilling out all over the floor and on everybody around me.

It was especially bad after Mardi would visit. I didn't think I was going to make it because I was filling long night hours with pictures in my head about how I would look if I hung myself. I imagined my eyes bulging and my tongue all black and hanging out, like when we were butchering a cow and hung it up. I spent hours and hours trying to figure out how to do it without that happening. I had a lot of time to think when I couldn't sleep because maggots were trying to eat their way out of my belly.

I had to fit into all that somehow. I couldn't separate myself from it. It's them things and what happens to you that makes you sick inside. You were forced to take a position and make it work for you, so you can survive. That's where I learned the most about people. You had to be able to read everybody. You had to know their attitude, then you knew how to react to them. You didn't make mistakes, because the pigs worked with that system too. There was nobody to run to for protection if you messed up. But it made you compromise too many things that you were brought up to respect. It's what made you hard inside. You couldn't care or else you found maggots crawling all over inside and you felt like maybe the maggots had more right than you to live.

For that reason, it was hard to see Mardi when she came. When she did, I listened to her talk and it seemed like she talked about a world that was far away in another place. A shiny bright world with real people who cared about other people. She talked a lot about things she was involved in. Sometimes I just sat there and stared at her like she wasn't real. I couldn't reach out to touch her, all I could do was look at her.

Toward the end of that second month, I walked out to the visiting area and saw her sitting there. So beautiful and so free. I felt like a hard burning thing was wriggling around trying to burst out of my chest. I walked over to her and said harshly, "Get out of here! I don't want to see you again. Don't come back!" I turned and walked away but I could remember the stricken look in her eyes. Like she was saying, "What did I do?" I couldn't explain to her. If I even tried, I felt like I would crumble.

Going back to the cells that night after the long day, I flashed on how I could die quietly without looking grotesque. I knew it would be easy because I already felt a certain coldness creeping outward from inside my chest. I thought, "I'll just wait up until everybody is asleep."

It seemed like forever before we were all settled into our cells and I sat at my bunk waiting.

I looked up and far away I could see the new snow on the tops of the mountain from the barred windows above me. The sun had set in a blaze making the snow look orange-pink with dark blue tinges. I could almost feel the soft cushioned brush of new snow against my shoes and feel the sharp wet bite of the fir and pine smells in the crisp air. Tracking deer in that snow would be easy. Tonight, I thought, I will go home to them mountains.

I knew it was close to Winter Dance time at home. Dad and my brother would be out tracking so there would be fresh meat for the feast. I could just smell the fresh fried deer steaks. Everybody would be talking and laughing while eating fried bread with lots of butter and all kinds of pies and cakes. I thought about that. I rested my mind on it wanting to remember every detail. I had to do that so I could go through with the whole thing. I knew I was ready.

I closed my eyes as the last light dissolved and the early winter night drew her curtain over my window. In my mind I heard the songs and smelled the fire smoke in the big room where the dances were held.

I heard deer hoof rattles shaking louder and louder and there seemed to be a soft roaring sound in my ears almost as though lots of people danced around me with their feet stamping, their eyes closed and their bodies sweating. The song vibrated through every fibre of my body like a light touch of wings, and the hard ball inside my chest seemed to melt and spread like warm mist across my chest and moved outward throughout my body.

I felt tears, warm and real, wet my cheeks and I heard someone singing Uncle Joe's dance song. All at once I heard my cell mate ask softly, "You okay, Tom?" and I realized it was me singing that song.

I couldn't stop for a long time. I just sang until there were no more tears and the song became happy and light. Kind of like how Uncle Joe gets when the dance feeling is on him and everybody can feel it with him at the Winter Dance, and everybody dances hard and shouts to release that happy feeling.

I did that. I shouted and I knew that everybody in the cell block heard it and felt it. I knew, too, that they heard me singing Uncle Joe's song. I didn't care. I felt okay for the first time in about three or four years. Even the pigs heard it because one of them walked over and stood outside my cell and looked in. I knew they had been watching me close. I guess they know the signs when a man isn't making it.

Anyhow, this pig looked at me and I smiled real big at him. He said, "Tom, seems like tomorrow the sun is gonna shine real bright, so you better get some sleep now." He smiled too. It was the first time I saw one of them as human.

After that I was okay. The tightness in my chest seemed to have gone. I guess you could say I felt free, kind of, even though I was in prison. Feelings like that made me decide that I should make the best of my stay there. I inquired about finishing my education. I had a heck of a time to get someone to take me seriously about schooling. I was helped out by the Indian Education Club that was formed to help inmates.

One of the reasons it was formed, I was told, was that about a couple of years before that, Indians had been given a really bad time when they wanted to get into training of any kind. The prison people had a pretty bad attitude about Indians. They thought they were all dumb, so they put them in dumb-work like making shoes or mopping. Anyhow this Indian Education Club had a sit-in where they made some demands about that and other conditions. That was before I got there, so I did get to have courses in Grade 12 and college level and also I got into an art class. After that I concentrated real heavy on the work and the time seemed to go pretty fast. I did some pretty good art while I was there.

When things are drab and ugly around you it feels good to paint stuff that's bright colored and full of light. You can get lost in it for awhile and forget what's around you.

I got out that spring when the leaves just unfolded and the air was damp and sweet. I felt really lost. I had on prison shoes but they issued me some normal clothes. It's just as scary coming out as going in. The first thing I did was I went to go to a restaurant to eat. I had wanted some meat, thick and juicy with baked potatoes and lots of butter. I had some money that I had made on different details while I was there. I had saved most of it because I didn't have any habits to spend it on.

Anyhow, when I walked into this steak house, it seemed like everybody was looking at me everytime I turned around. I thought, "Maybe they can tell I've just come out by my haircut or something." Then I thought of my shoes. I hurried out of there and walked on down the street to another place. All that time I kept feeling like somebody was either following me or watching me to see if I would do something wrong. Pretty soon I was almost running down the street. Shoot, I just wanted to get somewhere safe. I found myself studying everybody's faces to get a clue where they stood.

I didn't know jail did that to you. I wish somebody had told me because everything slammed me right in the face that first week. I guess I would have ended up back in jail one way or another because I started drinking real lots just to keep my balance about me. I didn't head home right away because I didn't know how I could handle that. I spent all my money and sold my art work that I had brought out with me. I didn't remember one day from the next for a while there.

I ended up at the Red Power Centre one night. This guy called Lenny had hauled me there. He was from the Okanagan, north of us. He was on Red Patrol when he found me. He kept me in a room until I sobered up. They fed me and never asked me too much.

It felt good to be with just Indians, young ones, who were seriously attacking a problem only they seemed to understand. One which I understood better and better. I finally began to understand why I had deserved to be punished for working in the dope business. The Johnny Johns and people who helped them just helped our people into the gutter. For that, I was sorry.

Exposure from *Brothers In Arms*
(Winnipeg: Pemmican Publications, 1989)
by Jordan Wheeler

Of Cree, Ojibwa, Irish, English, Scottish and French descent, Jordan Wheeler was born in Victoria in 1964. Jordan had aspirations to be a journalist since his high school days. He currently lives in Winnipeg where he works in video, film and popular theatre when he is not writing.

Brothers In Arms consists of three stories about brothers and their relationships with one another, stories of traditions, tragedy and caring. "Exposure" is a story about Kris and Martin Morris, two young Cree men from southern Saskatchewan. Martin, the younger brother, is dying of AIDS and has asked Kris, who works for an advertising agency in Toronto, to come home to the reserve. Martin wants Kris to help him fix up the old family home because this is where Martin has chosen to die.

Kris is shocked by the news of Martin's illness but tells himself that if they survived residential school, they can cope with this crisis, too. When they were children Kris used to be a great comfort to Martin and Kris remembers telling him a story about a green snake that lived in a slough when things were particularly difficult. He leaves his job in Toronto and as he becomes involved in his brother's problems he comes to terms with the disease and with his own abhorrence of his brother's sexual preference.

The airport was nearly empty. Kris sat in the waiting area leaning across his soft luggage. Martin was late, but this allowed Kris time to relax. He shut his eyes, trying to picture the reserve. Would the rolling hills still seem like hills? Would the road still be there . . .? Would the old house still be standing?

"Hey!" a voice said, "you can't crash here, this is a public place. Who do you think you are, Indian?"

Kris opened his eyes, squinting against the light. "Eh, Martin?" Kris sat up and examined his brother. "You're looking good," he said, lying. Martin's body was thin, strikingly thin, and it showed in his face. Only his eyes, deep brown and alert, seemed healthy.

Martin smiled, then grabbed a piece of luggage. "I've got a car outside."

Kris stood, suddenly aware of his advancing age. Was it more energy he had in his twenties, or an inability to relax? They walked out to the parking lot. The car was a wreck. A windshield-cracked, muffler-punctured, rusted out wreck. Kris sat amidst ripped upholstery and searched for his seat belt.

"Don't bother," Martin advised, "there aren't any."

The heat was asphyxiating. Martin's fingers danced across the hot, manual steering wheel as he veered the car noisily from the airport. A trail of smoke billowed in their wake. Kris sat sweating, wondering if he would survive the drive, or would the double greenhouse effect shrivel him prune-like. At least the electric windows worked. Kris watched Martin press the buttons, then heard the reluctant whir as the glass had a mind to protest, but thought Martin's need for heat might be because of his disease. For his brother's comfort, he grinned and sweated. Then came a miracle. Martin reached down and pressed a few more buttons. Amidst a cloud of dust, cool air filtered through the vents. Kris absorbed the cold with the lust of a voracious pig. He wallowed in it and opened his shirt to feel its touch against his clammy skin.

"How's that for luxury," Martin chimed, and then added apologetically, "It gobbles a lot of gas."

They drove past the city of Regina, content in their fridge-like comfort, then stopped on the outskirts to fill up; a thirty dollar fill up. They also stopped to fill up in Lestock.

"Maybe there's a leak in the gas tank," Martin suggested. When Kris didn't respond, he added, "Maybe it's a . . . car. A reserve car."

Then came Bonedry, the name written in bold, blue letters upon the ragged, grain elevator. They left the highway and crossed the tracks.

"Two more miles 'til we hit the rez," Martin said.

"I thought it was one," Kris countered.

It was only one. The road turned from provincial asphalt to reserve gravel; mud when it was wet. The houses they passed were distinctively reserve, cheap paint-covered, porchless square boxes without fancy trimmings. Often clustered together in three or four depending on the size of the family. They passed the Pow Wow grounds, the band office, and the school, then pulled onto a dirt road just beyond the Anglican church established by Charles Cowley Pratt. Bev Pratt was a part of that family. Her house, Kris noted, was a mile away. Would she still be there? They pulled off the main road onto a weed covered driveway that led to an empty looking shack. Martin stopped the car and the brothers got out, staring silently at the place where their earliest memories lay.

The prairie was silent, save for the wind and shimmering leaves. Flies and butterflies flew about the shack collapsing slowly in the shade of poplar trees and advancing bush. An impression, Kris thought, that's all it is. The windows were gone and weeds had forced their way through the floor inside the front door. The door itself lay out front, cracked and splintered. Exposure, Kris said to himself. The wood was grey, having suffered from years of exposure to the harsh, prairie elements. It used to be turquoise. He could remember when his father painted it. Their mother had brooded for days over what the colour should be. They bought the paint in Bonedry, and the three of them, Dad, Kris, and Ralph transformed the wood shell into a colourful home. There was a sidewalk, windows, and almost a lawn. In this place, his earliest memories formed. He wondered at the years which separated that home from the grey, cracked structure which stood before him, suffocating under the encroaching bush. It was a memorial to an earlier time, and now only an impression of its former self.

"It looks different," Martin observed, leaning against the car door, "but it's still standing."

Kris walked up and stood beside his brother, still contemplating the shack. It was still standing, he agreed. They still had something to work with. Something to salvage.

"It's about time you two came back," their aunt wailed. "You still got family here, people remember you."

Some things never change, Kris thought. Sure, their aunt's house was different. There was a washer and dryer now, a microwave, a carpet. A successful merger of technology and the old home. Quite unlike the shack they'd return to during breaks from school. Their cousins had done well. Two were on the band council and they had rewarded their mother with modern appliances for her years of child-rearing. Yet the house had the same feel. Both men felt this as they took everything in. Familiarity came slowly, but surely. Their aunt spoke with the same authoritative tone. The scowl, though buried under more wrinkles, was essentially the same. The grin still toothless.

"I got new teeth," she said proudly. "Tommy bought 'em in Regina. I put them in when I go out or if there's company." Her gums smacked noisily. "But you two ain't company, so I don't put 'em in. How long you gonna stay?" She spoke with a strong Cree accent.

Martin and Kris looked at each other.

"It depends," Kris said.

"On what?" she pressed.

Kris again looked at Martin. Martin nodded.

"On how long Martin lives."

The aunt stared at the younger brother. She shook her head and lowered it, then took a deep breath and looked across the table and out the window. The pain of three generations was clearly etched in the corners of her sad eyes.

Martin cleared his throat. "I've come back, Auntie, because I want to die on the reserve. I'm going to move back to my parents' house."

"You want to live in that old shack?"

"Kris will help me fix it up."

Aunt Peggy Jane turned to look at Kris. "This is what people choose for death when they get a choice?"

Kris shrugged.

"The place is still in your names, so the band'll fix it up for you if you want," she said, wiping the glaze from her eyes. "You'll find lots of changes here. The reserve ain't like it used to be."

Martin sat in his motel room staring at the half-full moon. It was a still night except for the wind, which blew dust and bits of debris past Martin's window. Any stronger, Martin thought, and it would blow away the moon. He sucked on the nail of his index finger as he stared, his eyes like a scared child's, his breath heavy and short. He glanced down to the fields of grain lit softly by the moon, and then to his feet. With the nail clippers loaded, he reached down to clip his toenails, grey and neglected, then stopped half way, his face wincing in pain. Slowly he sat up, his teeth grinding against the hurt. When the pain had subsided, he reached to the nightstand and grabbed a bottle of pills. He threw painkillers into his mouth, then grabbed another bottle and downed several antibiotics — septra, norfloxicin. There were three more bottles of pills he turned to before drinking a glass of water. He sat back, breathing deeply until the suffering passed, then reached down to his toenails again. This time, he made it, but he could feel the tumors despite the pills. Inside him, they were growing, unwanted invaders spreading through his body. He sat up and again stared through the window with the nail clippers twiddling between his fingers. His eyes glazed over and he lay down, his body limp.

In the bar, Kris sat with Frank Morris who was Aunt Peggy Jane's youngest son and a member of the reserve's band council. With a belly the size of a bread box, Frank was a comical contrast to his more fit cousin. Sharing a pitcher of beer and watching golf highlights on the big screen in the corner, the cousins chatted.

"You don't see many good looking girls in this bar," Frank complained. He cleared his throat and added, "Must be some hot looking babes in Toronto, huh?"

"A few," Kris admitted, his eyes were wandering the bar. "Aren't you married?" he asked.

"Yeah, yeah," Frank mumbled.

Kris watched Ben Crenshaw sink a thirty foot putt, then turned to his younger cousin and said, "Martin and I are moving into our parents' old house." His voice was serious. "Can we get the band to fix it up?"

Frank took a breath, then a swig of his beer. "There's a waiting list. . .," he said. "Everyone and his dog has put in requests for housing. . ." He paused as a woman across the bar caught his eye. "Wow! Check her out, she gets better looking every year."

Kris turned and looked in the direction that Frank's lips pointed. Across the room, beneath the golf highlights, Bev Pratt sat down. Kris' glance lingered, his eyes stuck on her. Bev's hair was long, perhaps to her waist. She was in her early thirties, but could pass for twenty-seven. If she had kids, you couldn't tell by her figure. She was beautiful, just as beautiful as Kris remembered.

"Your best bet," Frank continued, jarring Kris back to earth, "is to put in a claim for repairs, but go ahead and do them yourself. I'll make sure you're reimbursed for the costs. This way it gets done and you come out even. Otherwise, you could be waiting for months, even years."

"Could you put me at the top of the list?"

"Two years ago maybe, but not anymore."

"Fair enough," Kris said. "Have any tools I can borrow?"

Frank laughed as Kris turned back to the big screen, now showing football highlights. His eyes shifted to Bev, hoping to sneak in a stare, but she was looking right at him. For a moment, they stared at each other, dumbfounded expressions plastered on their faces. Then suddenly, Bev stood up and walked out.

Frank laughed. "Ha! You spooked her," he said.

Kris grabbed a beer and took a large gulp, hoping to wash his stomach out of his throat. . .

The big screen was a blur, as was the rest of the world. Kris tried to focus, his head wavering, his lips hanging. Occasionally, spittle streamed out.

"You drunk?" Frank asked.

It took some seconds for Kris' reply. "I'm not drunk, just feeling good," he slurred. Drops of spit spread across the table. "Are you drunk?"

"Yup!" Frank blurted. "I'm scared to stand up cause I might fall."

With determination, Kris stood up. "Nothin' to it," he burbled, struggling to keep his balance. "Goodnight."

Like a wet rag, Kris swaggered through the bar. The walk out took him past a forest of faces, many he thought he recognized. His eyes shifted slowly, trying to catch sight of the door with a red exit above it. He found three and aimed for the closest one.

The night was hot. Not like a Toronto hot, but a Regina hot. A dry, searing hot. And the night was dark, unlike Toronto, too. Kris walked into a small field beside the motel so he could see the night. Wavering, he stared into the sky and saw a brilliant collage of stars. In drunken awe, he stared. The sky was dotted with more stars than he had seen in twenty years. The effect was dizzying and Kris' legs gave out. He looked down in time to see the ground come up and smack him in the face. Then he rolled over and stared at the stars again. . .

The wind was rattling the grass and the weeds. Kris stuck his head up and looked around. The motel was some seventy-five metres to his left. In the other direction, there was infinite black. Above were the stars, the moon, the wisps of northern lights. Kris stared at the motel, then at the nearby vendor where dozens were milling about. A line from the vendor extended into the parking lot. Car trunks were open and there was a fight by a ratty Ford pickup. Kris' head sunk back to the ground.

Martin gargled and spat. The mouthwash spewed through the open window, landed in the hot dust, and formed little balls of mud at Kris' feet.

"Watch it," Kris yelled.

"Sorry," Martin replied. He lathered his face with shaving gel and started to shave.

Kris turned his attention back to the house and scrutinized a week's worth of repairs. The windows had all been replaced once the frames were strengthened. They stood out next to the rest of the house, though, still weathered and beaten. Kris sighed at the amount of work yet to do, then turned to the front steps. He paused there to inspect his carpentry. Overall, he was satisfied, despite having run out of lumber to complete the last rung. Trying to shake the morning's lethargy, he bounced up and into the house. Martin was fixing a bowl of cereal.

Kris walked past the kitchen and into the bathroom, little more than a closet with a mirror and wash basin. He took a new bar of soap and a toothbrush out of a little duffle bag in the corner and washed up.

"I thought we'd check out the health clinic and let them know I'm here," Martin yelled from the kitchen.

"Good idea," Kris answered. He was lathering his face with shaving gel. He looked at his razor pensively, then extracted the blade and threw it in the garbage.

[At first the brothers are accepted and receive money to repair the house. Kris tries to re-establish a relationship with his old girl friend, Bev, but fails. Their mother, Ruby Morris, comes to visit her sister and they find that she cannot accept Martin's illness. As his condition deteriorates, the discrimination and fear increases. Funding for house repairs is cut off, the medical clinic refuses to treat Martin, and their house is vandalized. Martin is viciously beaten so Kris takes him to a hospital in Regina. - *Ed.*]

Martin was quiet when Kris walked into the room on the ward set aside for terminal cancer patients. Kris sat down. The room was tubed. Tubes stuck out of Martin's body, out of the wall, from beneath the bed, and into machines. Surrounding the bed were machines monitoring Martin's pulse and respiratory rates. A bed pan sat under the bed and a box of surgical gloves were on the cupboard beside a sink. The sheets were white, hospital white. Covering Martin and the bed was a blue, wool blanket. Martin himself was blue. Welts and cuts covered his bandaged face and the sarcoma was clearly evident. It was the worst Kris had seen him.

Martin looked at him over the sheet. "I'm gonna stay in the hospital from now on," he whispered after several minutes. Kris' eyes shot up. He was about to object to Martin's decision, but thought of the pain they'd suffered on the reserve, the heartache, the antagonism, the embarrassment. "Anyway," Martin continued, "they won't let me leave." It's for the best, Kris thought, the reserve doesn't want us anyway.

It was late afternoon. Kris' hangover persisted. Martin drifted in and out of sleep. Still Kris sat in Martin's room leaving only when nurses changed Martin's catheter or attended some other bodily function. Then finally, the nurses quit asking him to leave. Kris stared out the room's window. Autumn was never more apparent. The sky was grey and drizzle fell. A tree's branches stretched by showing off its fall colours.

When Martin groaned or whined, Kris wanted to ask what hurt, but he knew it was pointless. Martin hurt everywhere. Later, Martin exhaled and relaxed. His eyes opened. Kris was able to produce a smile and Martin smiled back. "Make sure they bury me on the reserve, near Dad and Ralph," Martin said.

Kris nodded. "I'll make sure."

Martin nodded. Later still he said, between lips which were quivering, "I'm scared."

Kris watched his brother cry, then stared out the window fighting his own tears. A fight he was losing. He turned to Martin and saw him staring straight ahead as the tears streamed down towards his ears. The eyes were squinted and his mouth was open in a quiet bawl.

Let it out, Kris thought angrily. . . Tears spilled over and poured down Kris' face. Martin needed to be smoothed, to be loved, to be held. Hesitantly, Kris moved towards the bed and sat on its edge. Martin looked up, his eyes almost pleading. Kris shook, then reached out and wrapped his arms around Martin's shoulders. Martin's arms wrapped around Kris and he wept. Kris cleared his nose and throat.

"There was a snake," he began, "a green snake who lived in the slough. When it was dry, the snake stayed in the muddy wetness, but when it was wet, the snake would go for walks. Side to side it walked, wriggling like this."

And he wriggled his arm in the air to show how the snake did it. Martin looked up to watch, then stared towards the door. Kris turned the same way. In the room, ahead of Frank and Aunt Peggy Jane, stood Ruby Morris.

Kris became quiet as Ruby stared at Martin, then she stepped forward. Kris moved away to make room for her on the bed and she sat down, running a hand affectionately across Martin's cheek. She grabbed his other hand and kissed it, then lowered it to her bosom.

"The snake went for a walk," she began, grabbing the tissue to wipe Martin's eyes. Aunt Peggy Jane and Frank disappeared around the corner. Kris stood up and watched his mother continue the story. The tears still dripped and stained his eyes red, but he smiled as he left the room and wandered down the hall.

Outside, people were entering and leaving the hospital at a quick pace. Kris watched, wondering for a moment what their stories were, who they were visiting. Towards the street, trees stood tall on the boulevard. Cathedral-like, they stretched one by one on both sides down the street and out of sight. Kris noticed Frank's Bronco parked there. An officer was tucking a parking ticket under the front, left windshield wiper. In front of the truck stood a tall elm tree, its branches bare from dutch elm disease.

"Six to eight weeks," Kris mused quietly.

It took three.

Martin's wake was a boisterous affair, like all wakes on the reserve. What caught Kris off guard was that people came, in droves. Ruby and Aunt Peggy Jane cooked a feast and James Caribou told dirty jokes to old women, who giggled incessantly and flashed their gums. Serenely, Martin's body rested in the centre of the room. It was an expensive coffin, but Martin left behind enough money in his will to cover the expenses. He was buried on the reserve, right by his father.

Bev Pratt showed up about midnight.

"Quite a turnout," she commented as Kris met her by the door.

"Mom and Aunt Peggy Jane pulled it off," he explained. "But it was Martin who insisted we have it at the house. He figured we spent so much time fixing it up, we might as well use it." Bev looked the house over appreciatively. "You guys did a good job."

Kris shrugged.

"I know you're leaving soon," she said. "And I want to talk to you before you go." Bev motioned towards the door. They walked out into the night. The moon was haloed, and it was cold. Bev zipped up her jacket, Kris shivered. "Look," she said, "I remember what we had, and I remember that it was good, despite what happened at the end. It would have been so easy to start over. You were the first person I ever really loved. No matter who comes along after, the first one always remains."

Kris nodded his agreement.

"But I couldn't get into a relationship with you again," she said.

Kris watched her with questioning eyes.

"Just before I left Vancouver," she continued, shifting her gaze to the haloed moon, "I tested HIV positive. I have the AIDS virus."

Kris looked to the ground. After a while he said, "Thanks for coming to Martin's wake."

Bev's eyes warmed. "You're welcome."

"So what are you going to do?"

Bev stopped walking and stared into the stars. "I don't have the full blown disease yet. But I think I'm going to stay here. Being with you and Martin really helped me put things into perspective. I can handle it now. And you?"

Kris thought out loud. "Go back to Toronto. Convince my boss to take me back, convince Karina to take me back, then carry on."

"Think you'll ever come back here?" Bev asked.

"Oh yeah, I'll come back."

"Will you visit me?"

"Of course I will."

"Don't make any promises you can't keep, Mr. Morris," Bev laughed.

Kris smiled. "You think you know me so well," he goaded.

"Because I do."

Kris laughed. "Want to go for a walk?"

"I don't know," she said, acting coy. "Guys like you mean trouble."

They laughed and walked towards the road. The wind blew dead leaves as winter's breath hummed about.

"Maybe they'll find a cure," Kris wondered.

"Maybe you'll quit drinking," Bev countered.

"Maybe."

CHAPTER 7

Contemporary Poetry

Introduction

If you would seek to know a people, look to their poetry. It is in the most intense, controlled but emotionally honest statements that the natural eloquence of the group reveals itself.[1]

Poetry is inherent in the human spirit. It represents one way of ordering experience and making it meaningful. It is by far the most complex vehicle for communication that exists in a language. It compresses experience into a small set of symbols. Poetry helps the reader to hear distinctly, to see clearly, to smell acutely, and to feel keenly. Poetry springs from the depths of human need and gives an important dimension to literature. A true poem is endless in being; the reader never feels done with it but will come back to it again and again.

A poem is an attempt to give shape to an experience in words. It is the poet's verbal shaping of experience which leads to the readers' responses. Poetry achieves its power because its patterns are a combination of many elements such as rhythm, imagery, figurative language, word music, tone, and idea.

A poem has a slightly different meaning for everyone who reads it because no two people have had identical experiences. The poet's techniques, the form of the poem, as well as the actual words themselves are integrally bound up with meaning and effect. The concern of the reader should be to arrive at an experience rather than at a definition. Common cultural referents are necessary so that symbols have similar meanings to the readers. Externals like history, religion and culture may be directly relevant to the poem. Since true appreciation of poetry depends on the revival of memory imprints, the previous experiences of the readers are important.

1. Sanders, Thomas E. and Walter W. Peek: *Literature of the American Indians* (London: Collier Macmillan, 1973), p.43.

The value of a poem is dependent upon its ability to involve the reader; a poem that does not do this has little value. The poem itself is not beautiful — beauty comes when the reader experiences it and derives satisfaction from it. The reader should refrain from asking, — "What does it mean?" This kind of interpretation leads to rendering the poem into prose language, which destroys the aesthetic experience. The process itself that was originally the poem will have been forgotten. It is more satisfying to examine how the poem builds itself into a form out of images, ideas and rhythms.

Poetry is for everyone who has emotions and language. It is about life. Poetry is read and studied, not to define it, but to experience it. Analysis allows the reader to enter a poem more perceptively, but discussion must not lead away from the poem; rather it should lead further into the poem. The reader must examine how images, rhythm, and ideas blend; how elements become the meaning and how they cannot be separated from the meaning.

There is a fundamental human need for rhythm. The easy rhythm of nursery rhymes and ballads is familiar but there are many different kinds of rhythm in poetry, including contemporary poetry. All poems have rhythm — the rising and falling of the voice make a rhythmic sound pattern. The cadence of everyday speech, of the human voice in various situations, is the rhythmic base of many contemporary poems.

One way of classifying poetry is by theme. This method lends itself well to examining Native poetry. There are several major recurring themes in the poetry of Native people. This does not mean, however, that all poetry written by Native people falls into these thematic categories or that Native poetry can necessarily be recognized by these themes.

The move toward Native self-determination is manifested in all aspects of their lives today, so it comes as no surprise to find it in the poetry as well. In the following poem Sheila Erickson, a Cree, eloquently asks non-Native readers, writers, and publishers to allow Native people to write their own literature.

don't rhyme the words too closely
when you tell our story
leave time and space for us to install
our bit of truth
to add another line or word
each man his own
each nation its paragraph
leave room for us to chant and mourn
and mimic the roll of the buffalo herds
or shake the fish skin rattle
don't rhyme the words too closely

Many themes of Native poets cannot be separated from their history. The poetry reflects the feelings of minority culture groups who have been dominated by foreign invaders. This theme is the subject of a wide variety of Native poetry. It ranges from poems about the suffering of the Native people as their lands were confiscated, to the bewilderment of young Natives who have not had the opportunity to grow up in their own culture.

Another recurring theme, in common with poets of all cultures, is a nostalgia for a time that no longer is. There is a yearning for customs no longer practised, a mourning for traditional religions and beliefs that appear to be dying and a fear of an uncertain future. The poetry shows a great love for Native culture and an intense identification with values and beliefs that have survived despite hundreds of years of oppression.

Many young writers describe what it is to be a Native person today. In some cases the poetry expresses pain and despair at being Native in a society that still holds racial biases. In other cases the writing is a poetic reflection on what it is to be a young Canadian; race and colour of the poet have no bearing on the sentiments.

Whatever the theme, intent, or style of the poetry, universal truths are expressed. The ideas are intense, they are eloquent, they are controlled and they are emotionally honest.

Contemporary Poetry

Pauline Johnson (Mohawk)

When Pauline Johnson (1861-1913) died, flags in Canada flew at half-mast and Vancouver declared a civic day of mourning. In 1972 she was the first Canadian woman, the first Canadian Native and the first Canadian writer to be honoured with a commemorative postage stamp.

A mixed-blood from the Brantford Reserve in Ontario, she nevertheless identified strongly with her father's people, the Mohawks. She considered herself a Native by law, temperament, choice and upbringing. She received an excellent education at home from her English mother. Pauline Johnson wrote poetry of exceptional merit and popularity based on legends and folklore of her people but did not flinch from commenting on the social conditions of the Native people.

As an adult she made a living by giving poetry readings. Dressed in a white buckskin "Indian princess" dress she delighted crowds across Canada. Canada was then a group of loosely connected provinces, still in its early years as a country. Pauline Johnson united east and west as she crossed Canada several times giving performances. She was linked to Canada's past and had an unbounded faith in its future. Her stage career lasted for twenty years; she died of cancer in Vancouver where she is buried in Stanley Park. Chiefswood, her home on the Brantford Reserve, is now a museum. Her poetry is found in a book called *Flint and Feather* (Don Mills: Paperjacks, 1972).

THE CATTLE THIEF

They were coming across the prairie, they were
galloping hard and fast;
For the eyes of those desperate riders had sighted their
man at last-
Sighted him off to Eastward, where the Cree encampment lay,

Where the cotton woods fringed the river, miles and
miles away.
Mistake him? Never! Mistake him? the famous Eagle
Chief!
That terror to all the settlers, that desperate Cattle
Thief-
That monstrous, fearless Indian, who lorded it over
the plain,
Who thieved and raided, and scouted, who rode like a
hurricane!
But they've tracked him across the prairie; they've
followed him hard and fast;
For those desperate English settlers have sighted their
man at last.

Up they wheeled to the teepees, all their British blood
aflame,
Bent on bullets and bloodshed, bent on bringing down
their game;
But they searched in vain for the Cattle Thief: that
lion had left his lair,
And they cursed like a troop of demons - for the women
alone were there.
"The sneaking Indian coward," they hissed; "he hides
while yet he can;
He'll come in the night for cattle, but he's scared to
face a man."
"Never!" and up from the cotton woods rang the voice
of Eagle Chief;
And right out into the open stepped, unarmed, the
Cattle Thief.
Was that the game they had coveted? Scarce fifty years
had rolled
Over that fleshless, hungry frame, starved to the bone
and old;
Over that wrinkled, tawny skin, unfed by the warmth
of blood.

Over those hungry, hollow eyes that glared for the sight
of food.

He turned, like a hunted lion: "I know not fear,"
said he;
And the words outleapt from his shrunken lips in the
language of the Cree.
"I'll fight you, white-skins, one by one, till I kill you
all," he said;
But the threat was scarcely uttered, ere a dozen balls
of lead
Whizzed through the air about him like a shower of
metal rain,
And the gaunt old Indian Cattle Thief dropped dead
on the open plain.
And that band of cursing settlers gave one triumphant
yell,
And rushed like a pack of demons on the body that
writhed and fell.
"Cut the fiend up into inches, throw his carcass on the
plain;
Let the wolves eat the cursed Indian, he'd have treated
us the same."
A dozen hands responded, a dozen knives gleamed high,
But the first stroke was arrested by a woman's strange,
wild cry.
And out into the open, with a courage past belief,
She dashed, and spread her blanket o'er the corpse of
the Cattle Thief;
And the words outleapt from her shrunken lips in the
language of the Cree,
"If you mean to touch that body, you must cut your
way through me."
And that band of cursing settlers dropped backward
one by one,
For they knew that an Indian woman roused, was a
woman to let alone.
And then she raved in a frenzy that they scarcely under-

stood,
Raved of the wrongs she had suffered since her earliest babyhood:
"Stand back, stand back, you white-skins, touch that dead man to your shame;
You have stolen my father's spirit, but his body I only claim.
You have killed him, but you shall not dare to touch him now he's dead.
You have cursed, and called him a Cattle Thief, though you robbed him first of bread-
Robbed him and robbed my people - look there, at that shrunken face,
Starved with a hollow hunger, we owe to you and your race.
What you have left to us of land, what you have left of game,
What have you brought but evil, and curses since you came?
How have you paid us for our game? how paid us for our land?
By a *book*, to save our souls from the sins *you* brought in your other hand.
Go back with your new religion, we never have understood
You're robbing an Indian's *body*, and mocking his *soul* with food.
Go back with your new religion, and find - if find you can -
The *honest* man you have ever made from out a *starving* man.
You say your cattle are not ours, your meat is not our meat;
When you pay for the land you live in, *we'll* pay for the meat we eat.

Give back our land and our country, give back our
herds of game;
Give back the furs and the forests that were ours before
you came;
Give back the peace and the plenty. Then come with
your new belief,
And blame, if you dare, the hunger that *drove* him to
be a thief."

THE CORN HUSKER

Hard by the Indian lodges, where the bush
Breaks in a clearing, through ill-fashioned fields,
She comes to labour, when the first still hush
Of autumn follows large and recent yields.

Age in her fingers, hunger on her face,
Her shoulders stooped with weight of work and years,
But rich in tawny colouring of her race,
She comes a-field to strip the purple ears.

And all her thoughts are with the days gone by,
Ere might's injustice banished from their lands
Her people, that to-day unheeded lie
Like the dead that rustle through her hands.

Duke Redbird (Ojibway/Métis)

Duke Redbird's poetry was published in the 1960's, a time of social protest. His was one of the first Native voices to be heard in the literary field. Then in his twenties, his poetry had considerable impact and greatly assisted Native people in getting their message of self-determination across to other Canadians.

Duke had become a foster child after his mother burned to death while trying to rescue her children in a house fire. His father could not keep the family together. Duke met with the usual discrimination and the uncertainties of many moves. He reacted by living in a world of fantasy. His work reflects bitterness toward white society but, more significantly, it reflects his painful struggle in trying to understand and live with his identity as a Native person.

His poetry can be found in a book called *Red on White: The Biography of Duke Redbird* by Marty Dunn (Toronto: New Press, 1971).

MY MOCCASINS

My moccasins have not walked
Among the giant forest trees

My leggings have not been brushed
Against the fern and berry bush

My medicine pouch has not been filled
With roots and herbs and sweetgrass

My hands have not fondled a spotted fawn
My eyes have not beheld
The golden rainbow of the north

My hair has not been adorned
With the eagle feather

Yet
My dreams are dreams of these
My heart is one with them
The scent of them caresses my soul

Sheila Erickson (Cree)

Sheila Erickson was at one time the editor of the Canadian culture magazine, *TAWOW*. The magazine is now out of print. Her poetry is found in *Notice, This Is an Indian Reserve*, K. Gooderham, ed. (Toronto: Griffin House, 1972).

I HEAR THE GODS ARE CRYING

I hear the gods are crying in the night
I hear they've been abandoned and alone
it seems their glorious robes are melting
and their light is dying down
man the crystal ships we can't let them go
they're sad and crying amongst themselves
and wondering where to go
their beautiful heads are going down
bending with the loss
butterflies look slightly dazed
the sun is turning cold
the trees in silent goodbyes
are shedding leaves to mourn
Orion-in-the-sky is dead
no fawns are being born

MY CAMERA

my camera catch the light
freeze the flow
one sixtieth of a second it can capture
one sixty-thousanth I can know
my camera stop your walking
my camera freeze your feet
I dig my artsy pictures
I think my camera neat

Chief Dan George (Co-Salish)

Dan George (1899-1981) is most famous for his acting career. He starred in various CBC television programs and several Hollywood films. The one that brought him the greatest fame was *Little Big Man*. He had a normal childhood, attending residential school and marrying early. For many years he worked as a labourer and then went on the road, playing one-night stands with a group called "Dan George and His Indian Entertainers", a dance band. It was almost by accident that Dan George got his first acting job, but he was an instant success.

Throughout his triumphant years as a film star, Chief Dan George never lost humility. He was in great demand as a speaker and received honourary degrees from several universities. A deep spiritualism, a reverence for nature and a love for humanity, especially Native people, are reflected in all his eloquent speeches which have survived just as he delivered them. His poetry is recorded in two books, *My Heart Soars* (Saanichton, B.C.: Hancock House, 1974) and *My Spirit Soars* (Surrey, B.C.: Hancock House, 1982).

THEY SAY WE DO NOT SHOW OUR FEELINGS

They say we do not show our feelings.
This is not so.
Everything is within,
where the heart pounds out the richness of our emotions.

The face only speaks
the language of the passing years.

Rita Joe (Micmac)

Rita Joe is from Whycocomagh, Nova Scotia. She, too, was a foster child who was moved from home to home, from one reservation to another. She has special concerns for children, and writes so others may come to understand the right of Native people to education and dignity. She gives readings of her works wherever possible, often travelling long distances at her own expense to do so. She says she is always surprised to find that Canadians do care about what is happening with Native people today. Her poem "When I was small" is hanging in the Museum of Civilization in Ottawa. Her poems are found in *Poems of Rita Joe* (Halifax: Abenaki Press, 1978).

WOMEN OF PEACE

We make baskets of ash and maple.
Good wood.
Intricate designs, carefully woven,
  nothing crude,
Perfection binding.

Women of peace,
We weave each day.

MEN OF PEACE

There is a tale of the men of peace,
The quiet ones.
The wise elders
And modern sons.

Lnu
Left no records,
But his beliefs continue,
And his ceremonial dress remains.

The lore and legends
Are not to be lost.
To say they are vanishing is
Not true.

In accepting new ways
Native life has changed.
Yet, reattracted to the traditions,
They are practiced again.

These are still the men of tomorrow.
The proud races,
The men of peace,
The quiet ones.

WHEN I WAS SMALL

When I was small
I used to help my father
Make axe handles.
Coming home from the wood with a bundle
Of maskwi, snawey, aqamoq,
My father would chip away,
Carving with a crooked knife,
Until a well-made handle appeared,
Ready to be sand-papered
By my brother.

When it was finished
We started another,
Sometimes working through the night
With me holding a lighted shaving
To light their way
When the kerosene lamp ran dry.

Then in the morning
My mother would be happy
That there would be food today
When father sold our work.

Pauline Doore (Blackfoot)

MY NOKUM[2]

Scrape, scrape, scrape.
Oh! My Nokum
You try so hard.
Why?

Rest awhile.
It is not so important.
Ah, but it is.
If it were not for you, would I be here?

The skin you are preparing,
Brings warmth.
Moccasins, a dress perhaps
For the long cold winter ahead?

Soon the Great Manitou
Will be calling
To the hunting grounds there to join
The ones that left before.

Oh! My Nokum.
What will we do when you are gone,
For no more are the wise old ways of our people:
Legends, myths and guidance.

2 *Many Voices: An Anthology of Contemporary Canadian Indian Poetry* by Day, David and Marilyn Bowering (Vancouver: J. J. Douglas, 1977).

Tona and R.Z. Nobis, Jr.

The poetry of these two men comes from a book called *Native Sons* (Cobalt, Ont.: Highway Book Shop, 1977) which was written in jail. A group called "Native Sons" was organized to study Native culture at the Guelph Correctional Institute. This book of poetry was one result. The prisoners hope that in expressing their innermost feelings a better understanding of Native people will take place.

POTTERY

Fractured clay shards
Buried many years
Now uncovered

The ochre paint
Just a flaking hint
Begging to be seen.

This find implies
A truth oft forgot
Someone was here first.
- Tona

SOMEONE

My heart gets heavy
When I look around and see
What is happening
To my people and to me?
I feel thoughts presence
Creep slowly into my head;
Sorrow, confusion,
Lost feelings of someone dead
Questions about me
What's happening to us all?
Don't we care what we
Once were, standing proud and tall?
Comes a voice, "I care!"

From someone deep in my head,
"I always will care
Even until I am dead.
Am I the only one
Who cares? Tell me!
Please, someone tell me
That I am not."

- R.Z. Nobis, Jr.

ORDINARY MAN

He was just an ordinary man
And he played many roles;
His history has not been recorded
For children to study in school.
An ordinary man,
With ordinary fears,
Hopes and dreams,
And ordinary tears.
Songs are never written,
Stories never told,
No legends to remember,
About an ordinary man.
I am the evidence,
That he was once here.
My ordinary father,
For whom I shed my tears.

- R.Z. Nobis, Jr.

George Kenny (Ojibway)

George Kenny was introduced earlier in this anthology through his short story "On the Shooting of a Beaver." George Kenny lived on the Lac Seul Reserve in Ontario. He left the reserve at the age of six and grew up in small northwestern Ontario towns. His writing reflects experiences in both Native and non-Native worlds. He dedicated his book, *Indians Don't Cry*, to his father and mother. His father was a trapper and labourer, but he never discouraged George from becoming a writer. His mother encouraged him to finish school. In his dedication he acknowledges the contribution his parents made to his success. The book was made into a radio play and videotape called *October Stranger.*

SUNSET ON PORTAGE
(from the bus depot)

the Winnipeg sun dies
lastly

on the blue logo

of the Bank of Montreal.

Fluorescent and neon lights,
man's creation

surplants

God's technology.

OLD DANIEL

A wigwam, fire in the centre, smoke
rising, and the interior decorated with
children's laughter, grandmother's
soft comfort, and even mother's periodic
scolding instruction, and best of all,
huddling together in winter

seem now a lifetime away

said Old Daniel in gutteral Saulteaux.

Old Daniel (he's my mother's brother)

told me his memories

when I visited him, sometime last year
in the Senior Citizen's Spic and Span
tiled floor, flower-potted window,
highrise apartment building on Elgin St.
in Winnipeg.

I remember leaving, disengaging the
cold fingers of the old Indian's desperation

promising

when I find a place by the lake
you can come home to Dryden with me.

The next time I thought of Old Daniel
was when I got a notice asking,
as a near relative

Could I make funeral arrangements for

Old Daniel.

Roslea Prosser (Cree)

Roslea Prosser was born in The Pas, Manitoba. Her father worked for the Hudson Bay line so she was raised in Pikwitonei. Her father lived a traditional lifestyle but her mother had been raised in a residential school. The difference between her parents was always confusing for her.

Roslea has lived and worked in Saskatchewan and Ontario. At present, she is in Thompson, Manitoba, training to become a teacher. The following poem was written about her three-year-old son whom she had to leave behind with his father when she got work in Ontario. She says, "This is the same kind of feeling I have where my Indianness is concerned. Something I can never fully have."

MY LEIGHTON

My Leighton
in the midst of my
confusion and emptiness
I allow myself
the luxury of your sweet memory
but I pay the price
loneliness is always
it seems
an extension of love

Darlene Genaille (Métis)

Darlene was a grade nine student at Duck Bay School in Manitoba when she wrote the following poem. She presented it at the Duck Mountain Speech Arts Festival in 1988, where she received high praise for both content and delivery and was presented with a certificate of merit.

PREJUDICE HURTS

"Hey you!"

"Who, me?"

"Yeh, you. Come
here for a minute."

"What can I do for
you?"

"How about coming
with me to the
Basket Social tonight?"

"Yeh, sure. It would
be a great experience."

"Stop!"

"What?"

"Stop."

"What for, did you forget
something?"

"Yes."

"Well what?"

"I forgot to tell you
that this bas...,
well I don't know exactly
how to say this, but

this basket social is
for people like me."

"So you're telling me
that me an Indian is
not allowed to attend this
basket social!"

"Yes."

"Is this what you call a
right,

to this basket social?
Well, I call it prejudice."

"What are you telling me?"

"What I am telling you is
that:

Prejudice hurts,
for many people are fussy.
They choose the person,
that suits them best,
and leave the ones,
that don't fit in
all alone;

Prejudice hurts,
for many people are mean.
They make others,
think they belong.
And like the people at the social,
when the mean person,
finds out that the other
isn't exactly the same as he is
they just throw him out.
Like a speck of dust;

Prejudice hurts,
for many people are selfish.
All they think about
is themselves,
and not about others.
On the other hand,
that person who is left out,
just like me
ends up being very
lonely and hurt.

So I tell you,
my friend,
that prejudice
really hurts
on the outside
and on the inside
of a person."

"I am sorry I
even brought this up
about taking you
to the social.
I really am."

"It's Okay."

"How about you and I go
somewhere else,
where everyone
is welcome?"

"Yeh, sure."

Richard Delaronde and William Stevenson (Métis)

Both boys were grade nine students at Duck Bay School in Manitoba when they wrote the following poem.

MODEL T

It coughed
and coughed
while he turned
the starter,
sputtering
until it started.
The driver
leaped into the
smoke-covered monster.
As he drove down
the street,
his car
coughed and
coughed,
causing those in sight
to chuckle
at the ailing
creature.
As the day ended,
the driver
drove the car
to its den
to sleep
until tomorrow.
But for the Model T
there was
no tomorrow.

Dorine Cooper (Métis)

Dorine Cooper is a Métis writer from Selkirk, Manitoba. She feels that being Métis means being a divided spirit in one body. Métis people must look at both sides of their heritage and be proud, she believes. She has written a book about Native women called *Rubaboo* (Winnipeg, Pemmican Publications, 1981) as well as numerous short stories, magazine articles and poetry.

WHAT COLOUR IS LOVE?

What colour is love?

Love is red.
Red like apples in the fall and circus balloons and sunsets.
Red like new mittens and barns and old brick houses.
Red like people are.

Love is yellow.
Yellow like the sun in spring and daffodils and bright new pencils.
Yellow like a golden ring and autumn leaves and fresh farm butter.
Yellow like people are.

Love is black.
Black like earth in new dug gardens and soft nights and ravens' wings.
Black like smooth roads and polished shoes and wood stoves.
Black like people are.

Love is white.
White like snow and clouds and whitecaps on the water when it's windy.
White like gulls and Sunday shirts and sheets drying outside on the clothesline.
White like people are.

What colour is love?

Caroline Flett (Cree)

Caroline Flett received her teacher training in Winnipeg, Manitoba. She is presently teaching in northern Ontario. The following poem has been made into a poster in Cree, Ojibway, and English.

WALK SLOWLY, LITTLE ONE

Walk slowly through life, little one.
Stop to smell the wild flowers.
Stop to listen to the birds.
Stop to touch the animals.
Stop to look around you.

Walk slowly through life, little one.
Stop to smell the sweetgrass.
Stop to listen to the wind.
Stop to touch the raindrops.
Stop to look at nature.

Walk slowly through life, little one.
Stop to smell.
Stop to listen.
Stop to touch.
Stop to look.

Walk slowly through life, little one.

Lee Maracle (Métis/Salish)

Lee Maracle lives in Vancouver and writes from her own experiences as well as from the experiences of other Canadian minority groups. She says in the acknowledgement in her book that other minorities opened her eyes to the world of struggle for all oppressed people. She feels that a new humanity is being worked out that will destroy barriers caused by racism.

She completed the book *I Am Woman* (Vancouver: Write-on Press, 1988) from which these poems are taken, when she was thirty-seven, but she says it took twenty years to write it. Her children were denied extras like music and dancing lessons because she was writing, but with their co-operation and that of her partner, Dennis, the book was finally completed.

CREATION

I know nothing
of great mysteries
know less of creation
I do know
that the farther backward
in time that I travel
the more grandmothers
and the farther forward
the more grandchildren
I am obligated to both

ghosts

let's drink to the ghosts
in our closet
not one beer for unity
love,
or the right to be free -

here's a beer for the ghost
of jealousy
that plague of pain
that surly beast of doubt -

here, down a beer for the ghost
of insecurity
the ghost that interferes
whenever paths cross -

another round for the ghost
of rage
the one that boils over
each time a conflict we engage -

let's drink especially to the ghost
of terror
rage can't hold a candle to fear -
drink up then, drink to fear -

drag them out of the closet
march them up and down
before our eyes
drink to them, lest we forget
and bury them
in our dim and distant past -

let's not discuss a single thing
let us not be rational
that presumes we're human,
warm,
passionate beings,
in need of patience,
gentleness, and love -

the object is not unity
but win this fight -
retalliate - kick your lover's pride

dismantle his dignity
and drink,
drink,
drink - - -
to the ghosts
in your closet -

if we ever stop celebrating
the ghosts in our closet
we will be forced to face
the enemy
and really fight -

- - - TOGETHER - - -

Emma LaRocque (Métis)

Emma LaRocque was introduced earlier in this anthology through her essay on poverty. She also writes short stories and poetry and is particularly concerned about how Métis and Native people are portrayed in contemporary society.

WHEN I FIRST CAME TO THE CITY

And the streets!
Look at the streets
All in parallels and perpendiculars
Spawning concrete erectiles,
Straight-ups, phallus-powers
As if afraid of earth
And her Kiva gentleness.

And the people!
Look at the people
All in hustle and ghastly hassle
Spawning spurts and slapdash
Daze, dearth and spectral frazzle
As if afraid of calm
And her composed silence.

Do you know that sometimes still
I amble through the streets
searching for a brown face
for warmth
and loitering grace.

THE GEESE OVER THE CITY

In the city
one awakes to the sound
of man-made mobility:
    coughing motors,
    clanging truck boxes,
    wailing sirens,
    tire screeches.
There are the treadmarks on my soul.

But this morning-day
Very early -
Even before the sun
made it through the October grey --
I heard the Geese,
the Geese,
the Geese ---
and in my half-sleep
I jumped up,
ready to run out and see
Their V-formation
as was the tradition
of the great northern Cree
But sounds of some shifting gears
made me stop,
and aware that
the obstinate elm leaves,
electric wires
and too tall buildings
would not let me see,
let me see,
let me see --
so I fell back to sleep,
no, to reverie
I saw a little log-shack
full of family faces
all embraced
by a tangle tussle
of green-gold laces
And I smelled
the racy fragrance
of a widowed willow-leaf
etched with the earth
broken birch branch
and damp dew

ahh

Twice more
The Geese
went over the city
making me sad
that I could not see
making me happy
that I could not see
there was much Cree in me
despite
town height.

In Conclusion

Eva McKay (1920 -) lives on the Sioux Valley Reserve near Brandon, Manitoba. Many changes have taken place on the reserve in her lifetime, and she has been responsible in no small measure for many of these changes. She has been involved in establishing a locally controlled school and improving child care services in recent years. She is in frequent demand as a speaker. She rarely misses an opportunity to speak to young people and is particularly interested in helping university students.

In 1987, along with three other Native women, she was a speaker at a conference on "Women's Studies" at Brandon University. The following is a summary of the talk she gave that day.

We Are Here

I believe that each one of us has a goal. In traditional society the goal of women was to fulfill the role of motherhood. We learned at a very early age that we had to train for that role. We knew that we had a responsibility from the time the baby was born until it was grown up. But the role of mother and grandmother is never finished.

Life is a trip, a journey. Our foundation for this journey, our starting point, is the family. The mother is the foundation of this family, regardless of race. We can't talk about reaching a goal in life if we have not accepted our own identities. And that's a problem we have today, the loss of identity, not only for Native people but for other people as well. We are too busy to research our roots. And basically, if we are to find the rewards of life, we have to start by the roots.

Today we are here to talk about women's issues. The problems our young people are having today are a women's issue. As mothers we have the responsibility to train our children. It's the mother's shoulder where the child rests; that's where the young man rests his head. Our shoulder — we carry the load of our family; our shoulders are always there.

We want what is best for our children — that is why we are meeting today. Today we are sending our young women to university because we need Native teachers. Many of these young women are mothers and it is hard for them. Life in the city is hard. But family stories that have been passed down show that women are strong. A woman passes her strength on to her children. If young people can find comfort in a family they will be able to cope with realities outside the home. Without support from families we are doomed by problems of society.

Native people are very close to nature. When we come into buildings such as this we feel closed in, like budgies in a cage. The evening sunset indicates the end of the day, the early dawn when the birds start chirping tells us there's a new day, there's new life. The sunset and early morning give us a spiritual feeling. The world is a spiritual creation of the Great Spirit who has also given us breath.

We may take for granted that we were born like any other person. Our traditional people tell us that we were born in a sacred way. They say you are breathing a sacred breath of life. Should you become weak, strengthen yourself by looking at the world around you, and see that you are not alone in the sacredness of life which was, and is and always will be.

We are not alone. Life around is so busy that we don't take time to say thank you that I am alive this morning.

I think that we have drifted too far, so far from what we were in the beginning and what we were meant to be. We've drifted away from all that. Our spirits are weak today; the world around us, it seems, has no spiritual meaning anymore. The world situation we read about, see on TV, is unreal. This beautiful world with all the beautiful creations that are there for you and me are forgotten many times. Forgotten.

The Native women's issues or problems that we talk about stem from this loss of spirituality. The loss of our spirit — the loss that we are not aware, anymore, of the Creator who gave us our language, who gave you your language. And when another person tells you that your language is not accepted — that you will be punished if you speak your language — that your way of life is being taken away — then there is no more life in you to begin to look to the future.

We have tried our utmost to understand the ways of the white society. We have learned the language. It is hard for us people. We have tried to understand the different way of life. We have learned, we have tried to walk daily in the white mainstream, many times stumbling because we are weak, or become weak because of the many things we do not understand which were not a part of our way.

I have had the experience of being told that someone's God was better than mine. I was to step over to that side. And it made me sad. How many of our people have experienced that! But we have something in us that has survived.

The concerns of Native women are many. The mother has carried the load. The worries. The problems. We carry that load. And today we are beginning to see some changes coming about. For example, this morning and this afternoon. I have these four young Native women with me here. If we are given a chance, if you will step forward and we also take a step, then you will begin to understand why it has taken so long for us to become a part of society. Take a step closer and you will understand why we have so many Native issues, problems. Research does not do much for us. While we are still living, people like myself are the people with the stories. We are the people with experience. We are the people with the natural skills because the world and everything in it has a story for us. These are the natural stories. And this is why our people survived - long before Europeans came we survived and we are the descendants of those people. We're asking that you come forward, we'll meet you half way.

There are many problems that we face today. So if we can get together like this then we can begin to understand. We have learned about the people in your society, the speech which is a different language, who dress differently, who eat differently, who are spiritually different. We have learned. We are asking now that you will come and learn from us. We are here.

BIBLIOGRAPHY

Ahenakew, Edward. *Voices of the Plains Cree*. Toronto: McClelland and Stewart, 1973.

Armstrong, Jeanette. *Slash*. Penticton: Theytus Books, 1985.

Barker, George. *Forty Years a Chief.* Winnipeg: Peguis Publishers, 1979.

Batisse, Ken George and others. *Native Sons*. Cobalt, Ontario: Highway Book Shop, 1977.

Boulanger, Tom. *An Indian Remembers*. Winnipeg: Peguis Publishers, 1971.

Brass, Eleanor. *I Walk in Two Worlds*. Calgary: Glenbow-Alberta Institute, 1987.

__________________. *Medicine Boy and Other Cree Tales*. Calgary: Glenbow Museum, 1978.

Burton, Dwight. *Literature Study in High School*. New York: Holt, Rinehart and Winston Inc., 1960.

Campbell, Maria. *Halfbreed*. Toronto: McClelland and Stewart, 1973.

Carpenter, Jock. *Fifty Dollar Bride: Marie Rose Smith - A Chronicle of Métis Life Style in the 19th Century*. Sidney, British Columbia: Gray's Publishing, 1977.

Charette, Guillaume. *Vanishing Spaces: Memoirs of Louis Goulet*. Winnipeg: Editions Bois-Brûlés, 1976.

Clark, Ella Elizabeth. *Indian Legends of Canada*. Toronto: McClelland and Stewart, 1960.

Clay, Charles. *Swampy Cree Legends*. Bewdley: Pine Ridge Publishing, 1967.

Clutesi, George. *Son of Raven, Son of Deer*. Sidney, British Columbia: Gray's Publishing, 1967.

Colombo, John Robert. *Songs of the Indians I*. Ottawa: Oberon, 1983.

________________. *Songs of the Indians II*. Ottawa: Oberon, 1983.

Culleton, Beatrice. *In Search of April Raintree*. Winnipeg: Pemmican Publications Inc., 1983.

________________. *Spirit of the White Bison*. Winnipeg: Pemmican Publications Inc., 1985.

Day, David and Marilyn Bowering, eds. *Many Voices: An Anthology of Contemporary Canadian Indian Poetry*. Vancouver: J.J. Douglas, 1977.

Day, A. Grove. *The Sky Clears: Poetry of the American Indians*. Lincoln: University of Nebraska Press, 1951.

Dunn, Marty. *Red on White: The Biography of Duke Redbird*. Toronto: New Press, 1971.

French, Alice. *My Name is Masak*. Winnipeg: Peguis Publishers, 1976.

Frontier School Division. *Words and Images*. I, no. 4 (May, 1987).

George, Chief Dan. *My Heart Soars*. Saanichton, B.C.: Hancock House, 1974.

________________. *My Spirit Soars*. Surrey, B.C.: Hancock House, 1982.

Gooderham, Kent. *I Am an Indian*. Toronto: J.M. Dent, 1969.

________________. *Notice, This is an Indian Reserve*. Toronto: Griffin House, 1972.

Goodwill, Jean, ed. *Speaking Together: Canada's Native Women*. Ottawa: Secretary of State, 1975.

Grant, Agnes and Ingrid Makus. *Why Women's Studies?* Brandon: Brandon University Status of Women Organization, 1987.

Greene, Alma (Forbidden Voice). *Tales of the Mohawks*. Toronto: J.M. Dent, 1975.

Grinnell, George Bird. *Blackfoot Lodge Tales*. Lincoln: University of Nebraska Press, 1962.

Gunn, Hubert. "A Question of Rights" and "A Lamp to Read By". *Tawow*, I, no. 2, 1970.

Joe, Rita. *Poems of Rita Joe*. Halifax: Abenaki Press, 1978.

Johnson, E. Pauline. *Flint and Feather*.(1917 rpt.) Don Mills: Paperjacks, 1972.

________________. *The Moccasin Maker*. Tucson: The University of Arizona Press, 1987.

Johnston, Basil. *Moose Meat and Wild Rice*. Toronto: McClelland and Stewart, 1978.

________________. *Ojibway Heritage*. Toronto: McClelland and Stewart, 1976.

______________. "The Kiss and the Moonshine". *Tawow* 4, no. 4, 1974.

Johnston, Verna Patronella. *Tales of Nokomis*. Don Mills: Musson, 1975.

Kennedy, Dan (Ochankugahe). *Recollections of an Assiniboine Chief*. Toronto: McClelland and Stewart, 1972.

Kenny, George. *Indians Don't Cry*. Oakville, Ontario: Chimo, 1977.

Maracle, Lee. *I Am Woman*. Vancouver: Write-On Press, 1988.

Markoosie. *Harpoon of the Hunter*. Montreal: McGill-Queen's University Press, 1970.

Mélançon, Claude. *Indian Legends of Canada*. Toronto: Gage Publishing, 1974.

Norman, Howard. *The Wishing Bone Cycle*. Santa Barbara: Ross-Erikson Publishers 1976.

______________. *Where the Chill Came From*. Berkeley: North Point Press, 1982.

Oskaboose, Gilbert. "The Serpent's Egg". *Canadian Dimension* 22, no. I (February, 1988).

Ray, Carl and James Stevens. *Sacred Legends of the Sandy Lake Cree*. Toronto: McClelland and Stewart, 1971.

Redsky, James. *Great Leader of the Ojibway: Mis-quona-queb*. Toronto: McClelland and Stewart, 1972.

Sanders, Thomas E. and Walter W. Peek. *Literature of the American Indian*. Toronto: Collier McMillan, 1973.

Sealey, D. Bruce, ed. *Stories of the Métis*. Winnipeg: Manitoba Métis Federation Press, 1973.

______________. "Joe Bignell's Fight with the Weetigo", *Prairie Fire* 7, no. I, (Spring, 1986).

Sealey, D. Bruce and Antoine Lussier. *The Métis: Canada's Forgotten People*. Winnipeg, Pemmican Publications Inc., 1975.

Shipley, Nan, ed. *Wild Drums: Tales and Legends of the Plains Indians*. Winnipeg: Peguis Publishers, 1974.

Slipperjack, Ruby. *Honour the Sun*. Winnipeg: Pemmican Publications, 1987.

Speare, Jean E. *The Days of Augusta*. Vancouver: J.J. Douglas, 1973.

Swartz, Herbert. *Windigo and Other Tales of the Ojibway*. Toronto: McClelland and Stewart, 1969.

Tetso, John. *Trapping is My Life*. Toronto: Peter Martin Associates, 1976.

Thompson, Albert Edward. *Chief Peguis and His Descendants*. Winnipeg: Peguis Publishers, 1973.

Thomas, Dorine Cooper. *Rubaboo*. Winnipeg: Pemmican Publications Inc., 1981.

Vanderburgh, R.M. *I Am Nokomis, Too*. Don Mills: General Publishing, 1977.

Willis, Jane. *Geniesh: An Indian Girlhood*. Toronto: New Press, 1973.